07/05

The *YANKEE*® Way to Simplify Your Life

OLD-FASHIONED WISDOM
FOR A NEW-FANGLED WORLD

Jay Heinrichs

and the editors of *Yankee*® magazine

William Morrow and Company, Inc.
New York

It is the policy of William Morrow and Company, Inc., and its imprints and affili-
ates, recognizing the importance of preserving what has been written, to print the
books we publish on acid-free paper, and we exert our best efforts to that end.

Library of Congress Cataloging-in-Publication Data
Heinrichs, Jay.
The Yankee way to simplify your life : old-fashioned wisdom for a new-fangled
world / Jay Heinrichs and the editors of Yankee magazine.
p.   cm.
Includes index.
ISBN 0-688-14186-2
1. Simplicity.   2. Conduct of life.   3. Self-realization.   4. Life.
I. Yankee magazine.   II. Title.
BJ1496.H45   1996
179'.9—dc20   96-11152
CIP

Printed in the United States of America
First Edition
1   2   3   4   5   6   7   8   9   10
BOOK DESIGN BY EUGENIE SEIDENBERG DELANEY

To Harriet Beecher Stowe, who wrote
great literature to feed her children

———➤●◀———

Preface

THE STONE WALL

THE WALL LIES HIGH on the Lambert Ridge in New Hampshire. Anchoring a forest of birch and maple, it testifies to an old Yankee strength.

You have to climb a steep slope for a mile to see the wall, the relic of an eighteenth-century hill farm. You wonder how the people survived up there. The land seems more stone than soil. To use it meant removing the rocks—the great waste product of New England hill farming.

Instead of taking the rocks to a dump, the farmers made walls, dividing pasture and keeping livestock in bounds. The work is not easy, especially on a slope. The rocks are heavy, and the flies are hungry.

Still, the walls got built, and they lasted. Look down to the rich bottomlands along New England rivers; there is little trace of the original farms. It was the hill farmers who took the rocks and built a legacy.

Moral: When we do more than dispose of our obstacles, when we build something from what stands in our way, we learn a secret from the Yankees of old.

We learn what it is to simplify.

Acknowledgments

IT IS CUSTOMARY to thank people without whose help a book would be impossible. Bill Adler certainly falls into that category; this book was his idea. I am grateful to Sharon Smith for thinking of me as the writer, and for acting as lead cheerleader/skeptic. Jamie Trowbridge of *Yankee*, who was to the Puritan manner born, provided moral encouragement (and an occasional moral); William Morrow's Toni Sciarra edited with Yankee-like wisdom. Nancy Trafford offered the unflagging support that every author and self-improver needs.

My family—Dorothy Sr., Dorothy Jr., and George—did much more than put up with an author. They helped write the book. If there are flaws in it, I hope they improve the opportunity and write a better one.

Contents

Introduction

A Personal Tale of Nearly Disastrous Self-improvement

FOR A SHORT TIME WHILE WRITING THIS BOOK, I thought that simplifying my life might ruin it. Something seemed to go wrong with whatever aspect of living I happened to be writing about.

The first time it happened I was drafting the passage on the importance of "quantity time" with your kids when my ten-year-old daughter, Dorothy Jr., burst in. "The Bacons are taking me skiing," she said. "Can you come with us, Dad?"

"Beat it, kid," I said. "I'm telling how to be a good parent." Dorothy Jr. moped off and skied without me.

The very next day I was taking notes on how to argue effectively with your spouse when my wife, Dorothy Sr., and I had one of our biggest arguments in years—about Cub Scouts, I think. I ended up sleeping in my home office right next to my notes about simplifying marriage. In the middle of the money section in Chapter 10 some freelance business I'd been counting on fell through. That was followed by an office crisis while I was writing the work chapter. Then I lost my seven-year-old son, George, on New Hampshire's Mount Cardigan for an hour. He had charged on ahead of me and taken a different path. Guess what chapter I was working on? The one on play.

Call it "Self-improvement He Wrote." The very act of writing about simplifying your life seemed to be complicating mine. I became uncharacteristically superstitious, delaying work on Chapter 13, the one about the body, for fear of contracting some deadly disease.

Of course I didn't. It eventually occurred to me that I wasn't messing up my life, I was examining it. Screwups that happen all the time were just becoming more apparent. I was acting like a good Puritan, turning over the soil. Besides, the daily complications of my life proved how qualified I was to talk about simplifying.

My own attempt to simplify my life began a little more than a decade ago, when my wife and I decided to move out of the Washington, D.C., area. The one self-improvement habit we practiced back then was to go on a long walk every New Year's Day and talk about our lives. On this particular ramble I pictured an idyllic little college town in northern New England. She described staying home and caring for two children until she felt like returning to work. We strolled and mooned and then returned to reality.

A few weeks later a man offered me a job in downtown Washington. I thanked him and turned it down. "You can't stay in your job forever," he said. "What do you want to do?"

"I like what I'm doing now," I replied. "But since you asked . . ." and with a somewhat embarrassed smile I told him all about my squirrelly little vision.

"I'm a graduate of Dartmouth College," he said, "and there's an opening there for your sort of work."

I applied and got the job. My wife and I bought a house on ten acres a brisk bike ride from my office. Paths through our land hook up to the twenty-two-hundred-mile Appalachian Trail. I can walk north for twenty-five miles without crossing a paved road. When my wife isn't helping to run our little town, she is home with the kids. We're living our squirrelly little vision.

The day the call came telling me I had the job, the first real moral ever to occur to me suddenly popped into my head. It's not a profound moral, but it's true:

Sometimes you only have to know what you want.

My desire became fate, an outcome that fell into my lap without any goals, habits, targets, or deadlines. All I needed was a timely answer to a friendly man's question.

Since then I've met countless other people who have found a calling just by expressing it. Margo, a colleague at Dartmouth, once decided to spend much of the rest of her life traveling. She didn't have a whole lot of money but nonetheless envisioned a borrowed house in the south of France. Two weeks after she started dreaming in detail she came across a classified ad offering a house swap: a month in a cottage in Provence in return for a month someplace in Vermont. Margo happens to live in Vermont. The swap was a great success that led to more house-swap contacts, and Margo now frugally lives overseas during every bit of vacation time.

Stories like Margo's and mine have led me to believe that our lives actually can improve.

But it is one thing to dream your fate and another to tempt it. I never for a moment thought that my job offer was anything more than dumb luck. I learned that I could let my life change; it took me longer to discover I could improve it on my own. To do that, I had to undergo a process of Yankeefication, shedding my city ways and acquiring some of the attitudes of rural New England. That's another weird story.

Our land is in an area I had never visited before coming north, yet the moment I saw the place it felt familiar. The features had names I seemed to remember: Mink Brook, Goose Pond, Moose Mountain. I was beginning to think there was something to this business about past lives. Then one day I read a profile on the writer Corey Ford, who had lived in New Hampshire and written funny stories during the 1950s and early sixties for *Field and Stream* magazine. Ford invented a group of outdoorsmen called the Lower Forty Shooting, Angling and Inside Straight Club, in a fictional town called Hardscrabble. Turns out Ford modeled Hardscrabble after the very town I had moved to. I suddenly remembered reading *Field and Stream* in barbershops when I was a boy in Philadelphia. The residents of Hardscrabble had seemed to me then to live in a paradise, and for the rest of my life, even after I'd forgotten the stories themselves, I wanted to move to northern New England. I ended up buying land right under Moose Mountain in "Hardscrabble" itself.

That discovery inspired me to read about local history, and I branched out into biographies of old Yankees. I was surprised to find some common traits among the early residents of this region, including their belief in a person's ability to improve.

So I was inspired to try some improvement of my own by transforming myself into a morning person. Imitating nearly every admirable New Englander I'd read about, I devised a scheme to get up at 5:00 every weekday morning (you can see the plan in Chapter 6). I made a pact with myself to stand up automatically before the alarm watch stopped beeping (it has a long beep). I set a new habit of doing calisthenics and stretching first thing. Push-ups at 5:00 A.M. seemed masochistic at first, but we don't heat our house at night, and the exercise warmed me up better than the shower did. I actually started getting used to the routine. On some dark mornings I would find myself on the floor doing push-ups with no clue to how I'd arrived there. On the other hand, it took awhile to get used to actually thinking early in the morning. At times I found myself dozing over my work. But after a while even that got easier. And there was an added benefit: Sleeping in during the weekend meant getting up at 6:30 at the latest, which offered more time to play outside.

I was so proud of myself that I started setting other small goals: to run mountain trails, take more hikes with my children, exhibit more habits of grace with my wife, drink less beer, learn rock climbing. I'm far from meeting some of the goals, as my wife will be the first to tell you. But I'm better off than when I started. I have more time. Nice clothing and new cars and other fashion items seem less important than my more serious acquisitions of habit and physical ability. Even travel seems less of a big deal; a good mountain run is more exciting to me now than a trip to a city, because the mountain seems more attached to my desires. Most of all, I have begun to acquire that quintessential Yankee sense of superiority—not toward others but toward my former slovenly self.

My self-improvement passion has affected the rest of my family in different ways. At the age of forty-one Dorothy Sr. now runs the Appalachian Trail with a friend, and people say she looks twenty-five. Dorothy Jr. has developed goals to improve as a competitive cross-country skier. On the other hand, the day before George's seventh birthday Dorothy Sr. said to him, "You only have twenty-four hours left to be a six-year-old!" George paused on the stairs, stuck a sarcastic forefinger into the air, and said, "I will use the time wisely."

Every family needs a skeptic.

CHAPTER 1

The Simple Life

Regarding what makes a Yankee a Yankee

WHEN WE THINK OF A STEREOTYPICAL YANKEE, certain terms come to mind: plain speaking, ingenuity, hard work, stern morals. If we study them the right way, we can learn a thing or two from Yankees about making life more livable. The early New Englanders knew when and how to be satisfied. They rarely felt sorry for themselves. They had a clear sense of place and how they fitted into it. They knew that everything, especially themselves, can stand improvement.

Not all Yankees were that admirable, of course. Right from the start New England has included the gloriously fat, the lazy, the apartment-bound city dweller. But there is a grain of truth in the more rigorous stereotype. "Yankee" and "simple" go well together for a reason. The first New Englanders took pride in their unornamented religion, speech, writing,

1

dress, and government—simplicity that arose from the basic Puritan virtues of austerity, hard work, and denial of the flesh.

Austerity? Denial? Frankly, to want to return to the days of the Puritans, you'd have to be a little crazy. If instead you can just capture some old-time simplicity, you can become like John Adams, who, while still in his twenties, discovered heaven. Adams was traveling along the Connecticut River toward Hartford when he suddenly came across his idea of paradise on earth, which he duly noted in his diary: "The land will yield two crops of English grass, and two tons and a half at each crop with plenty of after-feed besides, if nicely managed and properly dunged."

Dung? In heaven?

Forget angels and lyres and heathen nectar; Adams's paradise looks a lot like home.

Which leads to two obvious questions: Why would anyone want to be a Yankee? Who wants to plow through the afterlife?

THE MOST PRODUCTIVE YANKEES

ADAMS WASN'T JUST A FARMER, of course; he was one of the most versatile of all American leaders. Throughout history there have been a number of people who, like him, led enormously complex lives and made them look simple. How could Ralph Waldo Emerson lead a grueling speaking schedule, write reams of poetry, and become the leading philosopher of his day? How could Daniel Webster draw crowds of fifty thousand, become the nation's top trial lawyer, and act as one of our greatest diplomats—all at the same time? How on earth did a runaway Boston apprentice named Benjamin Franklin juggle a printing business, studies of electricity, numerous inventions, political theories, best-selling books, and diplomacy while helping to foment American independence? Most impressive of all, how did Harriet Beecher Stowe write *Uncle Tom's Cabin* and help turn an entire nation against slavery while her six children were doing their homework practically on top of her?

If you read up on these and other amazingly productive people, you will discover that nearly all of them had several advantages in common:

1. Servants
2. Wealth
3. Understanding spouses

That leaves out a good many readers of this book, no doubt.

But then, what if it is possible to be more productive without the servants or money? (Understanding spouses have been rare in any century.) What if you could just spend less time on the parts of the day that don't make you any healthier, wealthier, or wiser—like getting up in the morning, commuting to work, sitting in meetings, fixing meals, watching television? How could you find more time for the things you love most—like playing with your kids, hooking a rug, or reading? And how could you have time left over for transcending your usual existence—by learning a new sport, or volunteering, or exploring the world?

The fact is, there are ways to do these things. They can be summed up as the simple life.

The simple life is a busy life, but one in which the pleasurable tasks far outnumber the odious ones. It is a life in which you make progress toward your most important goals and push the less important ones farther back.

In short, the simple life entails knowing the life you really want to live and then living it.

As Henry David Thoreau said, it means getting yourself out from under the details. That does not necessarily mean living like a hermit, wearing

Nostalgia the Way It Used to Be

P HYSICIANS ONCE DIAGNOSED a yearning for the past as a mental disease that could lead to severe weight loss or even suicide. Nostalgia first
seemed to afflict seventeenth-century Swiss mercenaries when they were
far from home. Dr. Johannes Hofer coined the term from the Greek *nostos*
(to return home) and *algia* (pain). He determined the cause to be "the
quite continuous vibration of animal spirits through those fibers of the
middle brain in which impressed traces of ideas of the Fatherland still cling."
Some scientists thought atmospheric pressure was to blame. Swiss soldiers
coming down out of the Alps to fight in the flatlands contracted the ailment when they subjected their bodies to greater atmospheric pressure.
Up until the early nineteenth century doctors thought the disease was
unique to the Swiss. Then other troops began suffering from it. During
the American Civil War medics attributed traumatic stress disorder, or shell
shock, to nostalgia.

Moral: You can't go "home" to the early New England of our imagination; you risk contracting nostalgia just by yearning for it. But with the help
of this book you can reproduce some of the comforts and disciplines of our
bygone small-town past.

homespun, and going without electricity or telephone. Some people do just
that, of course, but their lives seem rather complicated—not to mention
inconvenient, which is saying much the same thing. *You* try rearing babies
without running water.

Look at two friends, Jim and Bob.

THE STORY OF JIM AND BOB

SOME YEARS AGO Jim bought a tiny island on a lake in New Hampshire and built a log cabin on it with his own hands. He paddled a canoe to his car when the lake wasn't frozen. When it was, he skated. (When the ice was thin, he took his chances, falling in every now and then.) Inside his cabin were a gas refrigerator, a composting toilet, a woodstove, some wooden furniture, kerosene lamps, and some books. Many people would find Jim's life extremely complicated. He couldn't just pop around the corner for groceries. The temperature in his cabin would be forty degrees when he got home from work in the winter. Yet Jim lived simply—for Jim. He had exactly what he wanted for that time in his life: the outdoors, books, solitude, a couple of fine rocking chairs. He paid no mortgage, he never mowed his lawn (the island is covered entirely with blueberry bushes), and good swimming and fishing were right at his doorstep. While Jim doesn't live on the island anymore, he has not exactly moved to suburbia. He is restoring an eighteenth-century farmhouse that has never known electricity, and Jim, being Jim, has no intention of introducing it.

To Jim, his country life is simple. But Jim's friend Bob lives just as simply in the city. Bob moved from New Hampshire to live in a small Manhattan apartment and work as the entertainment editor of a big magazine. He has traveled all over the world, wears a killer double-breasted suit ("Hey!" he says. "It's Manhattan"), and accompanies his wife, a New York banker, to shows or parties or expensive restaurants almost every night. He doesn't have a car; he walks to work or takes a cab. He is an abominable cook, and he cheerfully keeps his refrigerator almost entirely empty. (Hey! It's Manhattan. He eats out.) He keeps in shape by running to the office through Central Park and has time for almost everything he wants to do.

While Jim and Bob have many similarities, neither would be caught dead living the other's life. These two guys show that there is no one simple life. The simple life is what is simple *for you*.

The simple life means creatively narrowing your choices so they don't overwhelm you.

It means having *time*—time to stay caught up with work, time to think about the future, time for your loved ones, time for yourself.

It means eating what you want, and not what your cravings force you to eat.

It means having enough money and possessions to live the way you want and being reasonably satisfied with what you have.

HOW DO YOU KNOW
IF YOU'RE LIVING SIMPLY?

IF YOU CAN SAY YES to each of these questions, yours is the simple life. If the answer to any or all of them is no, well . . . that's what this book is for.

1. Do you know exactly what you want out of life?
2. Do you have enough time during the day or week or year to do what you want?
3. Do your habits lead to goals?

As the next chapter shows, the early New Englanders were the first to come up with organized answers to those three questions. The aim should be to lead not the life of some old Yankee—just your own. But it doesn't take much to figure out that that can be the toughest, and the most rewarding, feat of all.

Eight Basic Morals to the Yankee Story

THROUGHOUT THIS BOOK you will find many morals, but they can be boiled down to eight essential ones (to simplify, you have to boil down). Some of them may not make perfect sense to you, but don't worry. If everything were explained right here, what would be the point of reading this book?

1. **Ignore the silver lining. Use the cloud.** Some of your greatest opportunities come from obstacles. Later we'll talk about the advantages of lowered expectations, bad habits, and noble failures.
2. **It's hard to set a course when you don't know where you are.** Our lives are complicated by the crosscurrents that buffet them. A couple of chapters will help you establish a sense of place and a sense of self.
3. **A well-chosen goal looks a lot like fate.** It is much simpler to meet a goal that seems inevitable than one that appears unattainable. We'll go into useful Puritan beliefs that helped inspire the Yankee approach to living.
4. **A wide target is easier to hit than a narrow one.** Goals often fail because they are hard to measure. This book will show you how to set the right goals and stay inspired by them.
5. **If the road to hell is paved with good intentions, the road to heaven is paved with habits.** The good habit is the best way to get free from the morass of day-to-day details. You will learn how to establish a habit and how to make a bad one serve you.

(continued on next page)

6. **Pleasure has more stamina than duty.** We mess up our lives when we swim against our own current.

7. **When you count your blessings, round up.** The best way to simplify is to know when, and how, to be satisfied. This book will help you use the techniques of artillery officers to "bracket" your expectations.

8. **Do nothing to excess, including doing nothing to excess.** "Simplify, simplify," wrote Thoreau, himself using twice as many words as he had to. He was a wise man who avoided simplifying to the point of complication.

CHAPTER 2

The Puritan Secret

*In which is revealed the Yankee's
most ingenious invention: the Yankee*

I F YOU DOUBT THAT YOU CAN SIMPLIFY YOUR LIFE, join the crowd. Although Americans spend billions of dollars a year in attempts to improve themselves—the diet industry alone rakes in thirty-three billion—it is unfashionable actually to believe that we can improve. Are we unhappy? Our childhood and parents are much to blame, and we can't fix *them*. Are we caught in the web of terrible habits? It's our addictive personality. Are we in debt to our credit cards and car companies? That's part of being an American. We even blame our faults on strange mental diseases. A woman recently brought her son to New Hampshire neurologist Richard Nordgren and announced that the boy was a lousy student because he had "work output deficit disorder." The mother had not made a new medical discovery. She had lost something, a faith that got its

9

start in New England and helped create an unprecedented burst of energy and wealth.

The secret behind the success of the Puritans was their belief in everyone's ability, even duty, to improve. They loved to tell the story of the Old Testament prophet Jeremiah, who one day visited a potter. The craftsman messed up a pot he was making, but instead of throwing it away he took the same clay and remolded it. At that point the voice of God popped into Jeremiah's head: "Have not I the right to deal with men and with nations as this potter has dealt with this clay?" (Think of Jeremiah when you despair of changing your own shape.)

The Puritans reshaped themselves with the help of some simple principles:

Examine thyself. Early New Englanders often took perverse pleasure in listing, and sometimes exaggerating, their faults. But they did it for a reason. By studying their faults, they hoped to learn how to eliminate them. They also gained useful self-awareness. In the next chapter we'll complete an important exercise in self-examination. Not being Puritans ourselves, we'll cover pleasures and admirable traits as well as faults.

Everyone is improvable. Regardless of family, childhood, or obstacles, a person could end up as one of the elect, especially favored by God. All it took, the Puritans thought, was a good education and the grace of the Almighty.

Every opportunity is an obligation. The Puritans, who believed in a strangely energetic form of predestination, taught that God gives you a set of innate abilities and then provides the circumstances for carrying them out. It is up to you to "improve your opportunities." If you work hard and do well, then your behavior might reveal you as one of the elect. On the other hand, if you blow your chances, you are probably one of those poor souls destined for hell. Some people have it in them; some don't. Needless to say, Puritans fell over one another trying to prove they had it in them.

A Town Not Named Dukakis

ADAMS, NEW HAMPSHIRE, changed its name to Jackson when Andrew Jackson beat John Quincy Adams in the 1828 election. The town had first been named in 1800, when John Adams won the presidency.

Moral: To a good Yankee, every event is an improvable moment.

Good things come from good habits. Early New Englanders knew how to set their lives on autopilot by establishing useful routines. One old Yankee technique allowed extraordinary accomplishments: the habit of getting up at five. In Chapter 6, I'll talk about why that's such an advantage (and how you can gain it, if you dare).

It's all right to feel a bit superior. What made early New Englanders hardest to bear also helped make them extraordinarily productive people. It was everyone's duty to believe that he or she was one of the righteous few who were bound for heaven. Low self-confidence was actually sinful; it showed a lack of faith in God.

Anything other than your calling is a distraction. You have a purpose in life, the Puritans believed, and it is your bounden duty to pursue it. Any extras—fashions, seductive pleasures, even fancy speech—could pull you away from the single-minded pursuit of your calling.

This explains why the Puritans didn't set the world on fire with their fashions. Contrary to myth, they loved colorful clothing. But they knew that the vagaries of public opinion can yank you from your calling. Fashion complicates your life by seducing you into living the lives of others. It isn't a sin to be fashionable, the Puritans said, but fashion can lead you

Even Fewer in
England Could Have Done It

B OSTON BECAME INFAMOUS for its citizens' belief that their city was chosen by God and therefore superior to every other community on earth. There is an old joke about an aged Bostonian who read Shakespeare for the first time. "There are not twenty men in Boston who could have written those plays," he said admiringly.

Moral: Confidence in self and place is not a sin, though it can get on other people's nerves.

into sin. The Puritans' quest to avoid distraction became the essence of simplicity.

This book does not show you how to be a Puritan. Very few people would want to be. Instead we will try to restore our forebears' canniest wisdom, the happiness that comes from living simply.

CHAPTER 3

Finding Your Calling

*In which the reader is led through a personal biography
and begins acquiring some advantages of early New Englanders*

MANY DESCENDANTS OF PURITANISM rejected the idea that some people were among the elect and the rest were doomed, but they still clung to faith in a person's calling. "Read your fate, see what is before you, and walk on into futurity," said Henry David Thoreau, who was no Puritan by a long shot.

If the notion of fate seems a little hokey in the twentieth century, take a look at your own calling—the unique set of skills and preferences that, properly understood, would head your life in the most desirable direction. Some things just come easily for you, while other forms of work or play seem like torture. You know you do best what you enjoy. The problem is, there's often too much white noise in your life—schedules, commitments, the vagaries of fashion—to let you determine your calling. Our lifestyles tend to fit our incomes and schedules (and then some), rather than our desires.

Have you noticed that some people don't appear to have this problem? They seem to be doing what they want to do. They don't look harried or pushed around, and some of them even have kids! And actually work for a living! Maybe there really is an elect, and maybe they're it.

Then again, maybe they're just lucky.

Consider the MacArthur "genius" fellows. The MacArthur Foundation is famous for its generous five-year grants to artists, scholars, journalists, and community organizers. The money frees its "fellows" from having to earn a living during the span of the grant. Anonymous judges choose the recipients in secret. You can't apply; the money just shows up, no strings attached. Newspaper reporters who tracked the lives of some of the genius fellows made a surprising discovery: Most of the recipients did what they were supposed to do. They wrote books, organized nonprofit groups, conducted research. Very few rented beach houses in the tropics and drank margaritas. For most MacArthur fellows, the money allowed them to do what they loved the most, which, for the most part, was what they were already doing. Is there any simpler life?

People who lead lives of good fortune tend to be extraordinarily skilled in going with their own flow. With unwavering dedication, courage, and ability, they commit themselves to what they want to do.

Luck, in short, comes most to those who know their callings.

RETIRE RIGHT NOW!
(The Catch: You Have to Keep On Working)

V ERY FEW PEOPLE get to be genius fellows, and that is a terrible shame. You may be a fellowless genius yourself. But there is an alternative that arises when people are sixty-five or so. They stop working and go on a permanent vacation called retirement. Most interesting about this group, however, is how few of them act like stereotypical golf-playing, sun-soaking, cruise-sailing retirees. The majority of people who retire do not go on what we would call a vacation. They work part-time, volunteer in their communities, run for public office, or continue their education. They often reveal their true callings for the first time in their lives. The sad thing is, most of us scheduled to retire in the next millennium will never retire in the traditional sense, according to the experts. We won't be able to afford it.

We may be doomed to live like Benjamin Franklin, who was eighty-one when he signed the U.S. Constitution.

Or like Paul Revere, who in his seventies began helping Robert Fulton make steam boilers that propelled boats and helped strengthen Boston's defenses in the War of 1812.

Or like John Kulish, who at eighty-five is a leading authority on the nature of southern New Hampshire. He can still carry a sixty-eight-pound canoe on his shoulders and hike all day without food and water. "I don't mind dying," he says. "I'm living on borrowed time as it is, but Jesus, how I'll miss the trout fishing."

Some people don't find their callings until they have "retired" from their careers. Other people do exactly what they want to do long before they're sixty-five, and then they just keep on doing it. Both groups have found their callings.

WHAT DETERMINES YOUR FATE

THE SIMPLE LIFE strays as little as possible from your calling, which in turn depends on three factors: what you have inherited, what happens to you by chance, and what you want.

You are stuck with your *inheritance*. This is the genetic makeup that gives you a prominent nose or overendowed rump. It is also the set of values and traditions you grew up with. Your inheritance is the life you have lived so far. We'll get to that in a moment.

Accident (and how you deal with it) is the second factor, such things as sickness, people you meet by chance, opportunities, catastrophes. You can prepare yourself for setbacks and moments of good fortune (this book will tell you how), but you can't count on them. Otherwise they wouldn't be accidents.

There is a third factor that can count as the most important of all, if you let it: your own *desires*.

If you can learn your calling from these three elements, you do more than simplify. You pursue happiness.

LOOKING BACK TO THE FUTURE

YOU CAN DISCOVER a lot about yourself by studying your inheritance. Your genes are visible to you every time you look in the mirror. First, though, let's talk about the part of your inheritance that is much less visible, your own past. "It is as hard to see one's self as to look backwards without turning round," Thoreau said.

To see yourself, you need to turn around and look backward.

One of the purest forms of your personality is your seven-year-old self. At the age of seven you have left babyhood and have acquired much of the personality you will be blessed, or stuck, with for the rest of your life. "Show me the boy of seven and I will show you the man" goes an old Jesuit saying, which works just as well with little girls. By the time we are seven our preferences are marked. Did you ask a lot of questions like a budding journalist, or have a passion for blocks like a carpenter or engineer, or prefer making up rules to the game itself (like a lawyer), or love the outdoors, or reading, or playing doctor? The child really is a parent to the adult; you are the living heir of your seven-year-old self.

But not the spitting image, of course. For one thing, your current self probably has front teeth. And you almost certainly have habits that would have been a scandal during childhood. But wouldn't it be great to return to the best parts of your seven-year-old state?

Imagine recapturing the simple, defining desires you had then, and consider everything else clutter.

One source of clutter is the praise and criticism we receive through life. While we hear a lot about the benefits of "positive reinforcement"—buttressing little egos with well-timed bits of praise—we don't often hear about its potential drawbacks. The world would have been spared many forgettable authors if their early attempts at creative writing had been accepted with a bit less enthusiasm. In his autobiography Benjamin Franklin recalls how as a young printer's apprentice he wrote two ballads that sold briskly. "This success flattered my vanity," he says. "But my father discouraged me by criticizing my performances and telling me verse-makers were generally beggars. Thus I escaped being a poet, and probably a bad one. . . ."

On the other hand, there is an old story about a psychology professor whose class conspired to use him as the subject of an experiment in positive reinforcement. During one lecture, unbeknownst to the prof, the students "reinforced" him each time he moved toward the classroom door. If he gestured or took a step that way, they would smile, laugh more loudly at his witticisms, look more attentive. If he went away from the door, they would frown, turn their gaze elsewhere, murmur among themselves, and look bored. By the end of the lecture the professor was speaking from halfway out in the hall, without even knowing it. And he was a *psychology* professor.

Beware of being damned through feinted praise.

Advantaged Childhoods

- Daniel Webster grew up on a hardscrabble New Hampshire farm. He suffered from childhood rickets, a vitamin D deficiency caused by malnutrition and lack of sun. The disease made his forehead protrude, giving him the prominent brow he was famous for later in life. It made him look brilliant, people said, even godlike.

- Back in the 1920s a gang of boys took to hanging out in front of Old Man Barry's place in North Cambridge, Massachusetts, much to the distress of Mr. Barry, who wasn't fond of loitering delinquents. One of the gang's most loyal members built on these friendships, made a great many more, and ended up as Speaker of the U.S. House of Representatives. "I'd rather be a lamppost on Barry's Corner than be with any of the people I've met from around the world," Tip O'Neill once said.

- Bostonian Amy Lowell suffered a glandular problem during adolescence and became unusually fat. Ostracized by children her age, she turned to poetry. Her first book, *A Dome of Many-Colored Glass*, published in 1912, established her as a literary powerhouse.

- Mary Baker was a sickly child, suffering from colds, fever, backache, lung and liver troubles, and, worst of all, dyspepsia. As an adult Mary Baker Eddy founded Christian Science.

- When P. T. Barnum was a four-year-old in rural Connecticut, his grandfather gave him his own farm, Ivy Island. At the age of ten his parents finally allowed him to see it. It turned out to be swampland. "The truth flashed upon me," he later wrote in his autobiography. "I had been the laughing-stock of the family and neighborhood for years." He went on, of course, to become one of the greatest hucksters in history.

◆ When Clara Barton was twelve, she fainted at the sight of an ox being butchered. From then on she was a vegetarian. She lived to age ninety.

◆ Richard Henry Dana suffered a serious ear injury when a schoolteacher yanked it. He grew up to be a lawyer whose court fights on behalf of sailors helped tone down the cruel discipline on American ships.

Moral: For some people, childhood difficulties turn out to be adult blessings.

EXPERIMENTING WITH YOUR FATE

TO EXAMINE YOUR PAST SELF and to learn more about your desires take a little experimentation.

Researchers know what the rest of us often don't consider: When you're studying something impossibly complicated, look at just part of it. Take, for example, two common items in a New England forest: chipmunks and trees. Any scientist will tell you that one of the worst ways to determine how many chipmunks there are in a forest is to try to count every one of them. Instead scientists will count just some of them within a small, plotted-out area and then make an educated guess about the whole forest. They call this a plot sample.

Trees are easier to count since they generally hold still better than chipmunks. But to examine an entire tree is trickier than studying a chipmunk. It is cumbersome to take a tree apart, and besides, it kills the tree. Instead researchers bore into the trunk and take out what is called a core sample. By examining the little cylinder of wood, they can tell the tree's age, its health, the types of nutrients in the soil, even the region's climate for as long as the tree has lived.

What have trees and chipmunks to do with your life? Nothing! Because of that, we miss a valuable technique for determining what you want. To simplify your life, you don't need to study your relationship with your parents or undergo psychoanalysis. You need only sample yourself, study the parts that can use simplifying, and record over a reasonably short period your habits and ways of doing things. So let's bore a bit into your life.

Don't think that you have to go through all the exercises below. Remember, simplicity means doing nothing to excess. You can tell something about yourself by the kinds of questions you picked. We'll get to that later. There is no real need to write down your answers either. (But you weren't going to, anyway, were you?) Later you'll "funnel" this self-examination into distinct likes and dislikes and eventually further narrow these preferences into a genuine calling.

CORE SAMPLE: YOUR BRAIN

DON'T WORRY. We don't mean an actual core sample, and the process doesn't require a drill. This part is painless.

Take the Shower Test—that is, take a shower or bath. What do you think of when you're bathing? If you don't think of anything, bathe at a different time of day.

What good is the Shower Test? It is a time when your thoughts spill over from other times. Many of us spend our bathing moments fantasizing, thinking of ourselves as improved versions of ourselves—superheroes, legendary lovers. If you're one of these people, think of that improved version. You'll want to remember it for later in this book.

Fantasize some more. Imagine that a rich aunt died tomorrow and left you a million dollars after taxes. What would you spend the money on? How would your life change? Now ask yourself: Could you do these things without the million dollars?

PLOT SAMPLE: YOUR DESTINY

"WHAT A MAN THINKS OF HIMSELF, that it is which determines, or rather indicates, his fate." So said Henry David Thoreau, who, like his ancestors, was crazy about the subject of predestination. We can learn a lot about our callings—and even hints of our destiny—by following clues to our own personalities and pasts. Let's start by taking a sample of your calling, the life you would live if you had the means to live it. Answer these questions:

What is the best weekend you ever had? Can you think of one that is even better?

What was the best vacation you ever had? How old were you? Whom were you with? How long did it last? What were the parts that made it the best? How likely is it that you'll have another one that good? Why? What would have to change in your life so you could have that vacation again?

Have you ever had times when you *weren't* on vacation that you enjoyed better than any holiday? What made those times so great? Could you get them back?

These times have something in common: When you are simply enjoying yourself, you are living your own life the most purely. The biggest source of stress in our daily existence comes from duties and activities that stray from that true life. What if instead we got to do entirely what we wanted to do during the day? What if our time was our own?

If you could retire right now, what would you do? Would you really want to do it for a decade or more?

If every day were an hour longer, what would you do with the extra hour?

If every week were eight days, what would you do with the eighth day?

If every year had an extra two weeks, what would you do with them?

Imagine the ideal country home. Picture it in your mind: the house, outbuildings, surroundings, people. Where is the house? Near a lake? In the middle of a farm field? In the woods? On the coast of Maine? Is it an old house or a new one? Do you think you could ever live like that?

If you could be as old (or young) as you want, what would your age be? Why? What would you gain (or, in some wonderful cases, lose) if you were allowed to be that age? Could you gain some of the same advantages without being that age?

What relaxes you most? Music? Being with friends? Reading a book? Watching TV? A drink? Exercise? Putting your feet up and doing nothing whatsoever?

What do you do when you're waiting in line?

When you eat a piece of pie, do you turn it before putting your fork into it?

If you can find any meaning in the last question, that alone says a lot about you.

CORE SAMPLE: YOUR DNA

L ET'S TAKE A LOOK at the part of your inheritance that is your genes through these questions:

Were all four grandparents alive when you were old enough to be conscious of them? Or do you still have pictures of them? Describe the looks you inherited. Now think of personality traits that you received: hot-blooded or even-keeled? A quick study or a still, deep pond? Affectionate or somewhat steely?

Which grandparent is your favorite?

What kind of person would you be if you had inherited all the best traits of these four people?

Can you describe ancestors who mean the most to you? If you don't have ancestors, try making some up. (Why not? It's a free country.)

Who was your favorite relative as a child? Why? Do you have any of the same traits?

PLOT SAMPLE: YOUR TRADITIONS

O UR FAMILY'S PASTS can have at least as much effect on our personal values and habits as, say, the news media or our current friends. Ask yourself:

Do you know any family stories?

What were holidays like when you were growing up?

How did your relatives express their religious faith or their lack of it?

Why does your family eat the way it does?

Are there old sayings that your family was repeating before you were born? This leads irresistibly to these questions:

Can you imagine your own grandchildren repeating something you like to say? Or fondly remembering a holiday tradition? Or passing on a recipe? Or remembering an anecdote you wish to blazes was forgotten?

Can you picture a statue on a town common of an ancestor that looks exactly like you? What noble feats did that ancestor accomplish to earn the statue?

What family stories are the most memorable to you?

CORE SAMPLE: YOUR CHILDHOOD

FOR THE LAST EXERCISE in determining your inheritance, let's get to the child-is-father-to-the-man part. This may be the useful way to find out the life that is most simple for you.

What made you cry when you were seven? Physical pain? Frustration? Fear? The failure to get the toys you wanted? Loneliness?

Can you think of your happiest moments when you were the same age?

What was your favorite childhood book? What is your favorite movie as an adult? Can you think of anything the two have in common?

What was your favorite game when you were seven? Was it a sport? Chess? Dolls? Capture the flag? Torturing plastic soldiers?

What is your favorite game today? Is it related in any way to the games you liked best when you were seven?

What were your greatest fears when you were seven? Today?

What was your most embarrassing moment as a child? Have you ever told someone about it? How did you feel while telling it? Is it a funny story or painfully revealing?

What got you in the most trouble when you were a kid? What got you in the most trouble in the past two years? Any pattern here?

What punishment did you hate most as a kid?

What is your favorite story about yourself as a child?

Which teachers meant most to you?

Who were your heroes as a child? What were the characteristics you most admired?

Who was your favorite relative? Why?

Was there a kid your age you looked up to? What was it about your friend that you admired the most? Are you a little embarrassed to remember this? Why?

Get a picture of yourself as a child; you at the age of seven would be ideal. What do you see? What does the picture have to do with the adult holding it?

FUNNELING THE DATA

A T THE END OF THIS CHAPTER we'll compare your biography with a new, improved version. First, though, let's establish some basic tendencies that help bring that picture of yourself into focus.

ADVANTAGES

What are your greatest strengths?

Friends
Words
Leadership
Mechanical ability
Morals and beliefs, and standing up for them
Athletics
Ability to withstand pain
Patience
Other

WEAKNESSES

Which of these are you worst at?

Friends
Words
Leadership
Mechanical ability
Morals and beliefs, and standing up for them
Athletics
Ability to withstand pain
Patience
Other

Think again of your main weaknesses. As you do, consider each of the following questions:

Which ones could you improve on, so they aren't weaknesses anymore? Which single weakness is the most easily fixed?

Which ones could you live with without feeling much the worse for them?

Which ones are you just plain stuck with, just can't be helped?

RISK TAKING

How true are the following statements for you?

My biggest regrets in life come from my failing to take risks and seize opportunities.

I'm a little too willing to jump into new things and not settle on something long term.

Sure, it's easy for you to tell me how to improve my life. You don't have my problems.

Better safe than sorry.

When I travel, I'd rather stay in a chain motel than an untried bed-and-breakfast.

Which of the statements above is *most* true for you?

Several years ago a Dartmouth student named Emily Hill got caught in a blizzard while on a bus tour in the mountains of China. Being an experienced outdoorswoman and the only passenger who could speak Cantonese, Emily helped lead the others to safety without serious injury, except for some pretty severe cases of frostbite. Two weeks later Emily was gored by a rhinoceros while hiking through Nepal's Royal Chitwan Park. As you might have guessed, Emily is a hardy young woman, and she recovered quickly. Within a week Jane Pauley of the *Today* show was interviewing Emily in Nepal and her relieved parents in Kansas City over a satellite link.

Emily later said the most interesting thing about her crises was the totally different reaction among friends of her parents in Kansas City and her fellow Dartmouth students. "See what happens when you let your daughter wander abroad?" her parents' friends said. Meanwhile, back on campus students were saying, "Man, I wish I'd had such a great experience!" And that leads to these questions:

Which reaction would your own be closest to?
Could you ever see yourself in Emily's situation?

Daniel Webster's Father Thought He Was the Laziest Boy He Had Ever Seen

GROWING UP ON A ROCKY FARM in New Hampshire, young Daniel would run off fishing at the earliest opportunity, leaving cows unmilked, stone walls unmended, gardens unweeded. As a U.S. senator he was notoriously lazy at committee work. Yet Webster produced a prodigious amount of correspondence, speeches, and unequaled legal argument. He was one of the most productive characters in American history.

Webster's secret: He knew what gave him energy and what drained it. Fishing gave him energy, and as soon as he could afford it, he bought a seaside farm in Massachusetts where he could fish whenever he had a vacation. Public speaking gave him energy, and he devoted enormous time to writing his greatest addresses. Argument gave him energy, and that was why he loved the law and sat enraptured whenever Senator Clay or Calhoun addressed the Senate.

Webster wasn't lazy. He was just choosy. We could do worse.

Moral: Pleasure has more stamina than duty.

What is the riskiest thing you have ever done? (Hint: It doesn't have to be physically dangerous. It could entail proposing a new idea, asking someone for a date, or speaking in front of a large crowd.) What exactly was at risk when you did it?

Suppose you are driving through your neighborhood when suddenly a car breaks down at the intersection in front of you. Traffic starts backing up behind you. What are you inclined to do first?

1. Talk to the driver and work out a plan.
2. Direct traffic.
3. Try to fix the broken car.
4. Go from car to car asking if one of them contains a mechanic.
5. Stay in your car until traffic can move again.

There are no right answers to these questions, except when you carry them out to their extremes. It is bad to be foolhardy. It is also bad to be controlled by your own fears. Between these extremes there is a lot of room for interpretation.

ENERGY SUPPLY

How true or false are the following statements for you?

Talking one-on-one with people makes me feel drained afterward, especially if we're disagreeing.

I feel a little charged up when I can check something off from a list of things I've had to do.

When I'm alone and concentrating on something—a memo, a plan, or a presentation—I feel as if I could work forever.

I'm at my best when I'm under pressure.

PRIDE

The early Puritans considered pride a sin, and the term "self-esteem" wasn't in their vocabulary. Pride is not a sin anymore. In a way that is too bad. Our forebears were taught to give God the credit for blessing them with any skill or attribute. If during a life of diligence and hard work they accomplished absolutely nothing and lived lives of poverty and misery, well, they didn't have themselves to blame. That's another luxury of the past most of us must do without. On the other hand, we can use our feelings of self-satisfaction as measures of the lives we most want to lead. Answer the following questions to see how dangerously humble you are:

What did you do over the past year that makes you proudest?

If a movie were to be made of your life, what would its title be?

List three things you did in the past that you're proudest of. What did you give up to achieve them? Were your achievements worth the sacrifice?

List the aspects of your life that make you proudest, in the following categories:

Family
Work
Athletics or physical activity
Crafts or hobbies
Community service
Romance
Friendship
Possessions and income
Other

DESIRES

Now we get to the crucial part of simple living: determining what you actually want to do.

Look at the pairs of opposites below and decide where you lie between each one. Take the pair "Company-Solitude." If you hang out with your friends every night and hate being alone, you should place yourself far over on the "Company" side. On the other hand, suppose you're pretty popular with your friends but like going on a solitary jog now and then. You might want to place yourself in the middle between "Company" and "Solitude." In the same way, place yourself somewhere in the continuum from "Noise" to "Silence," "Active" to "Sedentary," and so on.

Company	Solitude
Noise	Silence
Active	Sedentary
Responsibility	Independence
Caring	Dutiful
Variety	Sameness

Now think: What parts of your life are most important for you?

The respect of others
Family
Romance
Travel
The outdoors
Physical appearance
Friendships
Other

Think next: Which of those elements could most use improvement?
Ask yourself: Which of them is most easily improved?

And ask, finally: What would you be willing to give up to make the improvements?

- ✦ Time
- ✦ A quarter of your income
- ✦ A quarter of your family life

How much would you be willing to put at risk?

THE SUM TOTAL

HAVE YOU NOTICED how close you are to setting goals for yourself? Let's take a break from that and summarize all this reading you have been doing about yourself. In a bit you will describe your own "calling" as a basis for improvement.

Look at your favorite photo of yourself. Why do you like it? Has it flattered some part of you that you're proudest of? Has it nicely hidden some physical part you'd rather hide? Are you doing something you especially love? Are you with someone you love? Are you in a place that has special meaning for you? Does the picture represent a time of life that you remember fondly?

Describe yourself from these points of view:

1. Your lover
2. Your parents
3. Your kids
4. Your boss
5. Your employees
6. An attractive stranger

What makes you different from other people?

How are you like your astrological sign? How different?

Now look at the questions you chose *not* to answer. Why did you skip them? Did they simply look as if they would take too long, or are there questions in your life you'd just as soon avoid?

Just as important, which questions got the biggest reaction from you? Why? Were you surprised by any of your own responses?

Hang on to those thoughts. You may want to use them in a minute.

YOUR CALLING

IT IS NOW TIME TO DESCRIBE who you are and what you want as your calling. You have already collected data—taking the Shower Test, thinking about what you would do if you could retire immediately, listing your recent accomplishments, describing your seven-year-old self. Then you funneled the data, forming a picture of your strengths and weaknesses, the degree of risk you like to bear, what gets you charged up, what makes you proud, and what you most want.

Now it is time to translate this thinking into action. Think of yourself a year from now, as optimistically as you can. How does the picture change? Your calling might include:

Where you want to live

Whom you want to live with

What you want to do most of the day

What you want to do in your free time

What you would like to own

What you wish you looked like

Which of these changes is most important to you? Which are the least important? Which are the changes you can make most realistically, and which would be considerably more difficult? This just might be the time to pick up pen and paper. (You probably haven't so far, so stop complaining.) Draw yourself a chart that looks something like Mary's:

MARY'S PREFERENCES

CHANGE	DESIRABILITY	COST (TIME OR MONEY)	TIME IT WILL TAKE
Become noticed in my profession	Extremely high	High in time	Five years
Overcome my fear of public speaking	High	Low (but it sounds scary)	Two years
Create a home entertainment center	Moderate	High in money	Three years (to save the money)
Lose four pounds	High	Low (though I don't do diets well)	Four months
Learn Italian	Moderate to low, to be perfectly honest	High in time	Four years
Read good literature	High	High in time	Lifelong

Sometimes your preferences order themselves without your even trying. A change that is extremely desirable, involves little sacrifice of time or money, and can be accomplished quickly can take a high priority. As you can see from Mary's chart, however, the choices are usually not that easy. Still, some patterns emerge. Let's suppose Mary ranked the changes in order of the goals she wanted to start working on right away. She might list them in the following order, from "do immediately" to "put off until I win the lottery":

Overcome my fear of public speaking
Lose four pounds
Read good literature
Become noticed in my profession [she figures that overcoming her fear of public speaking gets her started on this goal]

The Hermit Who Got a Job

F OR ELEVEN YEARS Nathaniel Hawthorne wrote alone in his room in Salem, Massachusetts, seeing nobody. Then he moved to Boston, worked for a publishing house, and directed a customshouse. He married and became U.S. consul to Liverpool.

Hawthorne took stock of himself. He decided he was shy, but he wasn't crazy.

Moral: If a tendency becomes an obsession, then it is too extreme to be simple.

Create a home entertainment center [she begins to have doubts about the importance of this goal]

Learn Italian [*sure* she will, when Naples freezes over]

Mary figures she probably will take a crack at the first three goals right away. This is reasonable, but it will take some serious discipline. She will need:

+ Several ways to measure progress on each goal
+ Short-term targets to help her maintain her motivation
+ Extra time in her life, carved out from time-wasting habits she wants to break and from other daily activities she thinks she can quit
+ Good habits—i.e., habits that help her meet her goals

All these constitute the next several chapters. Like Mary, you are learning your calling and improving your opportunities. Already you are beginning to act like a good Yankee.

CHAPTER 4

Attempting Fate

*In which the reader converts desires
into goals that last forever*

T THIS POINT you may have many preferences but no solid
goals. Fine. The next step is to convert the preferences into
goals. As Thoreau said, "In the long run men hit only what
they aim at."

A goal is a preference with an education. It's taking your desires and
focusing them in a disciplined way. The Puritans knew about goals instinctively; their earthly duty was to take their circumstances and skills and
make something of them. We can do the same thing.

The Puritans could look ahead and see heaven, a goal that could really
get them motivated. Your own future might look less celestial. But there
is a trick to setting goals: The more deeply attached they are to your calling,
the more likely you are to achieve them.

IF YOU ARE WHAT YOU EAT, THEN DIET IS FATE

VERMONT-BASED *Eating Well* magazine made an interesting discovery about how people deal with goals. It once asked readers to send in stories about weight loss regimens that actually succeeded. The editors found a remarkably consistent pattern in the letters that came in. Almost every successful dieter recalled a kind of epiphany, "a point at which they decided once and for all to lose weight permanently."

For women, this critical point was the realization that their bodies did not match their self-images. The typical female dieter had a confrontation with herself in the mirror and decided that the blob in the size twelve dress simply wasn't the woman she knew. For most of the men, it was a medical crisis, a doctor telling them to diet or die. (It appears that men have fewer epiphanies in front of mirrors.)

Both sexes succeeded in losing weight over the long term because they attached their lives to this lifelong goal—literally in the men's case, figuratively in the women's (pun intended). All this should explain why nearly all New Year's resolutions, and 95 percent of all diets, do not work: They are attached to a date, not to your life.

Such resolutions are not entirely useless, however. They can be useful data for setting bigger goals, ones that become permanent parts of your life.

Let's list some resolutions and see where they lead.

Lose five pounds.
Learn French.
Travel.
Make more money.
Find a spouse.

Move to the country.
Become a hermit.
Do more community work.
Drink less.
Become a rock star.

How would any of these resolutions simplify your life? They probably wouldn't. But they could lead to some changes—new habits, new uses of time—that add up to simplicity. To do that, we need to take a closer look at each resolution.

Lose five pounds: Why would you want to lose five pounds?

+ If it's part of a larger goal to be healthier, then let's look at that larger goal. By cutting fat out of the diet, exercising, and eating smaller portions at mealtime, you probably could lose five pounds or more. Then the five-pound resolution serves as an interim measurement.
+ If you want to lose five pounds pretty quickly to fit into a bathing suit on your Florida vacation, fine. Just don't feel guilty when you gain the weight back. This kind of short-term goal doesn't simplify your life because it doesn't change your habits. But who's to argue against it?
+ Suppose you find the extra fat makes you feel and look older. You may be backing into another goal: to make your body match your self-impression. The best way to keep weight off permanently is to see the slimmer version of yourself as your *real* self. But why stop there? You probably want to look at other ways to bring your outward appearance down to your age: dress, hair, activities, and the like. (See Chapter 13 for more on bodily control.)

Learn French: What larger goal is implied by this resolution? Are you an avid traveler? Are you an intellectual who wants to read great works in their original tongue? Or do you simply feel inadequate when you order in a French restaurant? (It might be simpler to avoid French restaurants or at least the ones with snooty waiters.) In any case the larger goal should be linked with your view of yourself.

Travel: If you know you like to travel, then the question is simply how to afford the time and money. You need to weigh your wanderlust against other, competing preferences—a comfortable retirement, for example, or a challenging (and time-consuming) job. If travel is a consuming passion, then it can help lead you to other goals, such as a career that requires a lot of travel, or one that gives you considerable time off.

Make more money: As you have already seen, daydreaming about money is a great way to define your dreams. What would you do if you made twice the money you're making now? How could you do those things without the extra money? A 1994 poll by Roper Starch Worldwide for *Worth* magazine asked people how much they would need to earn a year to fulfill their dreams. The average answer: $102,200. Given that this was three times Americans' average household income, the poll adds up to a lot of unconsummated dreams. On the other hand, could some of them be fulfilled without the dough?

"Earning more money" is not the best of goals, in other words. But it can lead to some great ones.

Find a spouse: This resolution can be especially thorny because it requires a consenting partner. The cost of failure is great, and the spouse hunter puts rather a lot of pressure on dates. Nonetheless, a wish to get married can help lead you to more controllable goal setting. If you're just lonely, maybe you should look for companions, not a spouse. In a bit we'll deal with ways to set *targets* for measuring goals and how you can judge your degree of satisfaction.

Move to the country: Again the trick is to examine why this is your dream and then to ask if you can accomplish the same goals without the move. If you want to be close to the land, if you love the idea of waking up in a freezing house and trying to get the woodstove going, if you live for the day you can walk out your back door and head up a mountain, and if all these things are worth the sacrifice in career and money and convenience, then maybe you should prepare to move to the country. But if what you mostly want is quiet, a safe school for your kids, and a neighborhood where people know your name, you should seriously consider the alternatives: private school, a friendly co-op building, a bridge club, a soundproof den. Decide what is most important to you: the land itself or what it offers you. If it's the land, go for the land. If it's other attractions, you probably don't need to move to the country.

Become a hermit: Go on, admit it. The thought has crossed your mind, especially on your way to your umpty-umpth meeting. This is another useful daydream. It also makes a great idea for a vacation: Try being a temporary hermit for, say, a two-week vacation. Consider a retreat in a meditation center or monastery. Rent a cottage in Vermont's remote Northeast Kingdom. If you're an experienced backpacker, go on a "vision" quest, hiking alone and thinking about your life. When you return to work, your coworkers suddenly seem delightfully amiable.

Do more community work: Look into your motives. Are they sheer altruism? Do you like people to see you as a good person? Is there a cause that you burn to join? Or does a particular kind of work attract you, look like fun, promise some good friends? Fill in your dream with details. "Do more community work" is a vague resolution. "Work in the downtown homeless shelter" makes for more useful daydreaming. This is a goal you can research, something you can build your schedule and habits around.

Drink less: Does a two-beers-at-dinner habit give you a paunch that you'd rather not have? Then the goal should have more to do with the paunch than with the beers. Cut out one drink a night, eat less dessert, and start exercising. On the other hand, if you find yourself losing control at parties, or risking your marriage with nightly visits to the neighborhood bar, or driving after you've had several drinks, or feeling compelled to have a stiff one or two at lunch, then the drinking itself is a problem and possibly an addiction. We'll talk more about bad habits and addictions in the next chapter.

Become a rock star: It doesn't matter that you will never in a million years negotiate "Stairway to Heaven" on an electric guitar. Imagine yourself onstage in front of a jillion adoring fourteen-year-olds, or hopping to London on your private jet, or saying something outrageous on a late-night talk show. If any of this appeals greatly, ask yourself (in case you need to be reminded): Could I get it without being a rock star?

A mediocre saxophone player decided he liked appearing in front of big crowds and speaking on talk shows and jetting around the world. His musical skills made it unlikely he would ever go platinum. Instead, Bill Clinton got elected president of the United States. Some of the same desires, different goal.

ALL THAT GLITTERS IS NOT A GOAL

Y OU MIGHT WANT TO CONSIDER these four criteria to make sure your goal is a good one:

1. It should be achievable without a miracle or dumb luck. Deciding to win the lottery can make for a frustrating goal.

2. The idea of working toward your goal should get you excited or at least sound like fun. You are unlikely to say knowingly, "I think I'll torture myself for a few weeks and then quit after I lose my self-respect."

Make sure you're not saying that unconsciously. Your goal can be tough to meet, but if each step along the way sounds like an act of utter masochism, then you might think of a more attractive goal, one that fits you more closely.

3. The goal should be at the root of your desires. The best kind gets down to what is most basic about you. When you think of some way, large or small, that you want to change your life, ask: "Why do I want to do this?" Keep thinking, leading yourself from desire to desire, asking why? until you can answer: "I want to do this for its own sake. It will make me happier. It will match my vision of myself."

4. If your goal is basic enough, it should allow more than one measure for achieving it. Imagine for a moment that you're a forty-year-old weekend jogger with the notion of becoming a competitive age-group distance runner. You hardly dare admit it even to yourself, but your dream is to enter a marathon someday. In the meantime you set a yearlong goal to become a pretty good runner for your age. You decide that at the end of the year you should be able to run for an hour without stopping, you want to work up to four miles in less than forty minutes, you plan to enter one ten-kilometer race and finish it, and you hope to avoid hurting yourself.

A year later, after sticking fairly well to a three-runs-a-week schedule, you have several certifiable reasons to be proud of yourself. You can run for a whole hour. You are not quite down to a forty-minute four-miler, but you're making progress. You thrilled yourself by completing your first 10 K. And except for a little soreness in the Achilles tendon, you are injury free. Three out of four. Not too shabby.

Set interim targets to measure progress against your goal. Imagine, for example, that you want to learn to type so you can be more comfortable with computers. One of your measures of success is to be able to type fifty-five words per minute on a keyboard at the end of three months. Reasonable targets might include typing fifteen words per minute within two weeks, twenty-five within a month, forty-five within two months, and on up to fifty-five. (Other measures of typing success, such as accuracy and skill in composing letters, can be similarly targeted.)

The notion of multiple measurements can work in any other area of goal setting. Suppose your objective is to earn enough money to buy a little cabin in Maine. You tell yourself that in five years you want your income to be up 10 percent, not counting inflation. Or you hope to save forty thousand dollars over that period. Or you want to find a camp that costs a lot less than forty grand. Succeeding at any one of these measures could get you the camp in Maine.

Try this strategy in setting goals for work, for family life, for learning a new skill, for fixing up your house.

With most goals, the hardest part is knowing when to be satisfied. Targets help tell you when enough is enough. Some of the happiest people you meet have greatly simplified their lives by being skilled at contentment.

FOUR OF NEW ENGLAND'S MOST CONTENTED PEOPLE . . .

NORMAN ROCKWELL, who talked the way he painted, once said: "I have the best of all possible worlds and the best of all possible lives." He added: "I do ordinary people in everyday situations, and that's about all I do."

Joseph H. Choate was once asked who he would prefer to be if he could not be himself. "Mrs. Choate's second husband," he answered. Mrs. Choate's opinion was not recorded.

"My greatest skill has been to want but little," bragged Henry David Thoreau. When he was still living in a shack on Walden Pond, he wrote: "I intend to build me a house which will surpass any on the main street in Concord in grandeur and luxury, as soon as it pleases me as much and will cost me no more than my present one."

Benjamin Franklin congratulated himself as an old man that he had only three fatal diseases.

. . . AND ONE OF THE LEAST

Mark Twain was once bankrupted by his failure to know when enough was enough. In 1880 he invested in a typesetting machine invented by James W. Paige, an engineer at the Colt Arms Factory in Connecticut. Twain's original share was $2,000. He put in another $3,000 for improvements. A few years later Twain had invested a total of $13,000 when Paige told him that another $30,000 would easily finish the job. It was already the fastest automatic typesetter ever invented. Paige wanted to make it even better. By 1888 Twain was in for $80,000, but the machine was even more miraculous: It set type, adjusted the spacing, and even justified the margins, all automatically and at an unheard-of speed. But Paige thought it could stand some more improvements before it went on the market. He was still jazzing it up when the company went bankrupt. So did Twain, who was out $190,000. The typesetting machine was too complicated ever to work successfully, and Mark Twain spent the rest of his life writing and lecturing around the world, to pay off his creditors.

Contentment is a skill. It comes from setting the right targets and sticking to them.

USING ARTILLERY TO SATISFY

How do you acquire the skill of satisfaction while avoiding Mark Twain's kind of mistake? It all comes down to target setting. We recommend the following technique, borrowed from the military.

Suppose you actually find a lovely little camp in central Maine. Sure, the cabin is falling off its rock foundation, the privy needs a new hole, the lake is small, and the place is on a little peninsula accessible only by water. The good news is, it's up for sale and you think you can talk the owner down to a mere $30,000. Now is the time to bring in the artillery.

No, we don't mean a city lawyer. The artillery is for you. Ever since people started throwing things at each other, they have been using two principles of gunnery.

The first is easy to understand: **The bigger the target, the easier it is to hit.**

The second principle is: **When you miss, consider it information, not a failure.** It works like this: When you lob at a target, aim at the target, but don't expect to hit it right away. Chances are you'll be a little short, or a little long, or a little to the left or right. If your shot falls short, aim longer next time. If the next shot is too long, place your aim between the first and the second shot. Artillery officers do not call this bad shooting, they call it bracketing. Medieval soldiers used it with catapults. Cannon crews used it in the Revolutionary War. You can use it for your own aims: to buy a camp in Maine, get in shape, or just organize your life.

Let's go back to the fishing camp. You're beginning to fall in love with that little broken-down place. But then you begin to suffer from the classic buyer's anxiety: What if the owner won't sell it to you for a low price? What if he sells it to someone else before you can raise the extra money? Now is the time to fall back on the two artillery principles. First, consider a bigger target, such as every appropriate camp for sale within a half-hour radius of the first one. If you bid on three places instead of one, you are more likely to have a bid accepted. "Target acquired," as they say in the military.

But suppose none of your bids is accepted. You still have principle number two to fall back on: A miss is a source of information. Maybe you're looking at the wrong area; research might reveal a more isolated part of Maine where camps are cheaper. Maybe you need to stop looking until you've saved more money. You could consider sharing the cost of a cabin with a friend. Or you might set your sights a little lower, buying a much cheaper camp without the waterfront.

Artillery Bracketing

---><><---

WHEN YOU SET TARGETS to measure progress toward a goal, do what artillery officers do: Bracket your shots by aiming both high (your reasonable ideal) and low (the minimal effort you can get away with). Here are some examples:

Goal: To own a quiet retreat for relaxation and contemplation.
Target: Buy a camp in Maine.
High shot: A waterfront cabin that you buy within the year.
Low shot: A purchase price of thirty thousand dollars.
Range: You would be satisfied with a likable Maine cabin for thirty to forty thousand dollars within five years.
Plan: Search first for waterfront cabins in the thirty-thousand-dollar range.

(continued on next page)

Goal: To look as young as you think you are.

Target (along with finding a more flattering hairstyle and running three miles without collapsing)**:** Lose weight permanently.

High shot: Lose five pounds in a month.

Low shot: Cut out one dessert a week.

Range: You would be satisfied to lose two to five pounds in six months.

Plan: If you don't lose any weight after cutting out one dessert a week for one month, start jogging and changing your diet.

Goal: To enjoy your work more.

Target: Find a good job.

High shot: Within four months, get offered a new job with more responsibility, more creative tasks, and flexible hours.

Low shot: Get new responsibilities at work.

Range: You would be satisfied to get new tasks within a year, at either your current job or a new one.

Plan: Update your résumé; start researching other jobs; put out feelers; talk to your boss about your future in the company.

You have not failed—yet—to reach your goal. You have simply shot too long (seeking too fancy a cabin for your budget) or too short (arming yourself with too small a budget). This is information, not failure.

It helps to bracket your target when you plan the goal. First aim high: What would be the best realistic outcome you could hope for? Then aim low: What would be the minimum you would be happy with? What would be the greatest cost you could bear? Then work for something in between.

Sometimes you will find yourself coming up with targets before you even devise a goal. That's fine; one of the easiest ways to establish a goal is to back into it, to discover it lurking behind a decision. Think about the major choices you have made in the past few years. Whether you regretted those decisions or not, the side you came down on tells something about yourself. That is what happened to Rebecca. She applied for a job and discovered a life's goal.

REBECCA CHARTS HERSELF

R EBECCA LIVES IN MASSACHUSETTS. Some years ago she worked as a supervisor in a small software company. She walked to the office and went home every day for lunch. She loved her work, but her career wasn't going anywhere. She wanted a bigger working environment, one where she could learn from other people and improve her technical skills. She applied and got an offer for a job at a large computer company in Boston, an hour's bus ride away. She was excited about the prospects, but she wasn't sure it was the right decision. So she made a chart.

If charting seems bothersome and un-Yankee-like, keep in mind that the Puritans were masters at the craft. Early New Englanders constantly set up tests for themselves, experiments to confirm their heavenly destination. Their diaries are full of checked-off lists. Benjamin Franklin took charting to an art form. At the age of twenty-two he decided to become morally perfect. "I wished to live without committing any fault at any time," he recalled as an old man. But, he wrote sadly, "I soon found I had undertaken a task of more difficulty than I had imagined." Taking a sheet of paper, he listed thirteen virtues, ranging from temperance to humility, and then put down a mark for every day of the week he violated one of them. "Chastity" ended up covered with the marks of failure. He never did master that one; one of his sons, born out of wedlock, became governor of New Jersey. "On the whole," said Franklin, "I never arrived at the perfection I had been so ambitious of obtaining." Still, he ended up "a better and a happier man than I otherwise should have been if I had not attempted it." He was not as easily discouraged as the rest of us mortals.

Rebecca, being no Franklin, created a much less ambitious chart. She was not after moral perfection, but the right job. To compare the benefits of each job she was considering, she assigned points on a scale from 1 to 5. Her chart looked like this:

SHOULD I ACCEPT THE OFFER?

Benefit	Present job	Offered job
Career		
Prestige	2	4
Future employability	3	5
Mentors	1	4
Management skills	4	2
Enjoyment		
Nice office	4	3
Secretary	3	0
Travel	3	4
Independence	3	2
Daily challenge	3	5
Convenience		
Weekends free	0	5
Commute	5	1
Home for lunch	3	0
Flexible hours	5	3
Easy shopping	3	4

Note that Rebecca assigned only a "3" to "Home for lunch," even though this benefit applied only to her current job. She did this to assign less weight to lunch than she did to more important factors, such as "Commute" and "Flexible hours."

Now she added up the totals:

BENEFIT	PRESENT JOB	OFFERED JOB
Career	10	15
Enjoyment	16	14
Convenience	16	13
Total	42	42

"Well," Rebecca thought when she saw the totals, "*that* was a useless exercise." It was a dead heat. So much for the charting method of decision making. She considered flipping a coin—or, worse, calling her mother for advice.

But when she looked at the charts again, she found them more interesting. Her current job was probably more fun, and freer of hassles, than the other one would be. But the new job would clearly boost her career, and that was why she had applied in the first place. She thought about how she had given less weight to being home for lunch than she had to the commute. "Why don't I apply a weight to *each* of the benefits?" she asked. (Like many people faced with a big decision, she had begun talking to herself.)

Convenience was easily the least important benefit. Enjoyment was, oh, twice as important as convenience. And career? She thought hard and decided that given her long-term ambition, her career deserved twice the weight that daily enjoyment did. She scribbled these values on her chart and multiplied the "Career" totals by 4, "Enjoyment" by 2, and "Convenience" by 1. Her chart now looked like this:

BENEFIT	PRESENT JOB	OFFERED JOB
Career (x 4)	40	60
Enjoyment (x 2)	32	28
Convenience (x 1)	16	13
Total	88	101

The winner was perfectly clear. She took the new job and lived happily ever after.

Actually that's a lie. The commute turned out to be worse than she thought, and her new employers were reluctant to accept her ideas. She stayed less than two years and moved to western Massachusetts, where she started her own small software company.

Given the information she had at the time, she made a good choice. It just didn't turn out as well as she had hoped. The charts kept Rebecca from blaming herself. They also did something even more important: They allowed Rebecca to balance the importance of her career growth against other life goals, inspiring a series of thoughts that led to her starting her own company.

Decisions make some of the best mirrors. Rebecca's chart was better than any portrait. (She's a computer person. To her, a number is worth a thousand pictures.)

Rebecca has something in common with all the greatest New Englanders: *the sense that her goal is predestined.* "I realized, looking at those charts, that I was meant to be this ambitious," she says.

And that leads us back to one of our central morals: **A well-chosen goal looks a lot like fate.**

APPLYING YOURSELF

I T IS NOT ENOUGH to choose what you want and then assume that newly improved life will automatically follow. Like Rebecca, you should apply for it as well. We'll go through several steps to write résumés for life. Let's bring forward all the mental data you assembled in the previous chapter. If you are willing to commit yourself to one of the objectives you dreamed up, then you have already set yourself a goal.

Suppose it was to get a new job. What is the first thing you might do, especially if it were in an office? (Okay, what is the first thing you would do after you stopped imagining the things you would say to your current boss when you quit?) You probably would write a résumé.

This technique can work for noncareer goals as well. Suppose what you really want to do is lose weight and get in shape. Think up a résumé with which you "apply" for getting into shape. For "Objective," write: "To get less fat and stay that way." Below that, list your dieting and nutritional experience in the most positive way: the times you've lost weight; the exercise programs you have been through; the periods in your life when you looked the best; your greatest moments of self-control. (Again, it's not necessary to write the résumé down; just go over the objective and qualifications in your head.)

Sure, all the positive stuff you put in your résumé doesn't begin to give the whole picture. But remember, this is a résumé, not a signed confession. If you were applying for a job, would you feel compelled to reveal that you ate a crayon in kindergarten and got sick?

Winston Churchill had the right attitude. In his famous history of England, Churchill wrote magisterially about King Arthur, who may or may not actually have lived. "It is all true, or it ought to be," declared the statesman turned historian. Churchill would have written a heck of a résumé. He never let the facts get in the way of the truth. His declaration should

Job Résumé

Daniel Webster
c/o Office of the Secretary of State
The White House
Washington, D.C.

Objective
To be elected president of the United States

Experience
Secretary of state under three presidents
United States senator from Massachusetts
United States representative from Massachusetts
United States representative from New Hampshire
Practicing attorney

Accomplishments
Delivered more than four thousand speeches
Argued more than two hundred cases before the Supreme Court
Twice averted war with Great Britain
Opened diplomatic relations with Japan

Education
Read for the law in New Hampshire
Graduated from Dartmouth College near top of class

Fair health, married, enjoy hunting and fishing

References available upon request

Life Résumé

Daniel Webster
Marshfield
Massachusetts

Objective
To get rid of my nineteenth-century paunch and live long enough to be elected president of the United States

Experience
Was exposed early to involuntary dieting

Walked miles to school in New Hampshire climate

Showed stamina in delivering four thousand speeches, most lasting more than two hours

Accomplishments
Once took a trip without my portable bar

Have shown indomitable will with each goal

Walk every day into market for groceries

For reference you could talk to my first wife, but I outlived her.

be the motto of all introspective Yankees (unless he or she is writing a résumé that actually will be seen by a prospective employer, in which case the facts—the positive ones—are pretty important).

We're not just talking careers and dieting here, of course. Set as a goal the one part of your life that you most want to improve and that seems the most improvable: learning a language, getting your real estate license, doubling the time you spend with the kids, reading a good book every month, becoming a better lover, moving to some place you'd most want to live, learning to pray or meditate.

But this is not a diet book, or a time-management book, or a job-hunting book, or an enrich-your-relationship-discover-your-past-and-find-God book. This is a book about simplifying your life. To do that, you have already started thinking about your whole self and how you might gain control over it. You have thought about the advantages early New Englanders had and how you might acquire some of them yourself. You have started thinking about the choices you want to make. You may even have started making some of those choices, to move toward what you most want out of your life. Now let's figure out how to get those things for yourself.

CHAPTER 5

The Virtuous Weed

In which is revealed the simplifier's chief ally:
the obstacle in the way of a goal

I N 1622 A GROUP OF NEW COLONISTS arrived in Plymouth, Massachusetts, stretching an already limited food supply. Governor William Bradford wrote shamefacedly in his diary that the only meal he and the other hosts could provide was lobster. Today the critters go for as much as eight dollars a pound. Back in Bradford's time they would pile up onshore after a storm and stink the place up, causing major disposal problems. They were like weeds.

A weed, said Ralph Waldo Emerson, is a "plant whose virtues have not yet been discovered." Any gardener knows that a weed has its good points. If nothing else, it can tell what wants to grow on a plot. If left in the right place, it can help hold in moisture and soil. A good gardener doesn't merely throw a weed away; she uses it to her advantage.

Weeds of the Rich and Famous

✦ One hectic day in 1933 Ruth Wakefield, owner of the Toll House Inn in Whitman, Massachusetts, found herself too busy to melt chocolate for her butter dewdrop cookies. So she invented the chocolate chip cookie by accident. She cut large slabs of chocolate into pieces and dropped them into the batter, hoping they would melt in the oven. They didn't. Having no time to start over, she served them as "chocolate crunch cookies."

✦ Fifteen-year-old Chester Greenwood of Farmington, Maine, was missing all the fun. His friends were out skating on the town pond, and his parents had given him a brand-new pair of skates. But Chester's cold-sensitive ears kept him housebound by turning blue whenever he went outside. He got his mother to sew fur onto a doubly looped piece of wire, which he hooked on to a bowler hat, thus inventing the world's first earmuffs. He died a millionaire at the age of seventy-nine, having made Farmington the earmuff capital of the world.

✦ If a few riveters at the Fore River Shipyard in Quincy, Massachusetts, had been more honest, James J. Kilroy might have died a mere mortal. During World War II it was Kilroy's job to put a chalk mark next to every hole filled by the riveters, who were paid by the rivet. Some of them would erase the check marks to get paid twice. "One day," Kilroy's widow recalled when *Yankee®* magazine interviewed her in 1970, "just before he was going off duty, Jim heard his foreman ask one of these dishonest riveters if Kilroy had been there. When the man said no, my husband was furious, because he knew he'd already chalked that man's rivets. So he took his chalk and wrote 'KILROY WAS HERE' in letters too large and too bold to erase." From then on he wrote "Kilroy Was Here" next to every rivet. The ships went to sea bearing Kilroy's name all over the place. And "Kilroy Was Here" became a motto for the worldwide presence of the American military.

✦ When Fannie Farmer was a teenager in Medford, Massachusetts, she became seriously ill and was disabled for life. She turned to cooking and made it a science, encouraging accurate measurement and quality control. The *Fannie Farmer Cookbook,* first published in 1896 as *The Boston Cooking-School Cook Book,* couldn't find a publisher until Farmer offered to pay for the printing herself. The book became one of the greatest bestsellers of all time and is still in print.

✦ In 1876 Dr. Augustin Thompson of Lowell, Massachusetts, concocted Moxie Nerve Food to relieve "paralysis, softening of the brain, and insanity," along with "brain and nervous exhaustion, loss of manhood, imbecility and helplessness." The stuff sold pretty well. Thompson then created Beverage Moxie Nerve Food by adding soda water. The problem was, Beverage Moxie tasted terrible. So Thompson employed an old belief of New Englanders: If you don't enjoy it, it must be good for you. He dressed a respectable-looking man in a physician's white coat and had him urge people to "learn to drink Moxie." Throughout the twenties the beverage outsold Coca-Cola as America's favorite soft drink. You can still buy it in parts of New England.

✦ The man who inspired the Jules Verne novel *The Tour of the World in Eighty Days* was a Bostonian promoter named George Francis "Express" Train. In 1870 he went on a global tour to publicize completion of the Union Pacific Railroad. His trip actually took him eighty days plus one month (he spent the month in Paris helping out the Communards). Train

(continued on next page)

went on to beat his own record twice more. He also took time to be a successful businessman, builder of English street railways, radical advocate of women's suffrage, and candidate for president of the United States. His politics got him thrown into fifteen jails during his lifetime. "I have used prisons well," he said. "They have been schools to me, where I have reflected, and learned more about myself . . . and from them have launched many of my most startling and useful projects and innovations."

✦ L. L. Bean's first Maine hunting shoes were duds. The stitching came out of the rubber bottoms, causing them to separate from the leather tops. Bean earned lasting mail-order fame by returning every cent of the first order, a loss of $350. "Nobody ever won an argument with a customer," he said. That adage became the central wisdom of one of the most successful catalog businesses in history.

Moral: If you're lucky, you too can be blessed with a worthy obstacle.

HELPFUL OBSTACLES

THE BARRIERS THAT STAND IN THE WAY of your desires—your personal handicaps, your fears, your repeated failures, external factors, the odds against you—all have their uses:

✦ As information about yourself and your goal
✦ As pathfinders to help you fine-tune your life's direction
✦ As the very means of achieving your goal

And on top of all the other benefits:
✦ As a great way to lower other people's expectations

Let's start with the expectations-lowering part since that's the easiest. (One tenet of simplicity is to do first what is easy.)

You might want to share your goals with other people; the risk of embarrassment can be a great motivator. Or your goal may have been set in part by another person, such as a boss. In any case, set public expectations as low as possible; then exceed them as much as you can. Well-run hotels use this principle. Call room service, and it will tell you that your meal will come "in twenty to thirty minutes." But it intends to deliver within fifteen to twenty minutes. If it meets its own target, you're pleasantly surprised. If it misses, it's still on the schedule it gave you. Similarly, a good catalog company will set a generous deadline when it estimates delivery of your package. When you lower expectations, you cut yourself some slack. When you exceed expectations, you look like a hero. That is the wonderful thing about the obstacles that you face on your way to a goal. You're usually better off when you overcome them than if the obstacles were never there.

HOW TO CLASSIFY AN OBSTACLE

OBSTACLES CAN ALSO OFFER some important data for your own purposes. But you have to know how to read them. We mentioned earlier the most common barriers to accomplishing a goal:

- Personal handicaps (including fear or a lack of motivation on your part)
- External factors
- The odds against success
- Your own failed attempts to meet the goal

You have four choices with each type of obstacle: You can back down from your goal (this isn't necessarily a bad thing, as you shall see). You can overcome the obstacle somehow. You can figure out a way around it. Or you can use it as a means toward your goal. To make your choice, you should examine your obstacles closely. Are they permanent barriers? Will they go away by themselves if you wait a bit? If you can overcome them, will you succeed? Is the goal worth the effort?

High People with Low Expectations

✦ Paul Revere's first newspaper ad in the Boston *Gazette,* September 19, 1768, offered custom false teeth. Revere wrote that they looked natural and allowed "Speaking to all Intents." He did not claim that you could chew with them.

✦ Newspaper editor Horace Greeley was once asked what he called a successful lecture. "When more folks stay in than go out," Greeley replied.

✦ The New England Patriots had a long tradition of losing football games, but they were especially bad when Bill Parcells took over as coach in 1993. During his first year with the team it still had a losing season, but fans were thrilled that it had a few wins. The next year the Patriots actually made it to the play-offs. They got knocked off in the first game. Did New Englanders lament their lost hopes for the Super Bowl? Not on your life! They declared Parcells the best coach in the history of the world. In two short seasons he had taken the team from the cellar to, well, pretty high.

Moral: In lowering expectations, you turn disadvantages into advantages.

For illustration, let's consider Mary, who listed her preferences at the end of Chapter 3. She has chosen three goals that could in various ways simplify her life: to overcome her fear of public speaking, to lose four pounds (and keep them off), and to read good literature. She listed other preferences but decided that she shouldn't complicate her life by attempting to simplify to excess.

Before we get to the obstacles, we should ask how her goals lead to simple living. Wouldn't the effort count as a lot of extra bother? Mary's answer is that these goals should help *eliminate* some of the bother. She is rising in the advertising profession but finds that her terror of speaking in front of people is holding her back. She wants to lose some weight because she is tired of seeing a slightly misshapen person in the mirror. The Mary who steps out of the shower in the morning is not the Mary she knows; that's complication enough for her. Finally, she wouldn't admit this to anybody, but one of her motives for reading literature is pretty close to the one for losing weight: She finds herself a little less interesting when alone with her thoughts than she used to be and fears that the Mary she loves is becoming a bit shallow.

She lists the obstacles in the way of each goal:

Public speaking. Lack of motivation and time are the biggest barriers. She looks into acting lessons, considers hiring a speech coach, calls the local Toastmasters club. These alternatives gall her; she just can't see herself doing any of them. She prices some video cameras, thinking she might try taping herself in private. But she never gets around to buying one.

It occurs to Mary that she just doesn't see herself as a public speaker and that she should consider other ways of advancing herself professionally. She decides to compromise, agreeing to lead small meetings in the hope that she'll get used to it. She also buys herself a pocket tape recorder and starts dictating her letters. The practice can't hurt, she figures.

Will all this eliminate her fear? Probably not, but then, Mary is pretty sure she will always be anxious in front of a crowd. She can't eliminate that obstacle; she can just reduce it a bit. Should she feel like a weenie for failing to tackle the problem head-on? Not unless she enjoys belittling herself. Besides, she has learned something about herself, not a bad goal in its own right.

Losing weight. Here Mary knows exactly what the obstacle is. She adores chocolate. When she was younger, her body processed the fat and sugar pretty well, and she could maintain a reasonable weight even while eating chocolates in front of the TV every night. Since she turned thirty, she finds that her thighs are not quite so forgiving. If she can ditch the candy, she can respect herself in the mirror. But Mary just can't imagine a life without chocolate. So again she compromises. She limits her candy eating to the weekend, changes her television-watching habits to avoid temptation, and buys an exercise video for a ten-minute leg routine every morning.

This discipline becomes habit for Mary after a few months, and her thighs show their appreciation. This is not to say that she unfailingly keeps herself from weekday chocolate binges. Mary is no saint. But occasional lapses do not prevent her from her goal of losing weight; they just delay it a bit.

Reading. The biggest obstacle here is time. Mary decides to cut out half an hour of television before bed and spend the time reading. (This happens also to be when her craving for chocolate is strongest.) Occasionally, when she just doesn't feel like reading, she keeps the television on. But more and more she finds it difficult to fall asleep without a half hour or so of quietly turning pages.

Moral: The most achievable goals bring you back to yourself.

Mary's goals for losing weight and reading became natural appendages or parts of her life. Her public-speaking goal comes harder because she doesn't see herself as being a speaker. It's an appendage that does not attach easily.

Maybe it never will. But there is a technique Mary could use to try to change that mute impression of herself. It entails getting her head into training.

THE MIND BARRIER

A S MARY'S EXAMPLE SHOWS, one of the most intractable barriers to achieving a goal is the failure to believe you're capable. The Puritans saw self-doubt as a temptation of the devil. A lack of confidence showed a lack of faith, a sign that a soul was hell-bound.

Athletes leap the mind barrier with a skill called visualizing, a way of learning to believe in yourself. Olympians have proved its effectiveness. You can get into the habit of visualizing to attach yourself to your own goals.

One of the world's best visualizers is John "Morty" Morton, a former Olympic biathlon competitor and coach. When he was in his late forties, Morty decided to become the nation's top cross-country skier for his age. He spent a year working on his goal, and he met it. Morty quit his job and used his savings to compete all over the United States and even Europe. When he was done, he wrote a book, appropriately titled *Don't Look Back*, to advise and inspire other middle-aged athletes. Now in his sixth decade, he looks thirty, tops. He runs up mountains better than most college-age athletes. Yet he seems like a pretty laid-back guy. Maybe this attitude comes from the big sauna he built himself, heated with wood he cuts from his own trees in Thetford, Vermont. But a lot of his youthfulness is in his head. Morty visualizes young.

Visualization is nothing more than the disciplined imagination of success. A downhill skier stands at the top of a slope, eyes closed, skiing the course in her mind. A runner imagines the gun going off again and again and each time pictures himself breaking the tape ahead of everyone else. "The mind holds the key to achievements far beyond the generally accepted level," says Morty, who ought to know.

Visualizing is pretty simple, but that doesn't make it easy. Morty says it takes practice and mental conditioning, the way a sport takes physical training. Here are some tips, most of them interpreted from his book and applied to simple living.

✦ **It's hard (on you) to be humble.** If we do something well, we should be the first to admit it to ourselves—though not necessarily to others, of course. Yankees hate to brag—at least of themselves.

✦ **It's good to think about the future, so long as that future seems bright.** "For most of us it seems easier to imagine the worst-case scenario than the best case," Morty says. He attributes this trait to the Puritan ethic, but as we have seen, we shouldn't blame the Puritans. They imagined a worst-case scenario for everybody else, while keeping optimism to themselves. Not a bad strategy.

✦ **Turn obstacles into stepping-stones.** What seem to be disadvantages to some people are advantages to others. When it rains before a ski race, Morty looks up cheerfully and says, "Good! I'm a mudder!"

A pessimist acquires a self-centered boss and curses her fate. A visualizer thinks, "I know how to handle egotists," and imagines herself using this new supervisor as leverage to get herself promoted up and out of the department.

+ **Forgive yourself any temporary failure.** The Puritans saw their mistakes as exceptions that proved the rule, as we shall soon see. Follow their example.

+ **Constantly imagine yourself having met your goal.** Do you want to get a night school business degree? Picture yourself, in detail, devising market strategies for your employer, using your hard-earned knowledge long before you've actually earned it. Do you want a different job? Picture yourself in it. Morty says to use all your senses. Smell the carpet; hear the sound of the laser printer ejecting your latest spreadsheet; see your mahogany desk; feel the expensive flannel of your suit. You can picture yourself internally, looking out at your new improved world, or externally, as if watching yourself in a videotape. Try it both ways, though Morty claims the internal version gets better results.

+ **Attach yourself to someone who seems a little better.** Morty would "lock on" to a racer who passed him, hanging on to this faster racer's pace and looking for an opportunity to repass. We can do this outside sports. As Chapter 8 shows, the people we lock on to are called mentors.

+ **On the other hand, don't get fixated on the competition.** Morty imagines himself as an artist in front of an empty canvas. Every race is an opportunity to paint a masterpiece. "What any other artists do is totally irrelevant," he says. "The canvas I face is mine alone." What a great way to see a goal: as a work of art.

John Morton links this thinking habit with his goal of becoming a top age-group athlete. If you set the right goals, habits can take you a long way toward them, without much thought, and that, after all, is the whole point of a habit.

Noble Failures

→ Benjamin Franklin's famous kite experiment does not seem to have done him any harm. But he nearly killed himself trying to execute the Christmas turkey. He was holding both electrical wires in one hand when he touched a piece of metal, unwittingly turning himself into a conductor. After a flash and an explosion Franklin went into convulsions. No one knows what happened to the turkey. The inventor continued his electrical experiments after he recovered.

→ When John Ledyard dropped out of Dartmouth College in 1773, he returned home to Connecticut by hollowing out a tree log and paddling this homemade canoe down the Connecticut River. Impressed into the British Navy, he sailed with Captain James Cook to Hawaii and watched the indignant islanders butcher the explorer. In 1785, during a visit to Paris, he met American Ambassador to France Thomas Jefferson. Eighteen years before the Lewis and Clark Expedition, Jefferson supported Ledyard's idea on how to explore the American West. The plan was to travel across Europe and Russia, sail to the American west coast, and trek eastward. Ledyard got to within some five hundred miles of Russia's Pacific coast before Empress Catherine, thinking him a spy, had him arrested and dumped on the Polish border. Ledyard ended up that same year in Cairo planning to explore the African interior. While taking an emetic to soothe his nerves—it had been a rough year—he vomited so violently that he burst a blood vessel and died on the spot. Jefferson wrote later, "Thus failed the first attempt to explore the western part of our Northern continent." Nonetheless, in all his failure to finish anything, Ledyard managed to explore on foot more land than anyone else of his century.

+ Charles Goodyear was perpetually in debt and spent much of his time as a young man in debtors' prison. Then he heard that rubber manufacturers were suffering from their material's propensity to melt in hot weather. He could make a fortune if he could find a means of vulcanizing rubber—making it stronger and more flexible. His home in New Haven stank with the smell of cooked rubber. When he went to debtors' prison, he continued his experiments there. Then, in 1839, he was boiling rubber and sulfur on his brother-in-law's stove in Woburn, Massachusetts, when he dropped some of the stuff on the stove. The cooled rubber was—shazam!—vulcanized. It took him five years to get a patent, but by then his process was being pirated all over the place. In 1852 Goodyear fought a court battle in New Jersey, represented by Secretary of State Daniel Webster, who won the case but charged a fortune for the effort. When Goodyear died in 1860, he was two hundred thousand dollars in debt.

+ Richard Jordan Gatling of Hartford, Connecticut, was the son of a North Carolina inventor. In 1861, obsessed with the notion that a hugely destructive machine could be horrible enough to end all wars, he designed a gun with eight to ten barrels that revolved on an axis. The Gatling gun worked beautifully, except in its original peaceful purpose. Gatling went on to invent a tool that was more overtly peaceful, a motorized plow.

Moral: Some of the most accomplished people are those with the courage to fail.

ON SINNING AND FORGIVENESS

There are two basic problems with setting goals:

1. You might fail to meet them.
2. You might meet them.

The trouble with meeting a goal is the temptation to go on permanent vacation, to lose the incentive that the goal gave you in the first place. Suppose you "acquired" a target of losing five pounds. You already look younger! You've met your goal! You reward yourself with a chocolate cake and forget about dieting. Don't mistake a target—a temporary measure of progress—for a long-term goal. Losing five pounds is not the same as becoming permanently thin. The best goals are permanent ones.

Missing your targets, on the other hand, might not be such a bad thing. Suppose that instead of losing weight over a month, you gained it. You're going in the wrong direction! You're a sinner, headed for diet hell! One hot fudge sundae, and you've blown your diet. An evening in front of the television, and you've lost your plan to read a dozen books a year. A night out bowling is a betrayal of your resolution to learn a foreign language, or rewrite your résumé, or volunteer at a soup kitchen. We see these little side steps from our goals as permanent, irretrievable sins, proof of our inescapable fallibility. You curse the Puritans for burdening your culture with so much guilt.

But should you be blaming the Puritans? They believed you couldn't earn your way to heaven. Your behavior on earth was just an outward indication of whether you were destined for heaven or hell. If you were venal or lazy, that was the way God made you; you were one of the unfortunates doomed to inherit Adam's original sin. If, on the other hand, you were thrifty, honest, and hardworking, you were clearly one of the elect, one of God's chosen even before birth.

Needless to say, this belief made for some nervous moments on deathbeds. On the other hand, a Puritan who was convinced he was one of the elect didn't have to worry about straying from his goals. He plodded sturdily (if in something less than a straight line) toward sainthood because his success was predetermined. Who was he to second-guess his Maker? You would think this made Puritans a pretty somber lot, constantly checking to see if their moral flies were open. This is in fact the case. Still, their diaries show they could tell a joke, and to judge from records of alcohol consumption, they didn't hold back at a party. The Puritans knew how to sin properly. A little petty straying didn't mean you weren't perfect, for a human. This may be inconsistent philosophy, but it was wise living.

Contrast this attitude with our own. We slip a little in our pursuit of goals and think we're doomed from ever meeting them. If only we could be as forgiving about it as the Puritans!

We also have to believe ourselves capable of meeting our goals. This makes us able to allow a small detour now and then. So what if you gained weight in the first month of a diet plan? You've missed the target, not the goal. A month is a short stretch of your life. Maybe your plan was unrealistic. Maybe it will take different habits, less food, more exercise. Maybe you haven't yet made your goal an appendage of your life. Maybe you're not *supposed* to weigh that little. That missed target is valuable information, not eternal damnation.

CHAPTER 6

Lodes of Time

Regarding an unearthed treasure of simplicity: the ill-used hour

I T IS ALL WELL AND GOOD to talk about mental attitude, but even the most positive frame of mind isn't going to give you time off from your job or do the shopping while you pursue a simpler life. Remember the question asked in Chapter 3: What would you do if you had an extra hour in the day, or day in the week, or week in the year? That may sound impossible, but windfalls do come occasionally. Have you ever come across some unexpected cash while cleaning the house? Wouldn't it be great if you could find time in the same way? Actually you can. You just need to do some weeding, to root out pockets of time.

One such time pocket arises out of our own good nature. Much of our day-to-day clutter—a frantic schedule here, a small conflict there—comes from our having said yes too many times. We tend to take on time-eating social and family obligations as they come, without considering them

Nostalgia the Way It Used to Be

- Bostonian Ruth Stout became famous when she published her book, *Gardening Without Work,* while she was in her seventies. She practiced what she preached, which wasn't just gardening. She ordered supplies by mail and froze vegetables to get her through the winter. When she was ninety-five, she bragged that she hadn't visited a supermarket in fifteen years.
- You might say that Yankees invented fast food. One of the simplest meals in America is classically Yankee in origin and spirit: the New England boiled dinner, which you make by throwing a meal into a pot. The chief original ingredient was beef preserved by a long soaking in a brine of salt and gunpowder. In those days most people kept their gunpowder in cornucopia-shaped containers called corns. Hence "corned beef." You can make the dish today. Take a brisket of corned beef (gunpowder is no longer an ingredient, so the meat doesn't have quite the same zing). Boil it with potatoes and vegetables, stud the meat with cloves, and glaze it with maple syrup. Most people wouldn't find it the best-tasting food in the world, but it's easy to make and filling.

Moral: Saving time is a matter of weeding.

all together. If we're asked to serve on a committee or help organize a fundraiser, we do it. If our kids want to join a team, or take more lessons, or do anything else to add to our chauffeur's duties, we say okay.

We need to know how to make the big decisions that allow us to avoid the little ones. If you refuse your kids ballet on top of piano and soccer, will they grow up to write nasty books about your parenting? Do you really have to sell raffle tickets for the volunteer fire brigade, or is it enough that you serve on the PTA and organize the annual neighborhood food drive? Your willingness to say yes makes other people ask you all the more. And you're beginning to think you're something less than a saint; you're a sucker. You need to learn the noble art of saying no. This art consists of several techniques.

First, **list your functions.** Consider ranking your philanthropic activities. Agree to a temporary assignment more readily than a long-term assignment. Put family before community. Give priority to activities and causes that you genuinely enjoy and that give you energy.

Once you have rated this outside-the-home, nonpaying work, **give yourself a limit** to the number of activities or the amount of weekly hours devoted to them. Apply this principle to children by limiting them to, say, one sport and one other regular activity at a time. If a kid is dying to join the Scouts, first she has to give up weekend soccer.

If nothing else, a keen knowledge of the time you and your family spend, and how much you have to spend, can give you something to say when the call comes asking you to serve on another neighborhood committee. "Gee, I'd like nothing better," you can say with all sincerity, "but I'm booked solid for the next six months. I'd appreciate your considering me if a slot opens up next spring. By then the basketball league should be winding down."

This telephone technique leads to another suggestion: **Never say yes right away.** If the request for your time is not an emergency, ask for a day or two to think about it. Find out how much time it will take, and balance it against the time you have to spare. Consider your qualifications for the work, even if the duties do not seem terribly significant. Are you the best person for the job or simply the most available?

Ask yourself: What's the pay? Of course there isn't any of the monetary kind; that is the very definition of volunteer work. But to use your time wisely and to put your heart into the task, there should be some other compensation. Who benefits from your work? Are you enjoying it personally? What are you learning? What part of your life, or which member of your family, will benefit?

Have an arsenal of noes. Many times we say yes simply because we don't have a no ready. It's hard to turn something down, especially if we feel flattered that someone thought to ask us in the first place. Often the person on the other end of the phone is a volunteer herself, and the favor she asks can seem like a personal one. You need to have something to say. Try keeping little scripts by the phone: "Wow, [first name], I would really love to do that, but I'm right in the thick of [seasonal or temporary activity] and I just couldn't do justice to [request]. But I really appreciate your thinking of me, and if you need me for anything toward the [next season], I hope you think of me again."

This script doesn't burn any bridges. It makes you seem like a willing, friendly person, even while you're turning the job down. On the other hand, if you want to kill the request dead, you need more permanent-sounding language, like "Gee [first name], I wish I could, but I just don't see how I could give [request] enough time to do it justice." If you can volunteer another name without feeling guilty about it, this is a good time to do it.

DIGGING UP THE COUCH POTATO

THE ART OF SAYING NO is crucial for preventing additional duties from crowding out your life. But the biggest potential pockets of free time are actually *wasted* time: television, early morning, and the hours when you are on the move. Like Emerson's virtuous weeds, they can be put to good use.

Television may make the single biggest difference between family life today and as it existed in early New England. That may explain how people managed to be so productive. The average American family keeps at least one TV set on for more than seven hours every day. This doesn't mean that every member stares silent and slack-jawed at the screen the whole time. For many households the TV acts as a kind of picture window to the world outside. Family members talk, eat dinner, do their chores in front of the television, glancing now and then if something attracts them. This can't be great for sustained conversation, but it is not necessarily bad living.

Even if you do tend to sit mindlessly in front of the tube, maybe that is exactly what you want. You're tired after a hard day's work; you don't care to think for a while.

> # Channel Surfing and Eternity
>
> "As if you could kill time without injuring eternity," said Henry David Thoreau.
>
> **Moral**: Think what Thoreau would have said about television.

Or you switch on the public station and passively absorb some culture and science. Nothing wrong with that.

But if your TV watching is a regrettable habit, well, that's a good thing, too. It's a rich source of time that with a little effort you can convert into an extra daily hour or so.

Excess complicates your life. Anything done in excess offers an opportunity to simplify your life. Not that you have to throw out your television. That solution might be excessive and therefore not simple. Think of the ways you most want to improve your life, and the time you would like to have every day and every week to improve it. Then decide the best course to take with your TV watching. Some choices:

1. Keep the TV on as much as before. Just schedule your watching time so that you do other activities simultaneously. Here are some examples of what you might do in front of the tube:

➤ If one of your goals is to get fitter, try exercising or stretching, or both, while you watch television. Plan a routine around four of your favorite half-hour shows every week, so that the shows are linked to your exercise. This alone frees two hours of precious personal time weekly, without your having to give up any TV watching.

➤ If exercise isn't what you have in mind, try such crafts as knitting or rug hooking. Use television time to make gifts for family and friends. For some people, TV seems more pleasurable when they're making something in front of it. It seems a bit like a fireplace that way.

➤ Suppose you plan to give your family better meals, or you want to improve as a cook. Schedule a new recipe every week, and make it in front of an early-evening show. (Obviously it helps to have a TV set in your kitchen.) Try preparing meals that can be served the following day; this way you can schedule fancy-cooking time around your favorite shows.

➤ You can greatly raise the quality of your TV watching, and cut out the commercials, with a little advance planning. If you have a videocassette recorder, spend an hour or two with a notebook in a video rental store and write down all the movies you want to see in the next several months. If you get cable television, program the VCR to record the movies on your list. Or rent them, checking off the ones you see. (A list saves a lot of time in a store.) Good video catalogs allow you to make your list without leaving home. Try "The Video Catalogue" (1-800-733-2232), "Critics' Choice Video" (1-800-544-9852), or "Time Warner Viewer's Edge" (1-800-224-9944). An alternative to cable and rental is a friend with a video collection.

Ask coworkers and neighbors if you can borrow or swap tapes on your list. Public libraries lend videos for free.

2. Keep watching TV every night but cut back an hour. If you average two hours nightly, try just one hour. Spend that other hour on your goals. Here are a few ways you can use the extra time:

✦ Go to bed an hour earlier. Why? See the section below on the benefits of getting up early.
✦ Read books. Suppose you read a paperback at the rate of twenty pages per hour. If you switched an hour's TV time to books every weeknight, you could read a dozen a year. Schedule this reading time for the hour before you go to sleep, and do it in bed. After a couple of months you might find that you can't go to sleep without reading. Congratulations, you have acquired a new habit—one that enlightens rather than tranquilizes.
✦ Write letters; call friends.
✦ Do volunteer work.
✦ Study for a night course.
✦ Do some outdoor exercise like jogging.
✦ Schedule family time. If you have kids, set the time for the end of homework (a good incentive to get it done). Play video games on the TV, or Ping-Pong in the basement, or cards. Your family may balk at time away from television. Commit them to a month of this new routine. Do things that the other members want to do even if they give you a headache or bore you to tears. Make the time a family habit.

3. Put the television in an inaccessible part of the house, or keep it in a closet. Is there a guest room you usually keep unheated? That's the perfect place for a TV. Heat the room on the special occasions you want to watch something. Keep just one set in the house, and produce it only when the reason to watch it outweighs any other use of your time. At the very least, remove the television from your bedroom. When you are tired, you can fall prey to temptation.

4. Toss the TV. This is an extreme measure; it's up to you to determine if it's excessive. You could free up hours every day, time you could spend on yourself, your career, your friends, or your family. On the other hand, you could make lasting enemies of every TV-addicted housemate. Make sure you notify (and maybe get a consensus from) your tube-watching loved ones before you ditch the set.

MORNING GLORY

THERE IS ONE TIME OF THE DAY when the phone never rings, the world keeps getting brighter, and you have the whole day ahead: early morning.

Did that sentence just set your teeth on edge? You very likely had an instinctive reaction to the phrase "early morning." You said to yourself, "I am not a morning person."

Some people certainly get up early more easily than others. But if you feel groggy first thing in the morning, that does not mean you are biologically incapable of getting up. In the days when most Americans farmed, *everybody* was a morning person. A dairy farmer would not roll over in bed at 4:00 A.M. and mutter to his wife, "I'm sorry, dear, but I can't milk the cows right now. I'm not a morning person." We all wage a continuing struggle against biology. Who is genetically suited to sitting at a desk all day or driving a cab for hours? A woman who's thinking of taking up jogging doesn't determine whether her oxygen uptake and slow-twitch musculature

Plus They Were Healthy, Wealthy, and Wise

He that riseth late, must trot all day, and shall scarce overtake his business at night.

—Poor Richard

All memorable events . . . transpire in morning time and in a morning atmosphere.

—Henry David Thoreau

I never thought that Adam had much advantage of us from having seen the world while it was new. . . . We see as fine risings of the sun as Adam ever saw. . . .

—Daniel Webster

For fifty years he rose before the sun.

—President John Thornton Kirkland of Harvard, speaking approvingly of John Adams

make her a jogging person. Before spring cleaning we don't undergo psychological testing to see if we're cleanliness people. Yet we're perfectly willing to categorize ourselves as biologically unfit for dawn just because we're not one of those (extremely rare) people who bound out of bed, beam at their suffering mates, and shout, "Good morning! What are *your* plans for the day?"

Besides, if you need an alarm clock or a spouse to roust you out of bed, it probably isn't your genetic inheritance that makes you sleepy. Most adult Americans don't log enough Zs each night. If you are past the teenage years and under the age of sixty, you probably need seven or eight hours' sleep. If even seven doesn't seem enough—if you're drowsy after lunch or if getting out of bed feels like a death march—you should sleep an extra half hour to an hour at night. Most people who follow the same routine every weekday, going to bed at the same time and getting up at the same time, don't need alarms to get them up.

If you are getting enough sleep, you are more morning-adaptable than you think. You can fly from Los Angeles to Boston and cross three time zones, but you shudder at the thought of staying in one place and going to bed an hour early. Gaining a morning hour is a good deal easier, if you do it right, so easy that you might get ambitious and try for a little more. Here are four steps to becoming a certified morning person:

1. Mark Labor Day on your calendar as the beginning of your time-changing plan. On that day take stock of the amount of sleep you get at night. Before you begin rising earlier, make sure you're going to bed early enough on your old schedule. Spend a month getting used to a reasonable bedtime. Turn the television off an hour earlier, and read in bed for half an hour or so. Or close your eyes and listen to music. Establish a routine, a bedtime ritual. Unless television makes you sleepy, the routine probably should be tubeless; producers are masters at keeping you watching. Go to bed at the same time every weeknight. Don't stay up more than an hour late on most weekend nights. Avoid naps during this period, so you can feel sleepy when it's time to sleep. If at all possible, try to expose yourself to sunlight in the morning. It helps reset your biological clock.

2. On the Friday before the end of daylight saving time, go to bed on a weekday schedule. Avoid alcohol and caffeine; they interfere with effective sleep. Consider turning dinner on Friday into a minor family celebration. Exchange gifts—bedtime books, sleeping caps, herbal tea—that signify coziness and home comforts.

Morning People's Mornings

Benjamin Franklin

Got up at five, washed, said a prayer, took a "tonic bath" by sitting naked while he read or wrote. Breakfast at eight. Business from eight to twelve.

Margaret Fuller

Starting at age fifteen, got up at five, walked for an hour, practiced piano, read philosophy and French. From nine-thirty to noon, studied Greek, practiced piano, "lounged" for half an hour.

Went on to cofound the transcendentalist magazine the *Dial*, married an Italian count, and died, tragically and romantically, in a shipwreck.

John Quincy Adams

Starting as a child and continuing until he died, got up at five and timed the sunrise.

Salmon P. Chase

As a noted abolitionist lawyer, rose at four-thirty. Prayers, Bible reading, work on speeches. Breakfast at seven. Began meeting clients at eight. Court at nine, meetings afterward.

Henry David Thoreau

Rose at sunrise (he wasn't big on clocks). Took a bath in Walden Pond. Cleaned the cabin. Went off on an adventure.

Girls in the mills of Lowell, Massachusetts, during the 1830s
Up at five, cold bath, off to work.

Louisa May Alcott
When she was eleven, her father, Bronson Alcott, founded a commune called Fruitlands near Harvard, Massachusetts. Louisa's typical morning: Up at five, cold bath. Singing lesson. Washed dishes. Went for a walk. Did spelling and math lessons. Listened to a story.

Babe Ruth
At the St. Mary's Industrial School for Boys got up at five. To chapel for mass. Then breakfast. Then school. Then shirtmaking shop. Then baseball.

Daniel Webster
At his beloved Massachusetts farm, Marshfield, rose at three or four in the morning. Fed his cattle and then went to his library, worked until nine. Breakfast at ten. Afterward liked to say, "I have finished my day's work, written all my letters, and now I have nothing to do but enjoy myself."

In Washington rose at four, lit a fire, read or wrote until six, had breakfast, then walked to the city market for groceries.

Black abolitionist Charlotte Forten of Salem,
Massachusetts, when she was sixteen
Up at five. Homework until breakfast. School. Wrote in journal.

Moral: The most productive habits are early ones.

3. On the following night, turn your clocks back an hour to standard time, the way you're supposed to. Now go to bed an hour early by the clock, and set your alarm an hour earlier than your usual weekday time. If your habitual bedtime is eleven, set your clocks back an hour and go to sleep when they say ten. Your body will feel as if it's eleven anyway.

If you set your weekday alarm for 6:30 A.M., reset it for 5:30 Sunday morning. It may seem strange getting up long before dawn, and you may spark comment from family members who smell coffee at such an hour, but to your body it should feel like a normal weekday morning. Do something you especially want to do, like driving an hour or two to your favorite state park, or watching a video, or cooking a leisurely breakfast for the family, or writing letters to friends.

That first morning may feel a little rugged, but if you plan it right, you will have gained several hours of weekend. If you're used to sleeping in—to, say, eight-thirty—you'll have three extra hours without any obligation, hours to spend entirely on yourself.

4. Keep your alarm set to that new time every weekday for a month. The hardest part will be avoiding the temptation to stay up at night. If you have an answering machine, set it to answer quickly before you go to bed. After a month of this routine you should be able to wake up at the new hour even if the alarm doesn't go off—provided you manage your bedtime routine well. Even if you stay up late on an occasional weekend night, your definition of "late" should have changed permanently. You may be—dare we say it?—a self-made morning person.

WINDFALL HOURS

SUPPOSE YOU HAVE actually learned to get up early. You can congratulate yourself on being a highly disciplined person. Now reward yourself with still more time as you head off for work. One way might be to take the bus.

You will not hear many people say that public transportation saves time. How could it? Door to door it probably is faster to hop in your car and drive than it is to wait for a bus or train. But going faster does not necessarily mean saving time. When you drive, you limit your options to spend traveling time on activities other than driving.

Imagine that it takes twenty minutes to drive to work, but an hour door to door by bus, when you count in the time you walk to the stop, wait for the bus to show up, transfer to another bus, and walk from the bus stop to work. Which is the more efficient use of your time?

The answer isn't as obvious as it seems. Suppose you don't get any exercise but would like to start small with a daily fitness routine. Twenty minutes on a treadmill at a health club could take an hour out of your day, once you've driven both ways and showered. A brisk walk to the bus might be enough of a substitute workout. So, while the bus takes you an extra eighty minutes a day in transportation time, it could save you sixty minutes of club time. The bus then puts you just twenty minutes behind a car drive in daily freedom.

Now suppose one of your additional goals is to read at least a dozen books a year. You find you don't have enough time at night to meet that goal. So you bring a book on the bus and spend twenty minutes reading each way, or forty minutes daily. The walking and reading now put you twenty daily minutes ahead of driving.

Obviously everyone has a different use for transportation time. Some people like listening to abrasive talk show hosts on the car radio. Others play book tapes, "reading" as they drive. Still others bring along tape recorders and dictate letters or their thoughts. Or they spend the time daydreaming. Mass transportation may be impractical or nonexistent where you live. In that case, driving may be your best option. But you can't be sure that

But They Lacked Frequent Flier Mileage

———◆———

✦ Henry David Thoreau saved himself time and trouble by hardly ever leaving Concord, Massachusetts. His goal was to know thoroughly an area six miles square. "I have traveled a good deal in Concord," he asserted.

✦ Amherst resident Emily Dickinson was a fellow nontraveler. "To shut our eyes is Travel," she said. "The Seasons understand this."

Moral: What do you want from travel? Can you get it without going anywhere?

your own commuting time is useful until you do some accounting. If you drive to work, are you spending that time on meeting your goals? If not, deduct that time from your day; you're spending it just on driving. If there are alternative ways to get to work—including riding a bike, walking, or carpooling—does any of the resulting commuting time help you meet your goals? Subtract from this positive time the minutes that these alternative methods "waste"—time you have to spend showering or just plain traveling. Which form of transportation comes out ahead?

This approach can help you plan your longer trips better. Before you travel, estimate the amount of time you will have available to do what you want: reading, getting work done, watching an in-flight movie, taking a nap. If you find that traveling is a matter of waiting for the trip to end, try seeing it as personal time. If you take a long car trip alone, borrow some book tapes from your local library. Borrow or buy a cassette player if you don't have one in your car.

All these calculations assume you don't travel with spouse or children. A long trip with young kids cannot by any stretch of the imagination be considered personal time for you. In that case you have to consider the travel time as family time and plan accordingly. If you are used to family activities without television, then you probably know what to do already. Otherwise you will have to collaborate with family members and come up with a plan to keep children from killing each other. Or hope for an in-flight movie.

What are we doing when we see the potential of extra time in the parts of our lives—television, travel, our morning mental fog—that we once thought only *consumed* time? We have made a virtue of a weed. We have taken a hindrance, an obstacle, and made it work for us. In the next chapter you will see how the same notion can help us exploit one of the most useful obstacles of all, the bad habit.

CHAPTER 7

The Habitual Yankee

In which are revealed the virtues of the bad habit

B EING CREATURES OF HABIT makes us the planet's most adaptable species. Our bodies get used to things quickly. Cut way back on salt, and every restaurant meal and can of soup starts tasting salty. A Bostonian puts on a light sweater for the same temperature that drives a Miamian into gloves and scarf.

The body also plays the trick of habit with the sense of time. Stand next to a clock or watch that has a sweep second hand. Close your eyes, and count off twenty seconds as accurately as you can, saying, "one one thousand, two one thousand," and so on. Do this when you first get up, several hours later, after lunch, and at bedtime. If you are like most people, you counted too slowly first thing in the morning (if you could count then at all). You counted too fast at ten o'clock, slowed down at two, and then got more accurate before you went to bed. This little experiment can act as a kind of chronological mood ring, letting you see how keyed up you are at various times. (One drawback, of course, is that spouses and bosses tend to look askance at people who close their eyes and count when they're under pressure.) If every New Yorker performed this exercise on a regular basis, an entire city might begin walking more slowly, replacing the famous Manhattan stride with a leisurely stroll. "It is a great art to saunter," noted Henry David Thoreau.

What seems fast or slow depends on our perspective, a quality we can change.

Of course walking fast isn't necessarily a bad habit. A sin to one person is a virtue to another. But even those habits you consider bad have virtues of their own:

- If nothing else, habits reveal a lot about your inclinations.
- As we have seen, a time-consuming habit offers the promise of free time.
- Some bad habits aren't as bad as others and might properly be left alone—just as a good gardener doesn't try to remove every weed.

What makes a habit? Something you do regularly that you don't think about; something that would make you feel uneasy if you *didn't* do it. Good habits simplify. They boost you toward your goals, make your daily decisions for you, set parts of your life on autopilot. Bad habits complicate. The extreme versions, of course, are ruinous addictions. But even the less scary habits can sap time and push you backward, away from your goals.

Your body can get just as used to eating bran flakes as doughnuts every morning. It doesn't care whether you watch TV or read at bedtime. Either can be a habit that helps you go to sleep. In a bit we will talk more about bad habits and how to transform them into good ones. But you do not

---

Creatures of Habit

What maintains one vice would bring up two children. —POOR RICHARD

There is no more miserable human being than one in whom nothing is habitual but indecision.

—WILLIAM JAMES

Eat plenty of roughage and use your brains. —LYDIA PINKHAM, whose profile still adorns the Lydia E. Pinkham Vegetable Compound, the most successful and long-lived patent medicine ever sold. Mrs. Pinkham attributed her family's unusually good health not to her medicine but to her daily advice.

---

need to seek and destroy every bad habit. That just complicates things. Instead concentrate more on the habits you *want*.

To see how much a creature of habit you really are, consider this exercise:

✦ Think of every single thing you do out of habit in the course of a day. Include good habits and bad, from brushing your teeth to biting your nails. Now rank the habits from best to worst.

✦ Think of every decision you have to make in a day: selection of morning radio station, clothing, food, restaurant, business decisions, television shows. Could you turn any of them into habits?

✦ Think of all your accomplishments yesterday. It doesn't have to be anything important—just something that got you toward a goal, or advanced you toward a deadline, or somehow made you feel you made progress. Could you do any of these things regularly?

HABITUAL SIMPLIFYING

HERE ARE TWO HABIT-FORMING TECHNIQUES that might help unclutter your life and assist you in meeting goals. (More specific ones will appear in later chapters.)

Employ bad habits. Instead of trying to break all your unwanted habits, consider using some of them as cues to accomplish something else. Suppose you're a nail biter with gum trouble. The dentist warns you that root canal work is inevitable if you don't pay more attention to your gums. He tells you to improve your gums' circulation by "stimulating" them with orangewood toothpicks several times a day. Instead of writing little stick-um notes to yourself or tying a string on your finger, you "link" this new chore to your bad habit. Think of your nail biting as an

---

Or Was It Just the Nutmeg?

CONNECTICUT NOW CALLS ITSELF the Constitution State and the Nutmeg State. But throughout the seventeenth and eighteenth centuries it was known as the Land of Steady Habits.

The state has registered more patents per capita than any other part of the world.

Moral: These two facts may have nothing to do with each other. Then again, maybe they do. The most creative, productive people in history stood on a solid floor of habit.

alarm clock: Every time you find a finger in your mouth, grab a tooth-pick and start stimulating.

Ratchet up. A ratchet is a device that allows progress and prevents backsliding. When you use your human instinct for habits, you take advantage of your tendency to get used to things. Someone who has lived in the city all his life often finds it difficult to fall asleep in the country. A person who keeps the car radio tuned to the classical station usually finds rap music jarring. If you eat only vegetarian, a Big Mac can seem truly disgusting.

You can ratchet up toward your goals. Suppose you haven't had a lick of exercise in years. Running three miles may seem daunting, to say the least. But start walking a mile three times a week for six months. Two-mile walks start seeming doable. Then three-mile walks. Maybe you start jogging some of the distance, then all of the distance, and a three-mile run doesn't seem crazy anymore. It seems . . . normal.

A person accustomed to getting up at 7:00 every morning will probably find a 5:00 A.M. wake-up call, well, alarming. But a few weeks of getting up at 6:30 makes 6:00 seem possible. And if 6:00 becomes the custom, then 5:30 isn't so terrible.

Ratcheting up is a means of making your goal seem normal. Establish the right long-term goal, figure on the habits it will take to get you there, and then give yourself time to build up to them.

There are various kinds of habits that you can put to work for your goals. The *personal habit* is the easiest to maintain, because it has to do with our bodies, and our bodies have a lot to do with our lives. Successful goals are like appendages. Good personal habits—brushing teeth, eating breakfast, bathing—maintain your appendages. Most people wouldn't think of avoiding brushing their teeth; such a habit succeeds because it has to do with our bodies. If you want to get in shape or manage your household finances, make exercise or balancing your checkbook seem similar to brushing your teeth. Set aside a regular place and time, and keep it up until you do it without thinking.

The *household habit* is a chore you have put on automatic pilot. Doing the dishes, making the bed, putting clothes away, anything you do automatically to fix things up around you is a household habit. One of the best ways to annoy a loved one is to acquire habits that conflict. She drapes her clothes over the bedroom chair at night; he hangs his in the closet, carefully guarding the crease in his pants. She can't bear seeing pots in the sink; he thinks it the height of efficiency to let them stack up and wash them all at once. Ask your spouse what annoys him the most, and consider changing your habits.

A third kind of habit has atrophied in America or maybe just changed beyond recognition. Let's call it the *habit of grace*. In an earlier time it was called manners. A few graceful habits hang on, quaintly; many of us still say "please" and "thank you" and even "bless you" automatically. If you don't think twice before letting a car pull ahead of yours from a side street, if you could not bear the thought of making someone wait for you for a restaurant date, if calling your loved one is the first thing to come to mind when you have to work late, then you are blessed with habits of grace.

GRACE AND COMMUNITY

THESE HABITS HAVE BECOME LESS VISIBLE because of great changes in every person's social web. Until the rise of the automobile a person's circle of acquaintances was determined largely by geography. Your community was where you lived. These days it is not quite so easy to determine your community. Our families are not all in one place. Our friends

Two Graceful Yankees

✦ In 1977 McCoy Stadium in Pawtucket, Rhode Island, was starting to fade. Home of the Triple A professional baseball Pawtucket Red Sox, the park was attracting one sixth its former total attendance. Rowdies had taken over the stands. Then Ben Mondor bought the stadium. He stood outside the entrance before the games and shook the hand of every person who walked in. (He and the team president Mike Tamburro also threw out more than a hundred toughs the first game of the season.) By 1991 attendance had set a record of 362,000.

✦ In 1862 Clara Barton set out for Antietam with a wagon train of supplies for wounded soldiers. The teamsters refused to take orders from a lady. On the first night the men refused to stop and finally pulled into camp at 9:00 P.M. Instead of throwing a fit, Barton made dinner for them and treated them with elaborate politeness. It worked: The teamsters were duly ashamed, apologized, and promised to try to get used to answering to a woman.

Moral: Grace is the best revenge.

may be scattered. Our professional contacts may be thousands of miles away. Our social network can be a mix of coworkers, relatives, neighbors, even professional colleagues who converse over the Internet.

Life might be simpler if we still lived near the people we felt closest to. Wouldn't it be great to be able to go "calling" on a Sunday afternoon, driving around and visiting our friends? What if we could find out about jobs, advance ourselves in our professions, and talk to local civic leaders and politicians all in one visit to a local tavern? Of course most of us don't have time to drive around on a Sunday afternoon, and maybe it's best if our politicians don't hang out in taverns. But we miss something of the community that our forebears felt. Our nation was built on that sense of togetherness; the American Revolution was planned in taverns after all.

Technology has greatly simplified the effort of staying in touch with people, and geography is no longer a barrier. Still, there is a difference between *communication* and *community*. Communications technology throws information at us; community is what gives us our sense of place in the world beyond our home. Few people would want to substitute the convenience of the telephone and fax machine with the quaintness of Sunday visits and the camaraderie of the tavern. But what if we could combine the best of twentieth-century technology and nineteenth-century community? Maybe what we miss is not the low-tech small-town life but the *habits of community* that once were a part of that life.

Let's look at the chief means that gentlefolk had of keeping in touch with one another within a community: the calling card, the note, and the letter.

YOUR NAME ON A SILVER PLATTER

WHEN UPPER-CRUST NEW ENGLANDERS stopped frequenting taverns, they needed a way to keep their social connections strong. So began the practice of "calling." Most commonly reserved for Sunday after church, calling meant going to friends' houses and paying them short visits. If your friends were out calling as well, you left a calling card: your name, printed on heavy stock and left with a servant or beside the door. People had small silver plates to hold cards, as a kind of index of one's standing in society. The more visits, the more prestigious the visitors, the higher the social rank of the person being called on.

Most people these days would consider the practice an annoyance. Who has time to receive drop-in visitors, let alone go visiting?

On the other hand, the practice of calling has not disappeared. The telephone has replaced the horse and buggy, and the answering machine serves as a high-tech calling card platter. Through these devices people still "visit" with one another and leave evidence of themselves if no one is home. What if you made a list of, say, a dozen or so friends and relatives and reserved half an hour one evening a week for social calling? Assuming you were willing to pay the long-distance bills, you could call three or four of the people on your list. The following week you could call the next three or four, and so on. If you get their answering machines, you could leave messages saying, "I just thought I'd say hello. Nothing

---

And He Would Have
Loved Voice Mail

M ARK TWAIN was not enamored of the telephone, but in 1878 he had one of the world's first private home phones installed in his Hartford, Connecticut, mansion. When the line went in, he said, "The voice carries entirely too far as it is. If Bell had invented a muffler or a gag, he would have done a real service."

Moral: Some transcendent souls don't need technology. Twain's voice carried all the way into the next century.

---

important. Don't feel you have to return my call." That way you could ensure yourself of getting in touch with each of the dozen at least once a month.

A WONDER OF TECHNOLOGY: THE SHORT NOTE

THERE ARE OTHER MEANS of maintaining remote-control relationships, and they, too, involve a combination of postmodern technology and Victorian manners. When Margaret Fuller stayed as a guest at the home of Ralph Waldo Emerson, the two great transcendentalists kept to their separate floors during most of the day but wrote each other notes carried by servants. In those times it would have been scandalous for a man to be alone with a woman in a room; Emerson and Fuller saw each other mostly at mealtimes, when other people were present. The notes also allowed them to "visit" with each other while leaving time and privacy for their work. Miss Fuller and Mr. Emerson were not unusual. People sent messages to each other across town; a pair of friends would exchange four or five notes in a day.

If that seems strange to us, what would these two Victorians have thought about fax machines? Or electronic mail? They might have known exactly what to do once they got the hang of the technology. While offices often frown on socializing by fax, the machine is suited for just the sort of note exchanging that Emerson and Fuller did. You write a message, stick it into the contraption, dial a number, and the note is received almost instantly. The recipient can respond at her leisure.

Electronic mail works pretty much the same way, provided that all parties have a computer with access to the Internet. The Net allows people to send notes to individuals or to whole groups of people. Most professions

How George Bush Became Notable

$\longrightarrow\!\!\!\!\gg\!\bullet\!\ll\!\!\!\!\longleftarrow$

A S A BOY GROWING UP IN CONNECTICUT, George Herbert Walker Bush learned to write notes on every possible occasion. When he got older, the volume of letters increased, and his writing became a kind of reflex action. He banged away at his manual typewriter every time a friend or a relative (or even a distant acquaintance) got sick or had a birthday or an anniversary. When someone wrote him, he wrote right back, no matter who it was.

Bush gained an unusually large circle of friends that way, a useful resource in his business and politics. He developed a wide reputation for thoughtfulness. After he was elected president of the United States, the note writing continued, and it earned him an even better reputation: as a politician who was actually human.

Moral: George Bush was still writing notes long after letters went out of fashion. He carried out one of the great principles of simple living: He exceeded low expectations.

conduct ongoing discussions via computer, and with a little searching you can find endless conversation on nearly every avocation known to humans. Although computers are far from cheap, access to the Internet costs less than most people's minimum-service phone bill. As more people gain access to the Internet, we are likely to see the rise of "virtual taverns," electronic gathering places where people can share news, advice, and gossip—and engage in habits of community.

AND THEN THERE ARE
PERSONS OF LETTERS

ALL THIS TECHNOLOGY does not adequately substitute for the charm of the handwritten personal letter, which remains the most user-friendly, if slowest, form of modern communication. Letter writing is not a lost art. People still practice it; they just do it far less often than before. There is value in scarcity; the fewer the letters written and sent, the more their recipients appreciate them. Nothing is more courteous and respectful than a note. It requires time and thought to write, but little effort to read. And unlike a fax or phone call, it does not interrupt.

Habits of grace and community can be especially useful, as we shall see in the next chapter, in which we acquire helpmeets in our goals and allies to our calling.

CHAPTER 8

Helpmeets

In which the reader learns the art of superior attachment

TOO OFTEN THE PEOPLE AROUND US make our lives seem more messy than simple. They steal our time, burden us with guilt, boss us around. The only way to rid ourselves of human complications is to become a hermit. But being a hermit rarely brings a good salary.

Instead of daydreaming about an escape from people, we can seek helpmeets in finding our callings and meeting our goals. These useful people come in three varieties: heroes, mentors, and lovers. While lovers tend to get most of our attention, we are more likely to find our calling in heroes, especially those who seem like real, ordinary people, such as Rosa Parks or Paul Revere. "The hero is commonly the simplest and obscurest of men," Thoreau said. That makes it possible to apply their heroism to our own obscure lives.

Unlikely Heroines

- Prudence Crandall of Canterbury, Connecticut, allowed a black girl to enroll in her female boarding school during the 1830s. The town uproar over this unprecedented integration forced the school to close. So Miss Crandall created an academy for blacks only. In 1833 the state reacted by passing the Black Law, which forbade schools to educate out-of-state colored people. Miss Crandall was arrested and jailed. Mobs wrecked the building. She married and moved to Kansas, where she continued teaching African Americans. In 1886, lobbied by Mark Twain, an apologetic Connecticut legislature voted her a pension of four hundred dollars a year.

- The *Atlantic Monthly* reviewed Emily Dickinson's poetry in 1892: "An eccentric, dreamy, half-educated recluse in an out-of-the-way New England village—or anywhere else—cannot with impunity set at defiance the laws of gravitation and grammar. . . . Oblivion lingers in the immediate neighborhood."

- Emma Willard moved with her husband to Middlebury, Vermont, where he was headmaster of an academy. A nephew went with them to study at Middlebury College. Women were forbidden to study at Middlebury, so Mrs. Willard read all of her nephew's textbooks. She got enough of an education to start a school for girls in 1814, which eventually moved to Troy, New York. To this day the Emma Willard School pioneers in teaching academics, as well as independence, to girls.

Moral: Heroes often remain obscure during much of their lifetime because their heroism transcends their time.

The people who become your heroes help determine your own brand of heroism. When you follow their example, you are approaching your own calling. During the exercises in Chapter 3, did pictures of other people come to mind? Can you imagine yourself as a hero, boldly going where no one has gone before? Thinking in this way may allow you to attach some meaning to your habits. You might visualize yourself as the subject of a documentary or newsreel. ("He did twenty sit-ups *every morning* because his wife likes firm abs!" "She wrote all her thank-you letters *the day after Christmas!*")

A Dartmouth professor once agreed to teach a course in Greek to a single student. "Why are you wasting your time on just one kid?" a colleague asked the prof. "To save his immortal soul!" he shouted in reply. It is not a sin to think of your habits transcendently. The idea is a little dramatic, maybe, but it also gets pretty quickly to several central tenets of heroism and simplicity: Do your habits lead to what's important to you? Can you visualize the wondrous results if you continue with—or change—them? Are you saving your immortal soul?

The vision doesn't have to seem dramatic to other people. There is a small dose of heroism in the cleaning lady who sends three children to college, or in the man who fights to convert a town road easement into a hiking trail, or in the woman who gives up her worldly goods and enters a convent. By carrying out their callings with bravery and purpose, they may inspire just one other person, or maybe only themselves. They may be teachers with one student.

Then there are the helpmeets called mentors. You learn not so much from their accomplishments as from their knowledge. While a hero acts, a mentor *knows*.

You don't have to work very hard to get a mentor. You need only choose one.

CHOOSING A MENTOR

D O YOU WANT to get ahead in your profession? Then a boss, a colleague, or a member of the profession might provide ready-made mentoring.

Are you searching for some meaning in your life? Look around you for a spiritual mentor. Whole professions are devoted to this—the ministry and rabbinate, for instance.

You may want to become a better parent or lover. Good parents and lovers are everywhere (although their children and lovers may hesitate to admit it).

Or you may use a mentor to learn a new skill or become a better artist or musician or to become a better athlete or just get fitter. If you're of a certain age, it helps to acquire a mentor who is a bit older and has suffered the pains and injuries you're in danger of.

How can you pay for the advice and help? Sometimes the pleasure and plain ego gratification of mentoring someone are enough. On the other hand, an occasional invitation to dinner isn't a bad idea. You can also barter a skill of your own, from programming a VCR to clipping hedges.

A mentor may be below you in your office hierarchy or junior to you in age. If your first computer just landed on your desk, for example, a secretary may be the best person to teach you how to use it. Mentors show up among friends, relatives, teachers—anyone who does what you want to do. Early in their lives most people see a parent or two as mentors. This is fine, but an offspring needs mentor supplements. Too often parents look to their children as improved versions of themselves. They may fail to recognize when their kids actually succeed.

Spouses or lovers make equally good, if risky, mentors. It helps if each partner has something to teach the other. But close relationships can get touchy when the protégé has learned all that the mentor has to teach.

Mentors and Their Protégés

Susannah Wheatley and Phillis Wheatley

Slavers kidnapped Phillis Wheatley at the age of seven from her home in Senegal and brought her to Boston, where a tailor, John Wheatley, bought her. His wife, Susannah, took a shine to the girl and had her educated. Within two years Phillis was reading English and Latin literature and writing poetry. In 1773 Susannah sent her to England, where she became a darling of London society and published a highly acclaimed collection of *Poems on Various Subjects, Religious and Moral.*

Ben Franklin and Cotton Mather

When Franklin was a teenage Boston apprentice, he liked to visit Mather, who was ready with advice (and a few coins) for bright young men. One day Mather was seeing Franklin out when they passed under a low beam. "Stoop, stoop!" Mather said, but Franklin smacked his head against the beam. The old Puritan couldn't resist a homily. "You are young, and have the world before you," Mather said. "Stoop as you go through it, and you will miss many hard bumps."

Ben Franklin and the Gout

As an old man Franklin had no equals, let alone mentors. He found superior wisdom in his gout. He wrote a dialogue between himself and the ailment that admonished the man for complaining of the pain. "Is it not I who, in the character of your physician, have saved you from the palsy, dropsy, and apoplexy?" says the Gout. "One or the other of which would have done for you long ago but for me."

Athena and Telemachus

As every educated New Englander once knew, the first mentor was Mentor, an old man who advised Telemachus, son of Odysseus, in Homer's *Odyssey*. Mentor was really Athena, goddess of wisdom. Interesting how the first mentor was a woman. Here she was a goddess, and she had to dress as a man to get that boy to pay attention.

Moral: A great mentor sometimes looks different from you and comes without warning.

YOUR MENTOR: AN OWNER'S MANUAL

USE YOUR NEWLY ACQUIRED MENTOR for what you most want to improve in your life, including *technique*. Presumably your mentor is better than you are at what you want to do. Look for situations in which you find yourself blocked, unable to move ahead with your goal. Maybe you're having problems confronting a coworker, finding time to exercise, dealing with temptation. How does your mentor handle these situations?

Watch not just the mentor's technique but also her *attitude,* the expression on her face as she deals with moments that would be tough for you. Can you see yourself in her situation? A mentor can teach you without even knowing it. As Casey Stengel said, you can observe a lot just by looking.

Besides technique and attitude, you need to know how your mentor *manages time* and *disciplines* herself. You may need to ask some questions to get this information. How long did it take her to reach the point you aspire to? What did she give up along the way? How much time did she spend on achieving her (and your) goal? Per day? Per week? Per month?

Your mentor helps you most of all with *inspiration*. He shows you that it is possible to do what you want to do. It's been done! You don't feel alone with your goal. For every setback, every failure, every discouraging word, you can see a living refutation. You're not crazy after all (or, if you are, you have excellent company).

A good mentor is not always encouraging, however. You don't need just praise; you need feedback, someone to tell you in a positive way when you're screwing up. A mentor can be a yardstick or benchmark. You measure yourself against that person's example. Competitive people know this instinctively: If you want to improve your game, play a superior opponent.

With the right exemplars, you may do more than pursue your goals. You may even simplify your life. Who can help you set priorities better than the people you admire? They help anchor you, almost as much as a good family does. That brings us to . . .

THE EFFICIENT LOVER

"T HE IDEAL HUSBAND," wrote an elderly woman to *Yankee*® magazine some years ago, "is a man who is careful of his clothes; don't drink no spirits; can read the Old Testament without spelling out the words; and can eat a cold dinner on wash day to save the women folks from cooking."

As this wise woman knew, everything, even love, can be simplified—with the proper self-discipline. It is all well and good to get carried away, vow eternal loyalty and affection, and abuse the patience of friends and coworkers with testimony on the inamorata's charms. Such zeal is natural; some scientists think it may be hormonally dictated. But if you're looking for a lifetime relationship, you need to be more hardheaded about romantic acquisitions. Consider following this principle: **Acquiring a lover is like buying a camp in Maine.**

There are differences, of course. Camps require more taxes but less maintenance: You just take the dock out of the water, drain the pipes if the cabin has plumbing, and lock up for the season. Still, camps and lovers spark similar irrational emotions, and a simple strategy is essential to keep you from regretting your decisions. In Chapter 4 we discussed the principles of buying a camp in Maine:

+ The bigger the target, the easier it is to hit.
+ A miss is information, not failure.

And remember the "satisfaction" moral:

+ When counting your blessings, round up.

A woman could probably find a reasonable number of men who can read the Old Testament without getting stuck. The available population of nondrinking Old Testament readers is considerably smaller, but still a hittable target. Note that the elderly woman in *Yankee*® magazine did not set us up for disappointment by mentioning looks, bank account, or access to the information superhighway. With the wisdom of her years she limited the criteria and kept the target big.

The second camp-buying criterion, the part about the informative miss, is what single men and women employ when they go on dates. The Puritans weren't big on dating. They didn't have to go out to dinner to learn what they needed to know about a potential spouse. If we were looking only for Bible-toting teetotalers, we probably wouldn't have that much need for dates ourselves. But if we have set somewhat narrower targets, evenings out with the opposite sex produce two forms of information: whether the candidates hit your target and whether your target is reasonably attainable.

MARRIED BLITZ

IMMEDIATELY AFTER THE CIVIL WAR a group of women known as the Mercer Girls went to great lengths—seven thousand miles, actually—to hit their marital target. They were a strange cargo—five hundred young women from all over New England—that set sail from the East Coast in 1865 for Seattle, Washington. The genius behind the voyage was a merchant named Asa Mercer. Placing what must have been the world's most effective personals ad, Mercer got lonely bachelors to pony up three hundred dollars, enough for the voyage and a tidy profit. The first couple got hitched within a week of the women's arrival. Ecstatic residents elected Mercer to the Washington Assembly, but not before he had married one of the women himself.

If this story appalls you, consider that each lonely bachelor and hopeful lady undoubtedly started out with one of the prime ingredients of a successful marriage: low expectations. The main criterion was that the partner be unmarried and of the opposite sex, qualities in short supply on both sides of the continent. With expectations like that, a new spouse had every opportunity to be pleasantly surprised.

The most successfully married Mercer Girls and Boys also followed the advice of Poor Richard:

She Also Saved the Cost of a Personals Ad

THE TOMBSTONE for the late Jared Bates, erected in 1800, reads: "His Widow Aged 24 who mourns as one who can be comforted lives at 7 Elm Street this village and possesses every qualification for a Good Wife."

Moral: To a good Yankee, nearly every stroke of fate is an improvable opportunity.

They Did It to Their Credit

S HERMANS HILL, RHODE ISLAND, once had the local name of Shift Hill. Widows used the site to remarry while wearing nothing but their shifts. The weddings took place at night, and they symbolized the brides' "nakedness" in marriage, freeing their second husbands of the debts of the first.

Moral: While the symbolism would not go over big these days, the concept of shedding past encumbrances is a pretty good simplifying principle.

"Keep your eyes wide open before marriage; half shut afterwards." The time to be rational is before you make a major life decision. Once you have made it, you can be as sentimental as you want.

Most people, of course, take the opposite approach. Before marriage they see nothing but perfection in a future mate; after, the flaws become painfully visible. This is a foolish approach to life, but nearly everyone takes it. Scientists are probably right to blame it on biology.

This isn't to say that any marriage can't stand some improvement. A little positive change can eliminate some of the white noise in your life. But improving a marriage is not easy. It is hard enough for a person to achieve goals by herself; getting another committed to the same goals, and to acquiring the right habits to meet them, is something else again. It is like the old marriage counselor's version of the lightbulb joke:

How many marriage counselors does it take to change a lightbulb?

That depends. Does the bulb want to be changed? (A counselor would also ask, "Where's the other bulb?")

The bulb may not want fixing because it ain't broke. From your

---

She Suffered in His Silence

CALVIN COOLIDGE WROTE ABOUT HIS WIFE, Grace, in his autobiography: "For almost a quarter of a century she has borne with my infirmities and I have rejoiced in her graces."

Moral: If every spouse remained aware of his infirmities and rejoiced in his spouse's graces, there would be many more satisfied couples.

---

spouse's point of view, everything may be fine already. If that's not *your* point of view, you have some convincing to do. Or maybe your expectations are too high. Is your partner's figure less than Greek? Is his chin a little weak? Then, short of plastic surgery, maybe your spouse needs to change less than you or your attitude. It is extremely difficult to improve a spouse, who may in any case resent suggestions in that direction.

On the other hand, a marriage can be improved if both bulbs—sorry, spouses—want the change. Consider the procedures set out in Chapter 4 for setting goals. What exactly do you want out of a marriage? How much can you reasonably expect? What would satisfy you? How can you communicate these wishes without an explosion?

The chief answer is to go through the process together. But before you can do that, you should be sure that you both have an important skill for maintaining a good marriage: *Know how to argue*. It is a primary marital aid.

"Are you *kidding?*" asks the nervous reader. "I *hate* to argue. I spend half my time giving in just to avoid argument."

In New England right up through most of the nineteenth century you weren't considered fully educated unless you knew how to argue. Citizens devoted years of schooling to the subject, called rhetoric; it was foremost among the liberal arts. This is hard to believe today; we have an unfortunate aversion both to rhetoric and to the very notion of argument. Maybe we should reconsider this attitude if only for the reason that marriages don't last as long as they used to. (Rhetoric is not the only skill that sustains a marriage, of course, but bear with us for the sake of argument.) The Greeks invented rhetoric, and New Englanders adored the Greeks. Most of all they loved Aristotle, who wrote the book on argument.

ARISTOTLE'S PRINCIPLES
FOR GOOD MARITAL ARGUMENT

A CTUALLY HE WROTE A BOOK called *Rhetoric,* and his advice was directed toward the democratic management of a city-state. But his theories work at least as well with marital relations, and educated Yankee couples followed those notions to their benefit. After all, managing a marriage is no less difficult than managing a nation. So let us look at the *Rhetoric* as a marriage manual. To do so, you need learn only three Greek words. After employing them in marital argument, you can use them to impress your friends (and they come in handy in the workplace, as we shall see in Chapter 11).

Aristotle listed three basic elements to an effective argument. Being Greek, he listed them in his native language:

Ethos. This is the arguer's reputation. If your spouse trusts and respects you, he is much more open to persuasion. If you're lacking in ethos, that may be the main problem with your marriage. Why doesn't your spouse respect you? Is it because you have violated a trust in the past? Then you have to earn it back, a lengthy process. Is it because you always give in and never argue? Then it is time to begin arguing, standing up for what is important and ignoring the details (we'll get to that). Aristotle put ethos first because you can't get a good argument started without the listener's respect.

Pathos. This is your knowledge of the needs and emotions of your "audience," in this case your partner. What are the other person's needs? What does she want to hear? What is she likely to say in response? What will get her angry, or romantic, or frustrated, or make her laugh? *Pathos* is a root word for "sympathy." Recently whole books have been devoted to the difference in the ways that males and females communicate. Men tend to think in terms of winning and losing arguments. Women, on the other hand, consider a conversation successful if it brings two people closer. Men want to get to the point, to explain their overwhelming logic and then call it quits. Women often talk in a more roundabout way, gaining relationships rather than points. You give good pathos when you take into account your partner's way of arguing. The man should understand that the end point of most marital arguments is not winning the argument but improving the relationship, even when he's clearly right. The woman should look for the logic within the conversation and keep in mind where it's heading; that way she has a stake in solving problems.

Logos. This means the actual words of the argument in which logic comes in. Aristotle said the purpose of every logical argument should be not to win the battle but to discover what is best for all parties. He was not a great believer in compromise—that is, people giving in and coming up with some mutually unsatisfactory deal. Instead he argued for a consensus, which he defined as the "greater good." In a consensus everyone is supposed to win in the long run. A consensual marital argument aims its logic toward the good of the marriage, not toward the benefit of one or the other spouse. That should be the chief topic of every important argument between partners: What is good for the marriage? You compromise when you settle an argument over Saturday activities by devoting half the activities to shopping and half to a walk in the park. You reach a consensus if you agree to skip shopping and walking to dig up the garden. Compromise is give-and-take. It tends to focus on relatively petty details, on territory and who gets what. A consensus seeks benefit for everyone without regard to who benefits most. It focuses on what's important over the long run.

People took Aristotle's advice for more than two thousand years (even though there is no record of his having had a particularly successful marriage himself). As every educated Yankee once knew, two-thousand-year-old advice is worth listening to. Cultured New Englanders knew the difference between arguing and bickering. While bickering is pointless, a good argument comes to a point, a good relationship.

WHERE TO HAVE AN ARGUMENT

THE SIMPLEST OF MARRIAGES rests on a mutual sense of where the partners want to take the relationship and what they are willing to do to get there—goals and targets, in other words. But that is logos, and first you have to deal with ethos and pathos. Before you attack the argument itself, consider retreating. If you have kids, try to ditch them with a friend or relative. It might help to go someplace for a day and a night—an inn or a bed-and-breakfast, say—where you can go on walks and have some private conversation. If you stay at home, spend some time the day before fixing up a retreat area. Build a fire if you have a fireplace. Move the furniture around to make an enclosed nook. Change your surroundings to gain a fresh venue. It's best if both of you get involved somehow in the preparation.

Ethos is your first order of business, establishing the ways you like and respect each other. Don't dwell on the problems at this point. Count your blessings, and round up. List on a piece of paper what you like most about your partner physically, spiritually, mentally. Now list what you think are your own best assets that you offer your spouse. When each of you has two lists prepared, swap them (don't show anything until you're both done). How close are the lists? Any points of disagreement? Can you rank your spouse's attributes in order of importance to you? This is a great way at getting to the pathos: You tell your partner a lot when you rank what most turns you on.

How close does the list come to a description of the ideal Boy or Girl Scout? A Scout is supposed to be trustworthy, loyal, helpful, friendly, courteous, kind, obedient, cheerful, thrifty, brave, clean, and reverent. Add "good lover," and you have the ideal spouse as well, don't you?

For the logos, think about your goals for this year and over the next five years. Ask these questions:

Do you want to keep living where you are?
Do you expect the addition of any children?
Should either of you try to change jobs?
Over the next five years what do you most want to accomplish together?

It's often hard to talk about these things, so don't expect to launch flawlessly into a rational discussion. Think of the times you have had good, serious conversations, and try to duplicate the circumstances. Was it over dinner in a restaurant? A walk? A moment of delicious boredom? It also wouldn't hurt to decide on your agenda in advance. For your first retreat, consider just one item of discussion—say, how each of you wants to live five years from now and what it would take to get there. Build in plenty of time for silence, exercise, goofing around, or romance. Again, both of you should know what is on the agenda. If one of you secretly plans on romance and the other on a brisk hike, you could end up in an argument that has little to do with Aristotle.

MARITAL PRINCIPLES

WHETHER IN A RETREAT OR JUST TALKING with your spouse at any time, keep in mind the following principles for sustaining a marriage. **Know how to argue** is the first one.

Secondly, **always tell your spouse what you want.** Never blame your partner for failing to be a mind reader. Do you want flowers? Say you want flowers. Do you want cowboy boots for your birthday? Let it be known. Otherwise chances are good that you won't get what you want, and your loved one will have failed a test he didn't even know he was taking. Do you want to quit your job? Consult your partner first. Have you accomplished something you're proud of, or do you want your partner to notice your new clothing? Don't ever say, "Notice anything different?" Point it out. Silence is not always golden.

Thirdly, **count your blessings out loud.** If you see the slightest improvement in a partner, praise it. That positive reinforcement business actually works in some cases. If a husband gets rid of a small portion of spare tire, tell him how fit he is looking. If a wife changes a tire, praise her mechanical skill. Bring these improvements up when you hold your retreat. Discuss what brought about the change. Go into detail with your praise. Admire something specific about the improvement: the impressive outline of the pectorals or the fine detailing in a piece of sewing.

In Chapter 10 we discuss financial retreats, to help take the agony out of talking about money. Is there a big decision you need to make together: a possible move, or job change, or choice of school for a child? The point of a retreat is to take the pressure off decisions, to make your choices when the phone isn't ringing and no small person is hanging off your leg.

After you have been on a retreat, you need to do some maintenance, to check up on new habits and to see if targets are being met or have to be set back. If you've set a loose five-year plan, consider taking a few hours each year to update it. This could entail a retreat once a year. An alternative is to set a date—New Year's Eve, your anniversary, some obscure holiday—and go for a walk or huddle in some private space. Do the goals still seem realistic? Are your priorities in order?

DENYING THE SENSES

THIS THOUGHT MAY OCCUR TO YOU: What if you go on your retreat and discover you have nothing to say? What if you don't have any plans and don't care to acquire any? Worst of all, what if everything is going fine? Don't worry. You need only switch to another meeting technique: interspousal communication enhanced by sensory deprivation, aka pillow talk. When couples get together for a good time they often, out of sheer habit, look for stimulation—a movie, a restaurant dinner, bowling, that sort of thing. This works fine when you're seventeen; it is hard at that age to do anything with the opposite sex that *doesn't* stimulate you. Later in life, though, some couples find that the time they get along best is when they lie in the dark at bedtime and just talk. The reason many couples don't do this is that every minute of conversation is time spent not sleeping, and most of us get too little sleep as it is. Besides, there are few things more annoying than to have a partner drop off just when you're phrasing some profound thought.

Maybe we need something that gives us the advantages of pillow talk without the problem of exhaustion.

If both partners work, it might be a treat just to stay home. If you have kids, can you swap for a few hours with another family or pay the sitter to host them? An alternative would be to restrict the children to one floor—with a sitter, if possible—while keeping yourself to another. The ideal arrangement would be a soundproof underground bunker with a fireplace, but too few people have one.

Somehow ensconce yourselves in some quiet place. Once you get over the novelty of having quiet and privacy, you may find that you have absolutely nothing to say. This is perfectly understandable. If you're not in the habit of talking to each other, why would a quiet room make you start? There are several solutions:

1. Bask in the boredom. Limit the time to half an hour. Decide in advance that you won't mind the lack of stimulation. Sit next to each other, saying nothing if nothing comes to mind. Call it meditation.

Mather Glimpses Paradise

THE SUNDAY AFTER Cotton Mather married Katharine Philips in 1686, he preached a Boston sermon on "Divine Delights." Katharine bore him nine of his fifteen children.

Moral: Mather could find rapture on earth. Of course, it is not recorded what Katharine thought of the experience.

---

2. Get a good bottle of wine and a candle. Stare soulfully into each other's eyes. Laugh. Stare soulfully at the bottle.

3. Try reading to each other. Collections of letters are good because you can read them in small chunks. Does the whole thing embarrass you? Who cares? No one is watching! Nineteenth-century couples did this for hours,

and look how low their divorce rate was. (Okay, reading aloud probably had nothing to do with the divorce rate, but it's still an admirable activity.)

All this supports a fourth marital principle that can apply to other aspects of your life: **Boredom is a good antidote to stress.** Few things are more salutary for complicated living than the times when you deprive your senses of stimulation. Is your spouse particularly unstimulating? Perfect!

In fact, boredom is one of several excellent marital habits.

GOOD MARITAL HABITS

Savor moments of sweet boredom. We've already described the benefits (and don't wish to bore you; that's up to your partner).

Give gifts habitually. Call this habit permanent wooing. On regular occasions—from once a week to once a month—bring your partner something she particularly likes. Flowers are perfect, not just for women but for many men as well. Link the gift getting with another regular duty, such as filling your car's tank with gas. When you get gas, get flowers. The gifts don't have to cost much; even one flower will do. The point is simply to refresh the connection between you, to establish a small dutiful habit of grace.

Set bedtime ten minutes earlier than usual. Turn the television off. Spend the time talking—or not talking, as the case may be.

Listen for the sake of listening. When you come across a disagreement with your partner or a problem you both need to work out, schedule a special time for good argument. If you're the female partner, making an appointment gives the man the opportunity to feel he's not wasting time. If you're the man, try this revolutionary conversational technique: *Shut up*. Men talk a great deal more than women do, but they think they talk a good deal less. (Men compensate for this annoying trait by ensuring that everything they say is logical and to the point, but too few women have the perspicacity to notice.)

All this assumes that you can carve out the time to pay attention to your mate. If you have children, this mutual attention is even more important. But then your time is even scarcer. You're in serious need of management advice, which the next chapter offers.

CHAPTER 9

Offspring

On those factors of chaos called children

HARRIET BEECHER STOWE might have glittered even more as a literary star had she remained single. At a low moment she wrote her sister: "Since I began this note, I have been called off at least a dozen times; once for the fish man to buy a codfish; once to see a man who had brought me some barrels of apples; once to see a book man; then, to Mrs. Upham to see about a drawing I promised to make for her; then to nurse the baby; then into the kitchen to make a chowder for dinner; and now I am at it again, for nothing but deadly determination enables me ever to write. It is rowing against wind and tide."

Nothing complicates life so much as children, and Mrs. Stowe had six of them with her in that kitchen. Few of us are quite so fecund, but our parenting duties are no easier. Our own mistaken attitudes are partly to blame.

120

Modern society tends to hold parents solely responsible for their offspring's happiness and long-term stability. This is a very far cry from Puritans, who taught that infants arrived at birth already contaminated by sin. "In Adam's fall/We sinned all" are the first lines in *The New England Primer*. Back in those days no one thought to blame adults for juvenile delinquency.

In contrast, a modern primer slogan might read, "When your kid gets caught, it's all your fault." We wouldn't want to practice the Puritans' harsh discipline, but that original sin notion had its good points. If your kid is rotten, he's your begotten, but he also comes with the stuff of an original personality that takes you at least partly off the hook. So stop thinking blame and guilt. Instead improve your parenting opportunity. You need little more than the best of intentions and some simple principles.

> ## A Part Hepburn Turned Down
>
> ➤●◄
>
> B EING A HOUSEWIFE and a mother is the biggest job in the world, but if it doesn't interest you, don't do it. It didn't interest me, so I didn't do it.
> —KATHARINE HEPBURN
> in *People* magazine

THE FIRST PARENTAL PRINCIPLE:
If You Think You Know What You're Doing, Then You Probably Don't

T HERE IS ONE PERFECT WAY to raise each individual child, but it is impossible to know what it is.

There is a vast body of research on childhood development, and it is

Moral Authorities

✦ The Puritans had few sentimental attitudes toward their offspring. Even as late as the mid-eighteenth century John Adams was adjuring his wife, Abigail, to rid the evil in their little children's minds. "Root out every little Thing," he wrote her. "Weed out every Meanness." One way to do that, he thought, was to "raise their Wishes—Fix their Attention upon great and glorious Objects."

✦ Other Bostonians of the time took the opposite tack. One of the most popular books in the famous old Boston Athenaeum library is an autobiography by the notorious eighteenth-century criminal James Allen. The book is bound in Allen's own skin—at the request of one of Allen's victims, whose descendant donated the book to the Athenaeum. The volume was used for years to spank naughty children, "on the theory," according to Cleveland industrialist Nathaniel D. Chapin, "that the skin of a bad man was particularly adapted to warming [the backside of] a small child."

Moral: What weeds out "Meanness" in one child may have just the opposite effect in another.

good for new parents to read some of the literature, if only to assure themselves that the bizarre and demanding creature they have brought into the world is indeed a member of the same species. But the problem with child psychology is that it fails to conform with a basic tenet of modern science: that an experiment is valid only if the results can be replicated. You can learn a great deal from the careful study of a single child. But then the next kid comes along and you might as well throw the data out the window. Does one child blossom under a supportive but restraint-free environment? The same treatment turns another into a spoiled monster. Does one thrive in competitive sports, excel when the parent stands shouting on the sidelines? The other melts in embarrassment and shame. Would one benefit from being ordered to eat everything on her plate? The same rule could turn the other anorexic. And it's *all your fault*.

If every child were alike, this chapter could consist of a single set of rules, and you would be guaranteed happy and productive offspring to support you in your dotage. But because kids don't have the decency to conform, we will introduce:

THE SECOND PARENTAL PRINCIPLE: Principles Are Better Than Rules

A RULE IS MORE SPECIFIC THAN A PRINCIPLE; it tells exactly what to do. "Don't exceed fifty-five miles per hour on an urban highway." That's a rule. A principle, on the other hand, requires thought, not obedience. **Drive safely.** That's a principle. Principles are more flexible than rules. They allow latitude for us to select appropriate behavior and thus become principled.

Principles are essential to child rearing. You need something to fall back on when your kid suddenly collapses, writhing, onto a shopping mall floor in an attempt to extort a toy. A rule on this occasion might be: "Smile blithely, say brightly, 'That's not *my* child,' and pretend to walk off." After a few minutes' suspense the kid may very well get up and follow you, having learned never to repeat the offense. This rule has actually been known to work. The problem is what to do if the kid calls your bluff, screams even more loudly, and attracts the attention of mall security. To cover all contingencies requires a principle, not a rule. In this case a good principle might be: **Antisocial behavior doesn't belong in society.** Pick a screaming kid up, and make him sit in a quiet corner, as far from people as possible. Note how this principle can apply to an obnoxious child at home, at someone else's house, or on the playground.

A rule-based life is overly complicated. It takes an infinite number of rules to cover every situation. You can say, "When you take a test in school, don't look at your neighbor's answers." That's a rule, and a pretty sound one. But what if the kid accidentally discovers the answers in her own desk? Wouldn't she be better off with an overarching principle, such as **You're not a cheater?** A kid who believes in that principle can make up her own rules as she goes. Principles are easier to explain; rules are often harder to justify. If you find yourself saying, "Because I say so," a lot, it could be that you're bogging down in rules instead of principles. A rule implies punishment; if you think you're not going to get caught, then you have eliminated a major reason for obedience. A principle, on the other hand, can become an appendage, like a goal. It can become an integral part of the child, helping her define herself. "I am not a cheater," she says to herself. She may see other kids glancing at each other's tests, disobeying the rules, and maybe getting better grades. But they're cheaters. She's not obeying the rules. She's obeying herself.

Another good rule: "Brush your teeth before going to bed." This rule is even better if attached to a principle: **Keep yourself clean.** If the kid thinks of himself as a clean sort of person, he is more likely to keep up the good habit of tooth brushing and maybe even wash his own face by the time he's, oh, seventeen.

Other first-class principles: **Junk food makes you weak. The best things come with patience and work. The worst punishment for a bad deed is what it makes you think of yourself. When you fail something, learn something. Face up to bullies and your fears.**

THE THIRD PARENTAL PRINCIPLE:
Let Sleeping Babies Lie

DESPITE EVIDENCE TO THE CONTRARY, your child is a human being, a more or less autonomous and self-correcting entity. Even infants show an amazing ability to survive in a world that is not nearly as user-friendly as a mother's womb. This seemingly helpless creature knows at least as much as you do about child care: how much milk to suck, when it should sleep (not when *you* should, of course), whom to trust, and so on. The lesson for you is that *your child is not entirely yours.* She's on loan. She has a kind of autopilot that is already beginning to kick in, one that will be in overdrive in about fifteen years.

This is why children make terrible pets. Besides being enormously expensive and difficult to train (try making a four-year-old come to heel), kids really can't be owned. They go away when they grow up. Most parents eventually want them to. The hard part is understanding that all the preceding years are a process that prepares them to leave. The stages tend to be much more apparent at adolescence, a time when all parties may wish fervently for the separation. But children are getting ready to leave even at their cutest, most clinging stages.

If that thought bothers you—if you have children you'd love to keep around for a while—think instead how liberating it is not to own them. If your kids are helping to rear themselves, you're absolved of some guilt. You can *let them make their own mistakes.* Do they turn ankles on the sliding board? They're partly to blame! (Besides, a sore ankle is usually a less permanent injury than an acquired fear of risk.) A kid who thinks his parents will always catch him is in for a bad fall sooner or later. Then you're *really* talking about guilt.

This internal autopilot often controls the child's education more than school does and more than anything you can teach as a parent. World-renowned child psychologists look in awe as children blithely teach themselves without benefit of educational theories. Kids do the mental equivalent of push-ups, looking at the same book over and over and over, singing the same song until it's firmly embedded in *your* brain, taking apart valuable household equipment, exercising artistic license on walls and expensive books. Want to give a two-year-old educational toys for her birthday? Buy some cheap stuff at a yard sale and pack it lavishly in boxes and ribbons. The

Mother Liked Ezekiel Best

AFTER GRADUATING FROM COLLEGE and studying to be a lawyer, Daniel Webster turned down a lucrative government job that had been arranged by his father, Ebenezer. When Daniel came home and announced his decision, this is what his father said:

"Daniel, in the long struggle with poverty and adverse fortune that your mother and I have made to give you and Ezekiel an education, we have often talked over these sacrifices, and the prospects of our children. Your mother has often said to me that she had no fear about Ezekiel; that he had fixed and steady habits, and an indomitable energy. . . . But as for you, she did not know. Either you would be something or nothing, she did not know which. I think . . . you have fulfilled her prophecy. You have come to nothing."

Moral: Always take credit for your child's success. Hold yourself blameless for any failure. Ebenezer was right; at that point Daniel had come to nothing. Of course, when Dan eventually became the nation's leading constitutional lawyer and a member of Congress, Dad basked in the credit.

kid, who has not had the opportunity to read up on the latest studies of cognitive development, will invariably go for the packaging. *A toddler can teach you a lot about simple living.*

Not that you're entirely irrelevant, of course. You're a big influence on your offspring. But you can't determine how the kid turns out. That's *his* job. Think back to Chapter 3, where we talked about your inheritance of genes and family and personal experience. Think of your parents, and how they influenced you both genetically and educationally. They have a lot to do with how you turned out, but you're different in some ways from what they had expected or hoped. The same goes for your own parenting. *You can't expect your kids to be improved versions of yourself.* They just may turn out that way, but parents are usually the last to see it. If you want improvement, you just have to experiment on yourself. Your kids are sovereign territory.

THE FOURTH PARENTAL PRINCIPLE:
Story Time Is Better Than Private School

WHETHER OR NOT you provide your child with a blue-chip education, the single best way to make her grow up healthy, wealthy, and wise is to read a book to her every night before bed. If your schedule makes this impossible, set up a reading routine for a different time of the day, like early morning. Start a tradition at the earliest possible age, even before the child can talk. For most kids through the age of five the ritual—the snuggling, the reassuring sameness of the act—is even more important than the story. Every night put a few children's books on the bed, and leave the light on for a while. Good reading habits start before literacy. The act of holding a book, turning the pages, looking closely at the pictures segues right into reading the print.

This habit teaches an equally important one: the value of silence and solitude. Reading time can help recapture the family quietude that modernity has lost. In an essay, "Heating, Lighting, Plumbing, and Human Relations," in the journal *Landscape,* Albert Eide Parr speculates that the "era of candles and kerosene" helped foster close family ties. Lamps were too expensive to keep lit in every room, so activities were limited to a small space, mostly the living room. "Could it be pure accident that the generation gap does not seem to have been invented until after the invention of the electric light?" Parr asks. "Quiet, without complete silence, was naturally a condition particularly strongly insisted upon around the evening lamp, since you could close or turn your eyes, but not your ears."

Besides, books in bed create the cutest sight of all, a book lying like a tent over the face of a sleeping four-year-old, a scholar in the making.

Horace Never Did Learn Spinning, Though

Horace Greeley's mother was not known for her parenting skills; she was fond of the bottle and never could hold on to money. But she did practice one good habit with Horace and his four siblings: She read to them while she spun flax. As a result, the boy learned to read sideways and upside down, a useful skill for a printer and great newspaper editor.

Moral: If you just get story time right, you can compensate for a lot of mistakes.

THE FIFTH PARENTAL PRINCIPLE:
Sell the Call

WHEN THE UMP BEHIND THE PLATE sees a fastball whiz by the hitter somewhere between a strike and a ball, he yells, "STEEEEERIKE!" with more gusto than ever. The less sure he is, the more decisive he seems. He "sells the call."

An umpire should write a guide to child rearing. Manuals in the bookstores tell you that an essential trait of good parenting is consistency. The perfect parent always follows up a promise or a threat and issues the same judicial sentence to the same crime, every time. In other words, the ideal parent has a photographic memory, no emotions whatsoever, split-second reflexes, and a decisiveness that would earn a soldier a battlefield commission.

Aren't you sorry you're not the ideal parent?

Like the other two billion adults on this planet, you need a reasonable substitute for consistency when yours breaks down. You need to learn to sell the call.

All this means is that you must learn to act convincingly. Try hard to look sure of yourself when you discipline the kids, even when you're not. And take care never to contradict your spouse within earshot of the children. Think zone defense, not man-to-man.

How can you effect an unflappable demeanor when your child loudly demands a toy in a store at your most exhausted, harassed moment? Well, you probably can't. It helps to have had practice. Get in the habit of saying no properly when you aren't tired or harried (if you are lucky enough to have such moments around a kid). When conflict strikes, try for an appearance of disinterested objectivity, like a stern but fair judge. And remember:

THE SIXTH PARENTAL PRINCIPLE:
"No" Is Good Medicine

WHAT A STRIKE CALL IS TO AN UMPIRE, the word "no" is to a parent. Watch a baseball game during a disputed call; a batter who doesn't like a called strike often acts very like a young child. Unlike a professional baseball player, however, a kid benefits from a little negativity now and then. It is like the cod-liver oil of old, foul-tasting but healthful, and there is an additional moral benefit to the dosing. As a parent, "no" offers several opportunities for discipline:

✦ It gives your child the ability to accept a loss. It takes practice to take failure and rejection with equanimity. When the parent says no with sufficient frequency when the question is relatively unimportant, the kid gets into the habit of controlling her emotions over the more important matters.

✦ It sets comforting boundaries. Every kid wants a parent, whether she knows it or not. It's frightening being the leader of the pack at a tender age. Your saying no takes the leadership burden off the kid's shoulders.

✦ It gives you the chance to punish whining or temper tantrums. The worse your kid's behavior, the harder you must sell the call. On the other hand, allow yourself to change your mind if the child uses a rational and convincing argument. At the very least, you prepare your kid for a prosperous career in the law.

✦ It teaches the art of saying no properly. To a two-year-old, the word is magical, full of strange and wonderful powers. A toddler learns that a well-timed no can stop adults dead in their tracks. Your job as a parent is to teach a more sophisticated, less arbitrary use of the word. Whenever you say no, try to think of a principle to go with it. Are you denying the kid candy? Tell her that candy is not good for her and that she's had far too much of it lately. Does she want to balance on top of a high wall? Explain how difficult it would be to scrape her off the pavement. Your explanations need not be profound; you just want to get the kid used to hearing arguments associated with the word "no." If you can't think of a single reason why you have spontaneously denied your child something, well, you might just be wrong. Stick to your guns if the kid whines; be willing to change your mind in the face of his overwhelming logic.

➻ It makes the kid appreciate the times when you give in. Never say yes until the last possible moment; otherwise you could be in the embarrassing position of having reneged on a promise. (Kids who have not once remembered to close a door quietly somehow have total recall when it comes to promises.) Allow yourself to be persuaded. Cut a bargain. Say yes in exchange for a favor or a chore. Teach your kid the art of negotiating and the still nobler art of giving in properly. In any case, avoid power struggles. If your kid disobeys you after all, punish him for his sake, not your own. A saintly parent is one who can keep a stern face when she wants to laugh at a hilarious misdeed. She is saintly for her self-control and her sense of humor.

The ultimate lesson of good discipline is this: Although every child is smarter than her parents at some point in her life, her parents are always bound to be wiser. (This is not an unassailable fact of course, but hey, sell the call.)

These principles are easier to remember than to apply. That leads us to one of the most important principles to teach your children: It's all right to screw up. Parents do it all the time.

Jewels of Denial

✦ When Jacques Cousteau was ten, his parents sent him to summer school at Lake Harvey, Vermont. He hated it. One of the most domineering teachers, a German named Mr. Boetz, made him ride horses. "I fell a lot," Cousteau recalled as an adult. "I still hate horses." Mr. Boetz also made him clean up the bottom of the lake under the springboard. "I worked very hard diving in that murk without goggles, without a mask, and that's where I learned to dive," Cousteau said. "I became a good swimmer. So that was the beginning."

✦ Young Barbara Walters of Brookline, Massachusetts, also was denied the chance to go home after school. Instead she would take the MTA into Boston to her father's nightclub, the Latin Quarter, where she'd find a quiet spot to do her homework. She grew up able to concentrate easily in television newsrooms.

✦ Bookish Vermonter George Perkins Marsh did little but read until he was seven, when his parents discovered his chronic eye trouble. His parents banished him from books for four years and forced him outside. He grew up to become the nation's first great conservation writer with his book *Man and Nature,* and he was hiking in the Alps in his late seventies.

✦ Harriet Beecher Stowe's father forbade the reading of novels in his household. With a firm grounding in the Bible and philosophy, Harriet went on to write her generation's greatest indictment of slavery, *Uncle Tom's Cabin,* which also happened to be the best-selling novel of the century.

Moral: Denying a child what she wants can sometimes grant long-term wishes.

THE SEVENTH PARENTAL PRINCIPLE:
Don't Expect to Do Your Best

PARENTING IS A DISTANCE EVENT, not a sprint. Nobody can go all out twenty-four hours a day. Therefore, it is important to think like a Puritan: your good grace should outweigh your regrettable behavior. If you fail to live up to your ideal image of a parent, then you have given your child the blessing of having a human being as a caregiver.

This is not to condone any abusive or neglectful behavior. There is no excuse for treating a child as a possession. Regardless of what the courts say, morally you don't own your kid. He owns himself. But suppose you love him and take pretty good care of him and still feel guilty that you're not the parent you want to be. You see other parents cooking fabulous meals, going on lovely Sunday outings, working skillfully on craft projects, coaching kids' sports, buying the best clothing and toys, sending them to private school. You don't have that kind of time and money.

Well, go ahead and feel guilty. It's good for you, keeps you on your toes. At the same time consider these two sources of absolution:

Sunday's Child

EARLY IN THE eighteenth century, Israel Loring, a minister in Sudbury, Massachusetts, refused to baptize children who were born on the Sabbath. Puritans believed that anyone born on Sunday must have been wickedly conceived on Sunday. Then the Reverend Loring's own child was born on Sunday. He called in all the Sabbath-born children in the village and baptized them.

Moral: The ideal parent, if there is one, has the flexibility to make midcourse corrections.

1. Everything in your family is normal to your kids. They may compare you with other parents just because they see it gets a rise from you. But even if you don't do projects with your kids, they can still have a normal childhood. If you praise them, tell them you love them, yell at them for the best of reasons, and show yourself capable of forgiving and asking for forgiveness, your kids probably will have a better-than-normal childhood. They'll have a happy one.

2. Quality time is no substitute for quantity time. One of the greatest "activities" you can do with a seven-year-old is to lie together on a bed and stare at the ceiling. You may have the kind of kid who needs to be

---

But the Mare Might Have Suggested Whipping Them

IF DESPITE YOUR BEST EFFORTS, your kids still seem rotten, consider the saintly patience of Harvard tutor Henry Flynt. When he taught during the first half of the eighteenth century, the average age of a freshman was fifteen. It was a rare student who escaped fines for breaking windows, including Tutor Flynt's. One young charge put a live snake in the tutor's chamber; another cut the tail off his mare. After nearly every episode Tutor Flynt would rise in faculty meetings to argue for leniency. "Wild colts often make good horses," he would say.

Moral: It is easy in retrospect to see how the adult arose from the child. But it is impossible to predict the adult from the child beforehand. This should be a great comfort to every parent.

near exhaustion to hold still for very long. If so, start a bedtime ritual. Read from a book; then lie down for a while with the kid. Talk, or don't talk. Tickle, or just lie there. This is quantity time. If it seems a little boring, well, good.

One of the most important means of development is the childhood tradition of standing on a corner or in somebody's yard and saying, "What do you want to do?" The traditional response, of course, is "I don't know. What do *you* want to do?" Many overscheduled middle-class children are denied those exquisitely boring moments in which all life seems to be a rerun. Not only do periods of intense boredom teach a kid how to devise her own entertainment, but these empty moments also keep the kid from relying on others for her opinion of herself. Children don't need to be perpetually schooled. It's not natural. They need some downtime to school themselves. Boredom in a resourceful child is stimulating. And a good deal cheaper than ballet lessons.

EVERY DAY IS NOT CHILDREN'S DAY

ONE OF THE RITUALS of Mother's Day and Father's Day is the question that nearly every kid asks: "How come there isn't a Children's Day?" The only possible response, of course, is "Every day is Children's Day." The utter foolishness of this answer has failed to deter parents from giving it over the decades. The fact is, very few days are truly Children's Days. It is not easy to be a child, and what is more, kids rarely get a break from *being* kids, especially these days. Children are constantly being prepared for something; even their play tends to be purposeful and adult-supervised. Summer vacation can look a lot like school, what with camps or "recreational" programs.

Before the weekend was invented early in this century, holidays were much more common. The Sabbath was a day of leisure in America, with the rest of the week devoted to work. Celebrations were based around planting and the harvest. The Puritans did not celebrate Christmas; up until 1681 they outlawed it, considering it a pagan ritual falsely grafted onto Christianity. But they more than compensated with other holidays. They held Thanksgiving feasts whenever they felt like it, and they didn't stint on the food and drink.

The current American Thanksgiving festival has little in common with the Puritans' harvest festival, which they held in October, not November. We eat turkey and watch football. Families often come together at this time, and eating makes a wonderful ritual. But why not be like the Puritans and give thanks at other times of year as well? You could mark out a whole calendar of holidays simply by asking your kids what they're thankful for. Are they grateful that school doesn't last the year round? Why not celebrate the end of school? Toward the end of summer some kids are actually glad to go back to school. Hold a First Day of School Eve celebration. Consider honoring dates associated with family history: when you bought your house or when your grandparents became U.S. citizens. Go ahead and celebrate your wedding anniversary without the kids, but consider another celebration that includes them. In addition, try holidays associated with the seasons. The summer solstice, longest day of the year, is well worth celebrating. So is the winter solstice, when the days begin getting longer (after all, that's why Christmas is when it is). The first day of fishing season may deserve a holiday.

Small celebrations help focus the family, bringing you together for a common purpose. Little holidays also help take the pressure off big ones. Americans tell pollsters that Christmas is the most stressful time of the year. Americans make 40 percent of all their household purchases during the Christmas season, so there are budgetary stresses on top of all the other strains. We get mired in endless parties, eat and drink too much, and end up at the darkest time of year with a kind of holiday hangover. What is worse, our expectations for the holiday tend to be too high, and as you know, overly high expectations are anathema to simple living.

Maybe we're doing too much with too few holidays. Maybe we need to spread out our celebrating and do them all in a lower key.

THE EFFICIENT HOLIDAY

HOLIDAYS HAVE TO BE DONE PROPERLY in order to be simple. You must be efficient. The best way to explain this method of celebrating is to show a few examples.

+ **The caroling circuit.** Make the most of the winter holidays while expending the least effort. List all your friends within a twenty-minute drive. On a weekend afternoon, pack the car with hot chocolate, cookies, and little gifts if you want. Coax your kids or a couple of your most extroverted friends to come along. Drive to one friend's place and start singing. When the door opens, hand over paper cups of cocoa, a bag of cookies, and the gifts. Refuse to go inside unless you have time. Sing three songs. Leave for the next friend's home. You can easily hit eight families in two hours this way, without having a single muddy boot inside your house. Most local bookstores sell books of holiday carols; if you have a home computer, you can buy an inexpensive disk with lots of sheet music. Sometimes kids can borrow carol books from school or church.

There is no need to limit this neighborly event to the winter. Try doing it in the spring, with just about any repertoire you want: top forty hits, joke songs, camp songs, folk songs, work songs, anything that requires little teaching or sheet music. Caroling is too good an idea to limit to the traditional holiday season. Besides, at other times of the year you don't have to worry about keeping warm.

An ideal occasion for caroling, if your community hasn't left for vacation, is Fourth of July Eve. Sing patriotic songs; bring cookies and punch or sodas; give out paper Uncle Sam hats and little American flags. Kazoos make superb accompaniment.

✦ **A picking rendezvous.** Here is a great summer solstice (June 22) ritual: Invite friends to meet for a picking party at a farm within a forty-five-minute drive from town. Look up "Farm" and "Berry" in the yellow pages for prospects. Scope out the place before you invite anyone, and send directions with the invitations. Pack a picnic. Strawberries make ideal picking. Most farms will let you eat all you want without paying, provided you buy a box or two to take home. Blueberries are also good picking if you live in a region that grows them. Make room in your freezer before you go. Blueberries will last the winter in plastic freezer bags; just wash and drain the berries, and throw them into the bags. During a miserable stretch of winter take a bag out of the freezer before you go to bed. Put the berries on your cereal for breakfast for a bit of summery consolation. (Bags of frozen blueberries also make great holiday gifts. Just grab one out of the freezer, wrap it in aluminum foil and a bit of ribbon, and hand it to a friend who is bound to be grateful that it's fruit and not fruitcake.)

✦ **Motel pool party.** If you live in the North Country, try celebrating mud season. In late March and early April the snow melts, dirt roads turn to muck, fields become lakes, and a grim rain seems to fall ceaselessly. Cabin fever runs high. New Englanders enjoy boasting about the depth of the muck on their road and compare notes about years when it *really* rained.

If you aren't blessed with mud season in your part of the country, you can still celebrate. Find a motel with an indoor pool. Bargain for a special party rate. Motels often cater food at a reasonable price. If not, ask if you can bring your own. A few chains, such as Holiday Inn (800-365-3535), will set up the whole party for you. See if you can get special overnight group rates. That way, if you want alcohol for an adult party, nobody has to worry about driving.

✦ **Sports-TV party.** You can do this almost any time of year, not just Super Bowl Sunday, that great national football holiday in late January. Find a bar or restaurant that offers a wide selection of cable television, or call around and ask if a private room can't be provided with a big TV. Don't limit yourself to football. Consider organizing a party around televised synchronized swimming, a biathlon, or the Irish hurling championships. If no one knows the event, then everyone feels included. Borrow a book about the sport from the library so you can provide color commentary.

To keep costs down, arrange for a cash bar in which the guests pay for their own drinks. (Make sure you specify "cash bar" on the invitation.) You pay for the room and snacks.

✦ **Drive-in nostalgia.** Although the drive-in movie theater is dying out, chances are pretty good that there still is one within an hour's drive. For a wonderful end-of-summer party, invite friends to bring their cars, call the theater for that evening's show time, and plan to arrive an hour and a half early. Put blankets and pillows in the back of your car for comfort and small-child dozing. Pack a picnic dinner. Even the most video-jaded kids will be thrilled, and parents will find some pleasant (if secret) memories returning.

What do all these celebrations have in common? Not one of them is held in your house. The effort you expend is minimal. You maximize the number of people included, covering family and friends you may owe invitations to. You're being thoughtful, loving, and, best of all, efficient.

Note also that you have kept expenses low without being stingy. Being thoughtful does not necessarily mean spending a lot of money. This is a good principle to keep in mind as you read the next chapter.

CHAPTER 10

Weaning the Affections

*In which the reader discovers
the wealth that comes from shedding attachments*

T HE PURITANS HAD NO OBJECTION to acquiring wealth, but they thought spending it was sinful. You were supposed to pursue your calling, not riches. On the other hand, *being* rich was okay. It was a sign that you were one of the elect, those who were favored by God. This is the Protestant work ethic in a nutshell: Get rich, but don't spend it.

Being human, many New Englanders forgot the second part of the ethic and spent their fortunes wildly. But frugality has remained one of the enduring Yankee traits, and you can see evidence of it right down to modern times. In 1968 Vermonter George Aiken spent $17.09 on his successful bid for reelection to the U.S. Senate. A lot of people voted for him because of how little he spent. But Vermonters are pikers compared with their neighbors

Paragons of Frugality

✦ Boston installed streetlamps shortly before the Revolution. The city saved oil by leaving them unlit when the moon was bright.

✦ When members of the Trinity Episcopal Church in Hartford needed money to restore their organ in 1990, they found the answer had fallen from heaven. Pigeons had left a century's worth of droppings in the church bell tower. Enterprising church members organized the Pigeon Poop Brigade, packaged the guano as fertilizer, and sold it for a dollar a pound.

✦ Lydia Maria Child, author of the 1829 book *The Frugal Housewife*, recommended earwax as the most practical cure for chapped lips.

✦ In 1925 Calvin Coolidge cut the White House budget by replacing paper cups with glasses, ordering that all manila envelopes be reused, rationing food, and reducing the number of towels.

✦ During the mid-1700s John Phillips was the wealthiest man in Exeter, New Hampshire. He soaked the backlog in his fireplace every night to save wood. When he entertained clergy, he served cheap wine; only the minister who was to preach the next day got a decent vintage. During family prayers he would put out the candle. It's not needed when your eyes are closed, he explained.

✦ Author John Mitchell wrote in *Yankee*® magazine about a Vermonter named Porter who was "the most frugal man I ever knew." Porter lived in a makeshift cabin and used dogs to keep him warm. Total annual energy bill: one hundred to two hundred dollars, "mostly for dog food."

Moral: The Puritans believed they were blessed with frugality as a sign of being saved. Today New Englanders believe blessings come from saving.

across the river. The annual salary of New Hampshire legislators, $100, is the
nation's lowest. The state has the smallest percentage of public-aid partici-
pants in the nation. It even sells its road kill to the highest bidder—or did before a rabies epidemic shut the project down a couple years ago.

People make a mistake when they think modern Yankees have inherited a miserly prohibition against the enjoyment of things. Actually the
Puritans thought it was fine to obtain pleasure from worldly goods. They
just thought it a sin to let enjoyment get in the way of a person's calling.
People should live "with weaned affections," they said. Just as a toddler
enjoys milk but could survive without it, so the Puritans tried to live as if
they had been weaned from mere bodily pleasures.

This is not such a terrible notion when you think about it. To this day
many New Englanders believe that if someone works merely to obtain pleasure, he is a slave to pleasure. In such a case, as Poor Richard put it, "He
does not possess wealth; it possesses him." You can tell if your own wealth
possesses you by setting fire to your house and listing what you regret losing. Nathaniel Hawthorne thought neighborhoods should be burned down
after fifty years. Thoreau wrote approvingly of the Aztecs, who he said
would set fire to all they had every year. But that's a pretty drastic step,
and your insurance company would probably object. An alternative would
be to move. Benjamin Franklin said that moving three times is equal to
one fire. Besides all that gets damaged, you're forced to decide each time
what to leave behind.

THE MOOT MOVE

Y OU CAN TELL EXPERIENCED TRAVELERS by their luggage. A frequent flier travels lightly, taking just enough for the trip. A veteran
backpacker does the same thing. Both shed excess baggage over the years.

Each trip is a kind of move, in which you decide what to take and what to leave behind. We can apply this same lesson to our home lives. We tend to overpack for the lifetime journey. It is useful to leave some things behind.

One way is to rent a big truck, load everything in it, drive around the block, and then move it back in. Get rid of everything you don't feel like loading. (Just think of the interesting comments your neighbors will make.)

Well, of course you won't take this advice. But when you read it, did a picture begin to form in your head of what you would put in the truck? Can you imagine what you would leave behind, give away, sell, or just toss?

You can call that a moot move. In law school students hold make-believe courtroom battles and call them moot court (presumably because "let's pretend court" doesn't sound quite lawyerly enough). We'll steal the idea and apply it to an ersatz move. Consider making a list, putting everything you have into the following categories:

- ✦ Necessities (things that sustain life as you know it)
- ✦ Sentimental objects (things that connect you to loved ones, living or dead, or that are important to your past)
- ✦ Objects that help you toward your goals
- ✦ Objects that make you happy
- ✦ Objects that weigh you down
- ✦ Stuff that you'd just as soon get rid of

If most of what you listed in the last category is the junk of other family members, you might want to consult them before pitching it. First list your own possessions. What did you name as "necessities"? Did you include a car? A stereo? What would someone have listed in the nineteenth century? Is your definition of "necessity" a lot broader than what sustains life? Of course you want to have more than the bare necessities. But that is what the other categories are for: the possessions that help you toward your goals or that just plain make you happy.

Thoreau pointed out that most creatures need just two things: food and, in most cases, shelter. Humans in northern climates also need clothing. Thoreau pointed out that most of the work we do goes toward the extras: gathering or buying more food than we need for strength; accumulating clothes for modesty or social position as well as for warmth; building shelters that do far more than keep the rain off. Thoreau once toyed with the notion of living inside one of the boxes that railroad workers used to store their tools. Just drill a couple of breathing holes and you have a snug home for free. (He did not say what the railroad company would think of this plan.)

Thoreau made a good point even if he never actually lived in a box. We don't need much in the way of material goods. *Everything else is either something we want or something we don't want.* The person who knows the difference knows how to live simply.

Good Thing He Didn't Blow the Money on a Cruise

WHEN PAUL REVERE WAS IN HIS THIRTIES, he invested in his first personal extravagance, a luxury for a town-dwelling artisan who lived where he worked. The new possession was a horse.

Moral: Pleasure in a worldly good can lead to a calling.

ATTACHMENTS

W E KNOW WE HAVE TOO MANY DEMANDS on our time, income, energy, and loyalties. We often even know what to toss over the side if we could only bring ourselves to do it. But we can't bear to. The reason: *We're attached to these complications.* We identify ourselves too much with them. Consider these two scenarios:

Martin drives a sports car called a Testosterone (or something like that). Not only does it have a CD player and leather upholstery and an engine with power like it's on steroids, but Martin also looks great driving it. If he drove a less expensive car, with more affordable monthly payments, Martin wouldn't get a stomachache every time his credit card bills came in the mail. But he can't see himself in a cheap car anymore. He feels a lot more like *somebody,* the kind of person he wants to look like, when he drives the car.

Susan, a production manager at an ad agency, has two beautiful little girls. Both are in a good day care center, but she wishes she could stay at home with them. Actually she could. Her husband is a highly paid medical technician who has just been made supervisor. Between his raise and the money they would save on day care, she could quit her job without hurting their budget. Susan doesn't hate her work; she just finds it less inspiring than her younger daughter's drawings or her elder girl's attempts to read. The problem is, she's a *professional,* not a homemaker. Much as she would enjoy it, being a full-time mother would seem like a demotion. How would she answer the ubiquitous question, What do you do?

Both Martin and Susan are burdened with appendages that complicate their lives. Martin's is an overendowed car, and Susan's is a job she doesn't want or need. But because Martin's car helps define him as a person, removing it from his life—performing a carectomy, if you will—would be a painful operation. A jobectomy for Susan sounds similarly scary. So they both find themselves drifting away from their callings.

There is nothing wrong with liking your car, of course. Nor is it a sin to have a job and children at the same time. (For most parents the job is a necessity.) But Susan and Martin make a mistake when they allow themselves to be defined by job or car. Our calling comes from our roots and our preferences, not our titles and possessions.

When George Heinrichs (the son of this book's writer) was five, he went for a drive with his mother. They passed a sign in someone's yard. George, who couldn't read yet, asked what it said. "It says 'Estate Sale,'" his mother replied. "That's when someone dies and they sell what's left over."

George looked horrified. "You mean like their *teeth?*"

George hadn't yet reached an age when he identified people with their earthly goods. He had seen the remains of animals in the woods, so he knew what's left over after death. Maybe we all need to think a bit more like George. In fact, if you look at the requirements of a five-year-old, you can learn a lot about adult needs. The Compleat Kindergartner is:

Healthy
Physically comfortable
Interested
Loved
Secure
Challenged
Growing

And Virtue Is Cheaper Than Orthodoxy

ONE OF JOHN ADAMS'S favorite quotations came from a book called *The Independent Whig:* "There was virtue in the world before there was orthodoxy in it."

Moral: Fashion and other forms of orthodoxy often stray from virtue.

Could you do any better as an adult? It might be harder for you to meet all those criteria than to own the car of your dreams, but chances are the list itself is pretty complete. You can use it as a kind of litmus test for your possessions. If you own something that contributes to one or more of the criteria, keep it. If it does more harm than good to the list, consider pitching it.

Sort of makes you think differently about wealth, doesn't it?

HOW TO GET RICH

A SURVEY ONCE ASKED a group of millionaires how they made their money. Most said they had never set out to be rich, though they certainly didn't mind the wealth. They had just carried out an idea or followed a passion that ended up making money. Every one of them talked about working hard, taking risks, and focusing on the goals they set for their businesses, all of which they clearly loved doing. The wealth just followed.

Remember the genius fellows in Chapter 3, the lucky people who got grants for doing what they would have done without the money? The millionaires in the survey created their own genius fellowships. Wealth was the icing on the career cake. They didn't set out to own things. They pursued their own happiness.

Money is not the sole means to wealth. It can help a whole lot, of course. For one thing, it lets you avoid making some decisions, such as what to give up to obtain your goals. But what if you're good at such decisions? Then you don't need as much money.

To acquire this skill of becoming wealthy without the money, follow these three principles of wealth:

1. Think of money as means to your ends, not as an end in itself.

2. Avoid possessions that can make you poor by burdening you with expenses that keep you from your goals.

3. Take "plot samples" of what comes in and goes out. This is a simple way of determining how you spend what wealth you have.

Becoming rich requires discipline and courage, whether you have money or not. If you don't want to work too hard at getting rich, then congratulate yourself for not working too hard. In which case, are you really that poor?

Imagine what you could do if you were rich. Now think of the parts of that imagined life you could accomplish without all the money. (Sure, we've already asked this any number of times, but a frugal Yankee never lets a principle go to waste.)

If you prefer, think more modestly: How much more money would it take to make you truly happy? There are two ways to gain the wherewithal: You could get hold of the extra money by earning it or inheriting it or by some other means, or you could get rid of expenses you don't need. This

She Took the Rags with the Riches

——➤●◄——

S HE WAS KNOWN as the Witch of Wall Street for her tattered black dress
and her brilliant investments. Hetty Green inherited five million dollars
from her family in Medford, Massachusetts, and increased it to a hundred
million. She made a killing in the bond market but earned her greatest fame
as America's worst miser. Her son, Edward, lost a leg to gangrene when
Hetty refused to pay for a doctor. Both her children suffered from malnutrition. She forced her daughter, Sylvia, to become a nun to avoid a dowry.
Mrs. Green herself lived in a slum and once spent hours looking in the street
for a coin that Edward had lost. She died in 1916, paranoid and friendless.

Moral: Money and wealth are not the same thing.

second option makes us clench our teeth, but if we view it properly, we
might actually find greater luxury in fewer possessions.

Fashion often spurs us to burden ourselves with excess goods. "I say, beware of all enterprises that require new clothes," said Thoreau, "and not
rather a new wearer of clothes." Too often we spend money on things
simply because we think they're valuable, not because we value them. People in Connecticut tell a story about a man who decided to get rid of his
refrigerator. He put it out on his front yard with a sign saying FREE RE-
FRIGERATOR. Two weeks went by without a response. So the man changed
the sign to read: REFRIGERATOR $100. The next day it was stolen.

It is this kind of silly logic that makes us borrow money we don't have.
If we can't afford something, we tend to value it all the more. Credit cards
give us the means to let our reach exceed our financial grasp. Plastic al-

lows us not only to complicate our lives but to mortgage them.

Increasing numbers of American couples work not just one or two jobs but even three or four, moonlighting frantically to pay for their "lifestyle." American incomes have indeed gone down over the past two decades, and making ends meet takes more than it used to. But in addition to working harder, maybe we need to think harder about the ends. The more we believe we have to own, the more we must work to afford it. The more we earn, the more we pay in taxes.

> ## Why Thoreau Never Took Out a Home-Equity Loan
>
> ⸻
>
> T HE COST OF A THING is the amount of what I call life which is required to be exchanged for it, immediately or in the long run.
>
> —HENRY DAVID THOREAU

The more we pay in taxes, the more we have to work to make up the difference. Some lifestyle.

As Thoreau taught us, one way to save money is never to earn it in the first place.

THE HOUSEHOLD PLOT SAMPLE

U P TO THIS POINT we have used the word "budget" sparingly. As the federal government has proved, budgets are somewhat overrated. They won't make you rich any more than counting calories will make you thin. More important than tracking the money you spend is knowing what you're spending it *for*—not just how much but why.

That is not to say that budgets are useless; as you saw in Chapter 3, data and simple living go very well together. Taking a cue from that chapter, consider taking an occasional plot sample of your finances.

A plot sample is not a budget, although it might look like one. Start out by listing categories of income: salaries, tips, gifts, freelance or moonlighting money, anything you sell. An easy way to determine total net income is to look at your tax forms from last year and revise them for this year. Come up with an estimated total for the year.

Now list all the major categories you spend money on, for example:

Taxes
Mortgage or rent
Car
Travel and entertainment
Vacation
Insurance
Food
Clothing
Education
Medical expenses
Charity
Gifts
Savings
Pocket money

Take the last three months' worth of credit card bills and other records, and divide them into the categories you created. If you really want to be accurate, you could carry around a little notebook and jot down every expense. But most people find that more trouble than it's worth.

You may want to refer again to last year's tax records in order to calculate some of the expenses, such as insurance, taxes, and medical bills.

Just divide the year's expenses by four. Also keep in mind any major expenditure that can crop up before or after your sample period.

Now add up the totals, and see where you are. If expenses exceed a quarter of your yearly income, don't panic. Remember that your calculations are not costing you money; you're just testing. Besides, if you haven't noticed a large increase in your credit card debt or a decrease in your savings, it might be that some unusual expense is contaminating your plot sample—say, an unanticipated medical bill, a big repair, or an appliance gone hooey. Of course this sort of thing happens all the time, and you may want to allow for unpleasant financial surprises. Look at each category. Are you spending more than you think the category warrants?

ZEROING IN

IF YOU WANT, you can create a budget to adjust the spending in various categories and, if necessary, to reduce spending overall. For some people, this step is a necessity. But budgets can be restrictive and inflexible; they're not good at anticipating changes in your job or household, and they make you feel like a sinner when you stray. Rather than rules, let's concentrate on goals instead. If you're spending more than you want in any category, set a goal for that category. Suppose, for instance, your travel and entertainment are getting out of hand. The family goes out to a restaurant once a week, and every couple of weeks you and your spouse take in a first-run movie. Set a goal of eating out less and going to fewer movies. To avoid self-pity, treat yourself at home. Buy a good bottle of wine once a week, or take home a nice steak; rent a video on the night you would have gone out for a movie.

The same principle works for other categories as well. Don't set specific amounts as your goal; amounts are targets. Simply spending less is a goal. Try to establish new habits. If you're spending too much before the holidays, make a list of gifts for each family member, and try not to buy anything on impulse. Or if you want to spend less money on clothing, create a wardrobe plan and establish priority items—new shoes before a new blouse, for example, or a decent belt before another tie.

Coolidge Admits a Failing

AFTER DECIDING NOT TO RUN FOR REELECTION in 1928, President Calvin Coolidge told a member of his Cabinet: "I know how to save money. All my training has been in that direction. The country is in a sound financial position. Perhaps the time has come when we ought to spend money. I do not feel that I am qualified to do that."

Moral: The secret of frugality is to know not just how to save money but also how to spend it.

One of the plot sample categories—savings—makes you feel better when you increase the amount "spent" on it. If the rest of the categories aren't too far out of whack, some people make savings their first expenditure when they get their paychecks. Many savings plans, such as a 401(k), automatically deduct money from your pay. It's like paying taxes to your own future. This is one of the less painful financial habits since you're less likely to miss money you never see. If your employer doesn't offer a tax-deferred savings plan, talk to your banker about savings plans that help you with the habit, if not the taxes.

After you have set goals and habits for the categories that seem to need the discipline, you can determine reasonable targets. Plan a date three months or so from now for your next plot sample, when you'll examine your next three-month period to see if your habits are working. Your standard of measurement should be the targets you set for yourself.

In Chapter 4 we talk about the artillery method of setting targets. Keep in mind that *the bigger the target, the easier it is to hit.* Set multiple standards, and a range of standards, for each financial goal.

For instance, take the goal of spending less money on entertainment, including the expenses of eating out. Set several targets to help you measure your next three-month plot sample:

- ✦ Take a bag lunch to work at least twice a week instead of buying lunch.
- ✦ Go out to dinner no more than four times a month.
- ✦ Go out to the movies no more than twice a month.
- ✦ Spend 20 percent less on entertainment than you did in the last plot sample.

Notice that only one of the targets has to do directly with the goal itself; spending less money. That is because your *habits* are what will take you to the goal. The targets help you see whether the habits you set are doable—whether they fit you and how well you adapt to them.

What if you exercise astonishing self-control over those next three months and hit each of the first three targets but still end up spending more on entertainment than you want? What if you find that your expenses are down 10 percent instead of 20? Now our other artillery principle kicks in: *A missed target is a source of information.* It's clear that those particular habits will not save as much money as you'd hoped. You can either settle for saving less in that category or step up the habits: Take a bag lunch to work four days a week; go out to dinner just twice a month.

The point is not to save as much money as you can over a three-month period. Your goals should be for the long term, for at least as long as your income remains the same. Your plot sample is just that, an experiment, not a test of your moral fortitude. Even if you miss every one of the targets, you can't say that the experiment failed (or that *you* did, for that matter). You either have to come up with better habits or have to set a goal that seems more closely attached to your calling. It helps to carry out a two-part experiment, one simply to measure expenses over the past three months and the other to measure expenses against targets over the next three months. The process entails at least two sessions of sorting through bills and tax records. You might try scheduling the first session for the time you do your taxes. Then just make sure you put records of all your expenses in the same place so you can find them three months later.

STEADY HABITS

WHEN THE EXPERIMENT ENDS, you are ready to reconsider your habits. Habits are much simpler than budgets, and, if you can establish them, far more effective. Here are some good ones:

Get advice. Consult books, friends who are better at money than you are, and videos on money. Make sure you know the basics of borrowing money, buying a house or car, the differences between stocks, bonds, cash, and other forms of investment. A librarian can help you find reference guides. Consider assigning yourself and your spouse a reading list. Stay reasonably current with the world of finance. This doesn't necessarily mean reading the stock listings in the paper; just keep up with the news on interest rates, real estate prices, how the economy is doing in general.

Not a borrower be. If you can possibly help it, never borrow money unless it gives you a financial advantage. When you take out a loan, you force your future to pay your present.

Pay off credit card debts before they start accruing interest. Credit card rates would get lenders thrown in jail for usury in old New England. If you find it impossible to meet your card debts in time, do plot sample exercises over several three-month periods, setting targets for getting expenses in line. If you simply cannot live on your current income, you've got problems that credit cards can't solve. You need to work on increasing your income or finding another place to live.

On the other hand, if credit card debt is the result of impulse buying, take a pair of scissors and slice up every card. It's an awful pain to live without plastic. But debt is far worse. Ask your bank about declining balance cards, which work like credit cards without the credit. For a small fee, the bank will give you a plastic card that draws directly against your account. You get statements instead of bills in the mail, and you can use the card only so long as there is money in the account.

Never shop without a list of what you will buy. Or if you're shopping simply for recreation, set a firm limit on what you will spend. If you like to treat yourself, treat yourself with little things. A new book or CD can give you a much cheaper thrill than a large-screen TV you don't need.

Make a monthly list of things you need to buy for yourself and your family. Set a date on your calendar for sitting down and composing the list. Sort the items in order of (a) barely necessary, (b) necessary, (c) deeply desired, and (d) best put off for another time. Include an estimate of cost for each item. If you find something on sale, the low price might let you give the item greater priority. But if it's not on the list at all, don't buy it.

If lists don't work for you, **put a piece of paper in your purse or wallet with the following questions on it.** Allow yourself to buy something only after you've read the paper. (If you're easily embarrassed, pretend to be consulting a shopping list.)

Here's what the paper should say:

* Does this purchase meet or violate a goal?
* Do I want this, or is it my craving talking?
* Can I get it cheaper? Or is the convenience worth the expense?
* What would I rather have? Could I have both?

This habit works only if you're a reasonably obedient person, the kind who would never walk against a "Don't Walk" signal. Otherwise you might get heartily sick of that piece of paper and rebel against it, with disastrous results.

PLANNING

ONCE YOU HAVE your financial present in some order, it is time to work on the future. It may seem strange to talk about planning *after* doing the budgeting stuff. But remember, you weren't budgeting, you were only testing. Now that you have a good indication of your habits and preferences, you can think more clearly about the future.

Too many financial experts talk about finances as if they were separate from the rest of your life. The problem with this approach is that it tends to make money dictate everything else: "I'll make as much money as I can, invest it cleverly,

He Didn't Save Much, Though

———————

I WAS RICH, if not in money, in sunny hours and summer days, and spent them lavishly.

—HENRY DAVID THOREAU

and then decide what to do with it when I have enough."

How do you know when you have "enough"? Do you set a certain dollar amount? A year when you'd like to retire? What do you do with that nest egg? What's retirement *for*? These questions lead to all the non-financial issues that we've been talking about. The purpose of a financial retreat should be not to figure out how to get as much money as possible. You just have to plan how to link finances with the goals you have set for your life. The big money decisions should come last, after you have decided on the desires that you can fulfill *without* money.

If it weren't for family obligations, you could live like Thoreau, a man whose first true act of simplicity was to commit himself to a life of chastity. You wouldn't have to move into a cabin in a woods (which, what with property taxes and the cost of lakefront property, seems like a luxury today). You could live on less than ten thousand dollars a year in a suburban efficiency apartment, taking public transportation, eating frugally, spending leisure time in the public library. But you've got kids, debts, responsibilities, other plans. You have the future to worry about.

Good Thing Twain Could Afford It

⇥⊸●⊷⇤

"THERE ARE TWO TIMES in a man's life when he should not speculate," wrote Mark Twain, "when he can't afford it, and when he can." He should know. He lost his entire fortune in a single bad investment.

Moral: Twain's joke proves a New England proverb: "If you want to know what a man is really like, take notice how he acts when he loses money."

We've all been told of the rewards of hoarding money early and investing it for years. A little money does grow astonishingly large if invested properly for a long enough time. But before you start sacrificing for your future, you and your partner should first decide what that future is. Treat yourself to a financial retreat.

The idea of spending precious money and vacation time planning your future may sound only slightly more attractive than, say, boot camp. The whole notion of finances may make you more than a little nervous and guilty. But a well-run financial retreat should help turn down the anxiety volume.

As we saw earlier in this chapter, the chief advantage of wealth is that it keeps you from having to make as many decisions about what to give up. The flip side of this truth is, the more easily you can make financial decisions, the less money you need. A financial retreat can help make the choices seem less like torture. The trick is in treating yourself. If you can afford it, book a weekend in a local hotel, or drive to a bed-and-breakfast. Don't go so far that your weekend gets eaten up with travel. Choose a place where you can feel spoiled and luxuriant for a couple of days. Many hotel chains offer low weekend rates and even throw in meals. If you can't get away, prepare a retreat at home. (See the section in the Chapter 8 on retreats for couples.) If the weekend goes well, your finances will be better off for it.

> ## And He That Is Middle-Class Had Better Watch It
>
> ——————
>
> He that is rich need not live sparingly, and he that can live sparingly need not be rich.
>
> —Poor Richard

PREPARING FOR THE RETREAT

Six months before the retreat, gain a passing knowledge of your income and expenses. You might do a couple of plot samples before retreating.

Two months before the retreat, book the hotel. One night is sufficient; two nights are more fun. Assign some preparatory tasks to yourself and your partner. If you know absolutely nothing about managing or investing money, borrow a couple of books from the library. Don't let just one of you be the family expert. The one who knows the least about finances should do the most reading. That way the retreat won't turn into a lecture on economics.

In addition to reading, you and your partner should individually ask these questions:

- ✦ What do I want to do twenty years from now? When can I expect to stop working? What will I do then?
- ✦ Where should we live when we both stop working?
- ✦ What big expenses can we expect to incur before we stop working? College? House?
- ✦ What do I dream of doing in the next ten years? How much money would it take?
- ✦ Do both of us want to work? What would it take for one of us to quit and stay home?
- ✦ How much money are we saving? Am I happy with how that fund is growing? What are the savings for?

You don't have to discuss your answers with your partner. That's what the retreat is for.

When you pack to leave, include any data you might want to bring along, anything that tells you how much money you make and how much you spend. Plot samples are ideal.

After all this preparation you would think the agenda would be long and complicated. But it needn't be. Set yourself three purposes for the retreat:

1. To establish a reasonable level for savings and establish habits to get you there

2. To agree on how your income should be earned, spent, and invested

3. To tone down the nervousness either of you feels when thinking about money

If you meet any of these three targets, the retreat will have been worthwhile. Since they are fairly simple, set a simple agenda. An example:

SAMPLE RETREAT AGENDA

First Day

2:00   Check into hotel.

2:30   Set goals. You should be comfortable during this discussion. Have it while on a walk, in a café, or in the privacy of your room. Discuss:

> ✦ What you want to leave behind when you die
> ✦ Your ideal old age
> ✦ Worst-case old age
> ✦ Big-ticket items in the next five, ten, twenty years

4:30   Take a break.

5:00   Set up plot samples. Decide on the spending categories you want to reduce or increase. Don't worry about getting precise numbers to add up. You'll have another shot at this discussion.

6:30   Have dinner.

8:30–   This is your business.
bedtime

Next Day

5:00–7:00   Go for a walk or run. Read the paper. Or sleep.

7:30   Have breakfast. Eat in the room if possible.

8:00   Work on savings estimates. How much should you aim at saving during each three-month period? Just establish the amount you need to meet your long-term goals. If the figure you come up with seems impossible to meet, don't worry. That's what the next session is for.

10:00   Take a break.

10:30   Goals, part two. Now is the time to scale down the goals you set at the beginning of the retreat. The trick is to find a happy medium between what you want to accomplish in the future and the amount you can comfortably stow away in the present.

Are your travel plans worth a lot of current sacrifice? Are your retirement ideas too grandiose? Do you need to pay every cent of your kids' college education?

12:00   Have lunch.

12:30   Set up plot samples. Make sure all your spending categories add up to your current income.

2:00   Consider careers and future income. Given what you spend and what you want, what kind of work do you need to earn it? Discuss the future. If you need to get home, do this part in the car.

3:30   Done!

Well, not entirely. Just two more tasks:

✦ You might need to come up with an investment plan. If you're new at this, create the best plan you can, using available guides. Then, if you can afford it, ask a personal finance adviser to look at your plan and make specific suggestions. It may be too expensive to ask an adviser to write the plan itself; instead ask only for a critique of what you've done.

✦ Set another period for plot samples to test your spending categories. Give yourself a couple of months to settle into your new spending habits. Then establish your three-month plot.

When should you hold another retreat? Every two or three years are about right, unless your financial situation changes dramatically. You don't need to retreat to set new spending targets or take plot samples. But if you think you should change your long-term goals, it is time for another retreat.

Once this hard part is done, you can settle down to the pleasure of earning the wealth you have decided upon. That is what the next chapter is about.

CHAPTER 11

Work

On the life of leisure, and how to live it profitably

T HE CAREERS OF MODERN PROFESSIONALS would have been considered lives of leisure in former times. Up until the 1920s most people sweated for a living. A minority had the money and social position to keep them off the fields and shop floors. They spent their workdays attending meetings, writing memos, and traveling. In other words, they lived like the sort of people who fly business class today. People in earlier centuries worked just as hard as today's professionals, and travel was even less comfortable; but the gentlemen of old nonetheless called their careers leisure. That is because of the marvelous contrast between their lives and those of the common masses. A business meeting can seem grueling, but it's a piece of cake compared with wrestling a plow.

"A life of leisure and a life of laziness are two things," Ben Franklin liked to say. He was a leisurely man who worked like crazy.

Lures of a Happy Calling

---✦◆✦---

✦ Daniel Webster's son Fletcher reported that Webster wrote the famous address dedicating Boston's Bunker Hill Monument while he was fishing for trout. Dad didn't catch much at the time, said Fletcher.

✦ Another great work arose out of fishing when Massachusetts naturalist Clarence Birdseye caught a lunker in Labrador. The air temperature was twenty below zero, and the moment Birdseye pulled the fish out it froze solid. Back in camp he threw his catch into a bucket of water, where it quickly revived. Birdseye figured that flash freezing might be a good way to preserve food. So in 1925 he put the first frozen food on the market. It happened to be fish.

Moral: The life of leisure doesn't fuss with separating work and play too finely.

If hardworking leisure sounds alien today, maybe it shouldn't. We might learn something from that noble attitude. How can we parlay our lives so that they are filled with useful work and still feel leisurely? The answer is to find work so fulfilling and enjoyable that we would do it even if we didn't need the paycheck. As Thoreau said, "If the laborer gets no more than the wages which his employer pays him, he is cheated, he cheats himself."

"So," the reader replies, "there really *are* career opportunities for a professional sunbather?"

Not that we know of (unless George Hamilton is nearing retirement). If you haven't inherited a fortune, the life of leisure you envision is an ideal that must be modified by the need to earn money. Think of what you like to do, and combine that vision with a real job. If you think that you are working for yourself and not just for your possessions or for your employer, then you are living the life of leisure, which, not so coincidentally, is also the simple life. Follow your calling, and you live simply.

On the other hand, if what you love to do is not what your employer wants you to do, your life and your job are at cross-purposes. You have rented yourself out, selling your time to someone else. Lunchtime is a good test of whether your life and your job get along. Do you watch the clock waiting for the break? What do you do during lunch? Is it something you wish you could be doing all day? That could hint at your calling.

A failure to do what you want to do during the workday leaves very little time for living your own life. If you count in the time it takes to get dressed for work and to commute, how much free time does that leave you? Free time is time to do what you want. If you do what you want during the workday, then you have a lot more "free" time. Otherwise you have to squeeze in everything fun or fulfilling in too little leftover time, which tends to be when you're the most tired.

As we saw in earlier chapters, our lives are complicated by all the stuff we have to do. They're also complicated by regret over what we don't get to do.

THE KINDERGARTEN CAREER

CONSIDER THE COMPLEAT KINDERGARTNER from the previous chapter, the one who is Healthy, Physically Comfortable, Interested, Loved, Secure, Challenged, and Growing. If we denied a kid any one of these elements for a happy life, we'd hear about it—probably from the kid. Yet we don't pack many of them into our own workdays except during those fleeting hours of "free time." Suppose you could choose a career that met most of those kindergarten characteristics. Here's how it might look. (For the sake of our jobs, let's skip the "loved" part. Your coworkers may think you're great, but romance complicates the workday.):

Healthy. Your work doesn't hurt you.

Physically comfortable. There is adequate light, maybe even from a window. You get to sit or stand pretty much as you please. The work has enough variety to allow you to change positions or activities once in a while.

Interested. You can measure this by how much the time flies.

Secure. You feel appreciated by your superiors, paid what you're worth, and in little risk of losing your job in the near future.

Challenged. Your tasks are varied and pleasingly difficult; there is satisfaction in overcoming the obstacles.

Growing. You feel as if you're paid to get an education; you can see your career advancing as you work.

What else could you possibly want from a career? Vast wealth? Travel? Prestige? Power over legions of adoring staff? The sense that you're doing the world some good? There is nothing wrong with any of these desires. But they don't lead to elemental happiness hour by hour as much as the characteristics of the Compleat Kindergartner.

A magnificent salary is hard to spend at the office. The Ferrari sits in the parking garage; the mansion is a commute away; the vacation on the Riviera is just a memory; the thousand-dollar Hong Kong suit is mostly hidden behind a desk.

Business travel can be great—in moderation. Too much of it complicates life and wreaks havoc with the physical comfort category.

It feels good to name a prestigious job when someone asks what you do for a living. If you can get the prestige along with the kindergarten traits, go for it. But how often do people ask what you do? Is that worth giving up any kindergarten happiness?

If power is a means to making your job interesting and challenging, then it is great kindergarten stuff. But pursuing power for its own sake can turn your work into warfare; you waste time battling over territory and playing office politics. Pursuit of power can also become addictive, causing atrophy in other parts of your life, such as family and health.

Then there's the desire to do the world some good. It is hard to argue against a career that helps people or the environment. But if altruism is your sole motivation, you may not be able to keep up the enthusiasm over the long term. You do best what you like to do, day by day and hour by hour, unless you are one of those rare souls whose ardor for the cause sustains them.

The Pay Isn't Great, but Look at the Benefits

IN WESTERN VERMONT live the two legendary Galick brothers, aged ninety-four and eighty-three. They are famous throughout the region for their ability to fix anything—trucks, bulldozers, you name it. They charge a dollar an hour, not having raised their price since the 1950s. They love to work, but they manage to get a nap in during the day. In warm weather they sleep sitting in truck seats fixed to their porch.

Moral: The best kind of career is one you would never retire from.

YOUR CALLING

YOU CAN BUY DOZENS OF BOOKS on choosing a career. Most offer excellent advice on everything but how to discover your calling. Your career and your calling should be inseparable. When you think about pursuing a new line of work, don't ask yourself what kind of job you'd like. Ask instead what kind of day you want to live. The exercises in Chapter 3 might have given you some hints. Below are some additional questions that might help:

> Describe a perfect day. Can you figure out a way to make money having that kind of day?

If your fantasy looks a lot like vacation, ask yourself whether you'd really like to live that way year-round. Do you most enjoy sitting at poolside and talking on the phone? Which is the bigger thrill, the pool or the phone? There are many careers, from travel agent to stockbroker, that let you talk to people. The swimming pool part is trickier. Is it the sunbathing or the sitting that most appeals? Would it help to relocate to a warmer climate?

Your fantasy may go in an entirely different direction, say, a fancy conference room with beautifully dressed businesspeople listening raptly to your presentation. Again, break down the elements of this fantasy. Are the beautiful suits really important to you? Or does the idea of sharing your ideas with a group thrill you more? Happiness may lie in a teaching career at, say, an adult learning center.

Maybe you find ecstasy in your garden. This hobby suggests many kinds of work, but beware, making a career out of a hobby is as risky as letting a vacation inspire a job. You need to ask yourself whether you'd want to garden all day, every day. An avocation doesn't always make a good vocation.

> What sorts of things give you energy? Working alone? Collaborating with a team? Reading? Partying? Getting something done? What sorts of things make you feel drained?

These questions come closest to the themes of Chapter 3. Your calling gives you energy; distractions from your calling drain you. When most people dream about the simple life, they tend to yearn for a life free of distractions. The question you need to ask is: Distractions from what?

You may have done a double take at the mention of partying. What does that have to do with simple living? You may find the answer when you break your favorite activities down into root desires. If you like to party, what is it that most turns you on? If it's meeting new people and laughing at jokes, consider a career in sales. If you prefer organizing the party to the party itself, consider careers that allow you to organize, such as restaurant or hotel management, or meeting management, or catering, or even the moving business.

The essential principle of career fantasizing is this: **Take your dream and break it down.** Analyze your fantasy, dissecting it into the elements of a real-life career.

> What do you like most to do during the day: Play video games? Read? Schmooze? Eat? Tinker? Talk on the phone?

Happiness in a particular job has less to do with profound life meaning than with kindergarten characteristics. If you have a passion for video games, break it down: Do you love making a computer do your bidding? You might look into a career that lets you use computers or write software. On the other hand, if the chief stimulation of a video game is not the computer but the fast pace of the game, consider fields where you can be especially competitive or where the phone rings a lot.

Break down everything you like to do. If eating is a passion, what is it that most appeals? The infinite variety of food, the company at the table, the preparation of a meal? If you pride yourself on your discrimination, you might consider a career that has nothing to do with food—quality control, for example. A tinkerer does not have to be a mechanic. People who like to mess around under their cars often make superior problem solvers in places like business consulting firms.

Hobbies don't always make good careers, but if you break your hobby down into root desires, they can lead you in unexpectedly rewarding directions.

> Do you drive friends nuts with your lists and schedules?
> Or are you chronically late for everything? In school did you
> pull brilliant all-nighters and enjoy them? Or do you like
> planning things carefully in advance?

In choosing a career, you need to know not just your desires but also your personality. How do you behave when you're *not* working? Chances are very good that your character won't change all that much when you start a job. What were your chief strengths as a student? Your greatest weaknesses? When you think of careers, consider not just what you want to do but how well you could perform the individual tasks. What line of work plays to your strengths and minimizes your failings?

A weakness in one kind of job can be a strength in another. The student who chronically does homework at the last minute might make a lousy wedding planner but a great TV news producer.

EARLY BLOOMERS SYNDROME

I T TAKES MATURITY to become an adult kindergartner. One should not succeed at too tender an age. Pity the poor prodigies who get top grades in high school and go on to Ivy League universities, where they continue to excel. They're used to being the best at everything, and so when it comes time to think about life after college, they aim for the top notch.

Early Bloomers

"**F**OR PRECOCITY SOME GREAT PRICE IS ALWAYS DEMANDED sooner or later in life," said Margaret Fuller, herself a prodigy who died young in a shipwreck.

Zerah Colburn proves her point. As a small boy he could solve the most complicated mathematical puzzles entirely in his head. In 1812, at the age of eight, he went with his father from Cabot, Vermont, to tour the nation and Europe and perform before the king of England. But his genius seemed linked to his youth; the older he got, the longer he took to do the math. Zerah stayed in Europe for ten years until his father died. His mother didn't recognize the young man when he returned to the family farm. Colburn drifted from teaching to the ministry to languages. He died an obscure and disappointed professor at Norwich University in Vermont.

Late Bloomers

✦ When Sarah J. Hale was almost forty and a widow with five children, a publisher asked her to edit the nation's first magazine for women, *Ladies' Magazine*. She had never had a career before, or supervised anyone, or even worked in an office. She took the job and retired at ninety.

✦ In 1815 sheriffs threw thirty-two-year-old Frederic Tudor into debtor's prison. His dream of exporting ice to the West Indies had gone bust during the War of 1812 shipping embargo. Tudor pawned his way out of prison, built an icehouse in Havana, and received a shipload of New England ice. He introduced the first cold drinks to Cuba. After successful sales in the West Indies he sold ice throughout the U.S. South and allowed the felicitous invention of the mint julep. By the age of fifty he was a rich man. A year later he was back in prison for debt, having lost his fortune in a risky coffee venture. It took him fourteen years to repay his creditors. He died fabulously wealthy at eighty near the end of the Civil War.

◆ During the 1760s Abel Buell got caught counterfeiting. Connecticut authorities cut off the tip of an ear, held it on his tongue for a while, and then replaced it on the ear, where it eventually grew back. They branded him on the forehead with the letter *C,* holding the hot metal to his skin until he could finish saying, "God save the king." The talented young printer (an eavesdropper, not his phony notes, gave him away) went on to be the first in the American colonies to cut and cast native type. In 1769 the Connecticut Assembly gave him a subsidy of one hundred pounds to start a type foundry in New Haven.

◆ In 1857 Clara Barton was unemployed at the age of thirty-six. A Republican, she had lost her job in the U.S. Patent Office when the Democrats came to power. She moved back home to Worcester County, Massachusetts, where she unhappily kept house for her father. Then war came, and she hit her stride, becoming the greatest battlefield nurse in history. At the age of seventy-seven she was still working in hospitals in Cuba, aiding soldiers during the Spanish-American War.

Moral: People who hit their stride late tend to keep on striding.

When they job hunt, you rarely hear them discuss what they like to do during the day. Instead you see most of them trying to live up to their Ivy League degrees by going after money, prestige, power, impressive altruism. It is hard to make plans to tend bar and write a novel when your class-mates are making a killing or saving the world. It is especially hard to tell your parents that you have no idea how their sacrifices for your education will pay off materially.

Which would you rather be: a fast-track Ivy League grad or the uned-ucated P. T. Barnum, who, broke and unemployed at the age of forty-six, founded the Greatest Show on Earth? If you haven't done any impressive work yet, consider yourself a late bloomer. Your potential is before you.

SO WHO NEEDS EDUCATION?

ACTUALLY THESE DAYS Barnum could have a rough time. The na-tion's wealth flows toward college-trained workers, whom econo-mists call the cognitive elite. Harvard economist and Labor Secretary Robert Reich calls these people symbolic analysts because they manipu-late words or numbers or images. They may work in finance, the com-munications industry, or the law. They are trained as accountants, managers, software analysts, lawyers, or journalists, but they all have one thing in common: education. Nearly all have higher degrees. If you aren't one of these people, your standard of living is likely to decline over the next few decades. The contrast has never been so stark between the edu-cated elite and the rest of the country.

Does that mean you should run out and enroll in night school? Not necessarily. First, consider these principles of career education:

1. If the classes seem worth taking in their own right, take them. Enjoyment is the most important criterion. If the courses sound like tor-ture, don't take them. You probably won't do well. Consider something that sounds like more fun; your calling probably lies in that direction.

Even with the Degree,
Jeremiah, You're Still Dummer

—————⟫•⟪—————

IN 1703 HARVARD turned down Jeremiah Dummer for a job on the faculty because he was overqualified. He had become the first Harvard man to receive a Ph.D. from abroad. The college thought he had gotten a little above himself. Still unemployed two years later, Dummer returned to London and became a successful agent for the American colonies.

Moral: Pursue a broad education for its own sake, not for a job. If you need education for a job, get the minimum required.

---

2. Education is no substitute for experience. Avoid professional training if you could get the job you want without it. You'll hear people in technical professions complain that they don't have the precise knowledge they need to hit the ground running. Years later, when they are promoted to management positions, they bemoan their lack of communication skills and their ignorance of sociology, psychology, and history, information they would have gotten in a liberal arts college. That leads us to the next principle.

3. Get a broad education for the long haul; get the minimum specific training needed to land a job. Once you have a job, you may need more educational credentials for promotion. But companies will often pay at least part of the tuition.

The point is not whether you're thoroughly qualified for a job. The questions are, Do you like the job and can you get the offer?

People Who Forged
Their Own Education

✦ If you think you don't have time to get a broad education on top of all the other things you do, consider Elihu Burritt of Worcester, Massachusetts, famous as the Learned Blacksmith. Early in the nineteenth century he translated Longfellow into Sanskrit and learned more than forty languages. He studied at the forge and after work. Here is a passage from his diary, quoted in Van Wyck Brooks's *Flowering of New England:* "*Monday,* June 18, headache; forty pages Cuvier's Theory of the Earth, sixty-four pages French, eleven hours forging. *Tuesday,* sixty-five lines of Hebrew, thirty pages of French, ten pages Cuvier's Theory, eight lines Syriac, ten ditto Danish, ten ditto Bohemian, nine ditto Polish, fifteen names of stars, ten hours forging. *Wednesday,* twenty-five lines Hebrew, fifty pages of astronomy, eleven hours forging. *Thursday,* fifty-five lines Hebrew, eight ditto Syriac, eleven hours forging. *Friday,* unwell, twelve hours forging. . . ."

✦ One of America's first great generals was a plump bookseller named Henry Knox. He figured out how to move a hundred artillery pieces from captured Fort Ticonderoga to Boston, helping to drive out the British. Where did Knox learn his military science? From books.

Moral: You don't need to attend classes to be educated.

It is hard to convince a twenty-two-year-old of this, but a new college graduate's greatest resources are health, energy, and relative lack of commitments. There are few times in life when there is so much personal freedom (of course, only if the recent grad isn't buried in college loans). Too much focus on the future can waste these resources. Imagine a young woman who goes straight to graduate school after college, spends several years qualifying herself for a respectable profession, works like a slave to pay off her loans, and then gets married and acquires husband, kids, and mortgage. All that is fine if she loves grad school and her work. But if more schooling is just an unpleasant stepping-stone, then she is throwing away her youth, committing the unpardonable offense of failing to lounge on a beach.

THE SIMPLE JOB HUNT

EVENTUALLY, THOUGH, the beach gets old, and thoughts of wearing clothing every day and earning a real paycheck actually start to sound appealing. Don't worry about seeking employment. You're already employed, beginning what you hope will be a short-lived career as a job hunter.

The chief goal of a job hunt doesn't have to be a job. For a new career, your main quarry should be information. If you fail to land a position right away and can keep from starving in the meantime, your career may be better off in the long run. Your pocketbook may need a job, but a career needs contacts. To get them, look beyond your first job and hunt for a career. Remember the habits of grace, and employ the following eight techniques:

1. Research each prospective employer. Don't waste interview time asking questions that you could answer with a little advance research. An employer can tell when an interviewer has made the effort.

2. Fine-tune your résumé and letter to each company. Don't make many copies of one résumé. Rewrite it for each employer, making it look as though your entire life had destined you for a job there and there alone (as, for all you know, it has). This technique is much easier if you have access to a personal computer and a laser printer.

3. Show up early. If the prospective employer can see you right away, you get more face-to-face time. At the very least you're less likely to show up late, an unpardonable job-hunting sin.

4. Ask about salaries, qualifications, how an applicant can stand out from the crowd. Ask the interviewer about her own career, how she got where she is.

5. Ask each contact for new contacts. Whom else should you be talking to in the profession or industry? Ask each contact if you can use her name to call the others. That way you don't have to make what salespeople term a cold call, in which you telephone someone out of the blue. Instead you can say, "Ms. Fatcat suggested I call you."

6. Immediately after each interview write a thank-you note. Tailor it to the individual person, and mention some part of the interview, preferably something you learned. Keep the note short, and send it so it arrives just a day or two after the interview. You'd be amazed how few people write such notes. A good, prompt letter makes you stand out from the crowd. It worked for George Bush, after all.

7. Develop good files. Put in everything you know about each company

---

And If You Can't Get There, Sue

A STUDENT ONCE ASKED Daniel Webster whether the profession of law was full. He answered, "The lower storey is crowded but there is always plenty of room upstairs."

That was one of P. T. Barnum's favorite sayings.

Moral: Don't think about the odds when you look for a job. All you need is one opening.

and each person with whom you interview. Jot down notes right after each conversation, and place them in the appropriate folders. Write neatly, and organize everything. The better the files, the more useful they will be throughout your career.

8. Keep up your contacts. When you land a paying job, send a letter to everyone with whom you interviewed thanking them for their help and encouragement. Whenever you can find a legitimate excuse to talk to them, use it. As you get to know them better, put them on your card list during the holidays, or perhaps send them cards on their birthdays. Work to acquire new contacts. When you visit a different city, consider dropping in on other members of your profession or industry. This is cheaper than attending conventions and can make for a higher-quality contact.

These techniques work for almost every kind of job. And you don't have to be just out of school to hunt down a new career. Use the simple job hunt if you are switching careers, are going back to work after raising children, or have been laid off.

Once you're established in a career, don't miss the chance to help out a job seeker yourself. That person is a contact for you. Most successful employees have formed the good habit of developing and maintaining contacts at all levels.

"But that's unfair!" you say. "Jobs ought to go to the most qualified, not the ones with the best contacts." Well, what is it that qualifies someone for a particular job? Technical skills, education, organization, an ability to work hard and meet deadlines? Sure, all those things. But every job also entails being part of a community—a member of a profession, a worker among workers, a supervisor who must motivate workers. Someone who shows skill in making friends, in doing favors and asking for favors is valuable at every step of the organizational ladder. Does that person sound like a politician? Yes, indeed. But there are good politicians and bad politicians.

THE PROFESSIONAL

S UPPOSE YOU FINISHED THE HUNT and landed the job of your dreams. The next step is to wake up because the job of your dreams usually isn't. Your boss is a jerk, everybody in the organization spends more time protecting turf than getting the job done, the hours are long, and promised promotions don't come through. Even your chair is uncomfortable. Other than that, it's a good job.

It's time to simplify.

You have many good reasons to feel sorry for yourself. But ultimately you have to think like a Yankee, an outlook that does not include self-pity. It is a wasteful emotion. Worse, it is unprofessional.

The main difference between a true professional and nearly everyone else is that a professional focuses on goals, while everyone else does not. If something gets in the way of goals, there is a problem. If not, no problem. Who sets the goals? Your boss is supposed to (unless you're the boss). Higher-ups are supposed to determine the broader goals. If they don't, it's up to the peons. We'll get to how in a minute.

There are goals that you should set for yourself as well. A good place to start is the Compleat Kindergartner: healthy, physically comfortable, interested, secure, challenged, growing. If your job does not meet all these criteria, you need to fix it, or it's time to work on your résumé again. Your workplace goals should go well with your bosses' goals, or at least you should couch your own desires in terms of those higher goals.

You usually see territorial battles at work when people aren't inspired by a central purpose for the company or institution. If you and your fellow workers are doing something particularly innovative or high in quality, something that makes you stand out from the competition, then you have a *cause*. That is how Egyptians got other Egyptians to build the pyramids, according to archaeologists. Representatives of the pharaoh went into vil-

And He Hadn't Even Started the Feature Presentation

I N 1911 AN EX-JUNK DEALER named Louis Mayer opened the Colonial Theater in Haverhill, Massachusetts, to show moving pictures. "The Colonial is the zenith of my ambition," he told the crowd. Thirteen years later he was the head of Metro-Goldwyn-Mayer, the nation's largest movie company.

Moral: The most successful people allow their ambitions to ratchet up.

lages and picked out strong young men to join the crew. No one is sure about the job incentives. The pay probably wasn't great. But once they got to the building site, the men found themselves engaged in the greatest act of their lives. There is every reason to believe that morale was okay. How many people get the chance to perform a living devotion for a visible god who happened to be the pharaoh? How many can be involved in building the largest, most impressive structure ever created up to that point? Sure, there might have been some backbiting among the bureaucrats at headquarters. But when people believe they are part of something larger, office battles seem exactly as petty as they are.

How do you establish a cause in your work? Unless you're in management, that may be impossible. But it is a rare organization that at some point hasn't stated a mission. Your job (if no one else has done it) is to accept that mission and attach relevant goals to it. Suppose you're a management trainee for a fast-food franchise that dishes out fat-laden, mass-produced garbage to ad-dazzled customers who sit in uncomfort-

Great Causes

- Late in the eighteenth century Timothy Dexter of Newburyport, Massachusetts, made a fortune and created a business legend by selling coals to Newcastle. The English coal region had been suffering a miners' strike. Dexter went on to sell bed-warming pans to the West Indies, where they were used as molasses ladles.

- George Flanders is the reigning king of beans. Founder and president of the Flanders Bean-Hole-Beans Company, Inc., of Pittsfield, New Hampshire, he has revived the New England institution of the bean hole supper. A legume version of the clambake, the beans are slowly baked on coals in a hole dug in the ground. Flanders's dinners attract as many as eight hundred people at a time. "The beans keep me young," he told *Yankee*® magazine.

- When James T. Fields was a clerk in a nineteenth-century Boston bookshop, he earned local fame by his ability to tell in advance which book a customer was going to request. Fields's shop became a hangout for Longfellow, Emerson, and Stowe. He went on to cofound one of the great publishing houses, Ticknor & Fields.

Moral: True professionals can find glory in the mundane.

able chairs and masticate to insipid piped-in music. What's the cause in *that?* Well, if you think your job actually hurts people, you might look for another line of work. But you can justify fast food by saying that it provides convenience to people who don't have time to cook, that it offers hot meals at a low price in a clean, safe setting. That's the mission. Your goal as management trainee? To learn how to make the place as efficient and clean—and profitable—as possible.

Why do you need goals when what you're really working for is a paycheck? Two reasons: First, goals are wonderful allies in office politics. They allow you to fight your battles as a loyal employee. They help you measure the accuracy of criticism of superiors. They keep you from going crazy.

Second, goals give you a chance to measure your own performance. They give you confidence when no one else around you seems to recognize your work. They help you to focus on what's important and to eliminate the white noise. In short, they simplify.

As previous chapters have shown, goals help you structure targets as yardsticks of your performance. Make sure your goals match any your superiors set for you. Consider even putting them in writing and giving the higher-ups a copy.

THE HABITUAL WORKER

A S YOU CERTAINLY KNOW BY NOW, you can't simplify without habits. It would be impossible to list here every habit you need for your particular job. You might want to seek out a mentor for that; find a colleague or coworker who seems to be doing especially well, and study that person's habits. Ask for some pointers. At the very least, even if you don't learn anything profound, you will have neatly flattered a rising star.

In the meantime, consider some general work habits to make your work life more leisurely:

Set weekly targets. Managers will often give you targets and deadlines. If not, you can set them for yourself. In fact, it isn't a bad idea to set specific targets on a monthly, weekly, or even daily basis. Some work experts call this time management. But time does perfectly well on its own, without your involvement. The hours would pass whether you supervised them or not. You don't manage time. You manage yourself.

Sum up. Before you leave work at the end of the day, write down what you want to accomplish the next day. When you arrive in the morning, go over your plan. It could consist of three or four tasks written in pencil on the back of an envelope, nothing fancy. Check off the tasks as you get them done. Each month go over your targets. Don't think you have to meet all of them (unless your boss says you do). Set broad and varied targets, as we suggest in Chapter 4. Congratulate yourself for meeting a high percentage of them. Your targets should have dates or numbers attached to them, so they can be specific and measurable. They should be geared toward your goals. Ultimately they should help show progress in your career.

Set your priorities. Do what's most important first, least important last. Avoid the temptation to put fun tasks first. Save "dessert" for last; consider your most pleasurable duties virtual breaks.

Bundle your tasks. If possible, set regular daily times for each task; then the tasks themselves become habitual. While you probably can't eliminate interruptions, avoid interrupting yourself. Turn purposefully from one task to another.

Hit the morning running. Establish the day's momentum early. Don't spend excessive time socializing when you arrive at work. Arrive fully alert and ready to get started, even if that means getting up earlier and making your own coffee. Supervisors tend to watch employees most closely in the morning; early diligence could improve your reputation. In most office situations, interruptions are fewest in the early morning. If you're not a morning person, devote your first hour to what you hate doing most. What the heck, you feel crummy anyway.

Use clock watching as a sign. If you find yourself following the time so closely that it creeps, turn the habit into an experiment. When do you watch the clock the most? If it's a particular time of day, such as the hour before a break, save a fun task for that time. If you tend to watch the clock during a particularly boring duty, see if you can't change your circumstances. If you can't pass the duty on to someone else, consider doing it differently. If you usually sit, stand, or vice versa. Every now and then skip the break. Just work through it. By disrupting your break habits, you can eliminate the clock-watching habit. On the other hand, if you do little *but* watch the clock, you might need to change jobs.

Compensate for homework. If you have to bring work home at night, try to save it for a time when your family doesn't especially want your company. Five o'clock in the morning is ideal, as we note in Chapter 6. Early homework can give you superb momentum when you arrive at the workplace. (It can also make the afternoon a trial, but no routine is perfect.) If you must work at night, do everything you can to be flexible in reverse: Leave work early occasionally to be with your family. Let your kid visit you in the workplace. It's no sin to let work slop over into homelife. Nor is it a sin to let homelife come into work occasionally. Both habits let you slip into a life of leisure.

Play politics. Some workers announce proudly that they have nothing to do with politics. They're wrong. They may ignore the politicking around them, but they're very much a part of it. Workers who politic badly feel out of touch, betrayed, and confused. Avoiding politics does not lead to simple working. On the other hand, you don't have to be slimy and manipulative to be good at workplace politics. You just have to remember your Aristotle.

Chapter 8 offers Aristotle's advice for arguing with your spouse. (Actually, the advice he gave was supposed to apply to the management of a democracy, but let's not quibble.) The same rhetorical principles are good for the workplace, whether you're the boss or a peon. Let's review those three Greek words again and apply them to your career.

Ethos, your reputation among the managers and other workers. Remember how we said a Boy Scout makes the best husband (when he grows up, that is)? The Boy Scout oath isn't a bad set of criteria for the ideal employee either. Pick from these qualities the ones that seem most important to you: trustworthy, loyal, helpful, friendly, courteous, kind, obedient, cheerful, thrifty, brave, clean, and reverent. It's interesting how these words aren't often used to describe trial lawyers or corporate moguls. Maybe that is why we don't feel too sorry for them when they fail. Remember, Aristotle listed "ethos" first among the essentials of good argument.

Pathos, your knowledge of coworkers' and bosses' needs and emotions. Never make a proposal at work in your own terms. Always make it in terms of the people you're pitching to. Don't suggest how a change might affect you; show how it will benefit *them.* If you don't like a decision, show how it will hurt the decision maker, not you. Whining is death to a worker's ethos.

Logos, words and logic that lead to a consensus. In a good consensus everyone wins. A memo or presentation is a form of argument. How well it works depends not just on your language but also on your reputation and your understanding of the organization's (and higher-ups') needs.

THE VIRTUAL MANAGER

SHOULD YOU WORRY about management techniques if you're not a manager? The fact is, you *are* a manager, responsible for at least two people, yourself and your boss. You can tell yourself what to do whenever you want. You need to be more subtle with your boss. Help him meet his own goals, and in a way you're managing him. If he's not a good manager, he needs you all the more.

If you can organize your job to take on more duties, do it. Even if your pay doesn't go up, if you're unrecognized for the extra work, the experience alone may be worth it. Go for duties that give you new skills and contacts. In the worst case, draw up a plan that gives you the résumé and contacts to qualify you for a different job—in another company, if necessary. Most successful careers are endless job searches, helping colleagues find jobs, using colleagues to meet new colleagues, using colleagues to find jobs of your own. Become good at this, and you are halfway to becoming a member of the cognitive elite, composed mostly of people with good contacts. If in addition you can persuade people, know your way around a computer (a skill that, as computers improve, is getting easier all the time), and have the right education, then you *are* a member of the cognitive elite. You have a good shot at a great salary. Even more important, you have an improved chance at living where you want, doing what you want, and possibly even working *when* you want. You aren't merely managing your time. You're managing your life. That (need we say it again?) is what living simply *is*.

But wait. What about the working-when-you-want part? Increasing numbers of professionals—in the investment business, law, publishing, and a myriad of other fields—are finding it less necessary to spend eight hours a day, forty hours a week in the office. It started when people got personal computers at their jobs. They worked on the computer and talked on the phone, tasks that could be performed at home if they got computers. Then came modems, devices that hooked their computers to the phone, allowing people to communicate by electronic mail and send files back and forth. Then came the laptop computer, and professionals could turn a plane seat into a private office (which, for lovers of mystery novels and other aerial diversions, was admittedly a mixed blessing). What people once predicted would be the most amazing result of computers—the paperless office, in which information is created and stored electronically—became an even more amazing concept, the officeless office. Increasing numbers of professionals are using technology to free them from offices. Instead of working at jobs, many of them work on projects, getting hired by a variety of companies for specific, limited tasks. They diversify their employers the way an investor diversifies a portfolio. If they lose a job, they're not unemployed; they're just *less* employed.

More important, they own their time. When the fishing is good, they fish. When the working is good, they work. They merge work and play. They lead the life of leisure.

EDUCATIONAL PLAY

MOST OF US still don't have the luxury to knock off work and fish when we want. But that shouldn't keep us from having a little fun during the workday. Play can be productive. Look at a little kid playing alone in a room, working out social relationships with dolls, learning engineering with blocks, developing a sense of power and self-worth by trashing the bedroom. All this is educational, as the toy makers like to tell us. Why don't we take a cue from kids and use playtime to practice some of the skills that come hardest to us? Why don't we play "job interview" after dinner? Or a rousing game of "office politics"?

Well, maybe not. But too few managers encourage playtime for their employees at work. If workers have to learn a new set of skills—say, a computer program or a fancy phone system—the standard way to teach them is to send them to a seminar or hire an expensive consultant. Consider playtime instead. Ask employees to spend some time messing around with the equipment (under some supervision, if the equipment is easy to break). Has a new spreadsheet program come into the office? Have a computer person devise a puzzle that the software can solve, and offer a prize for the first solution. If the new program is a fancy word processor with built-in graphics, encourage people to create cards for the holidays. A new copier? Hold a party with a contest for the most original (G-rated) photocopy art.

"Yeah, sure," the harassed reader thinks. "Try playing around with *my* deadlines." But even crunch times can be playful. If a lot of clerical work has to be done in a hurry, hold a mailing bee, or a copying bee, or a run-the-envelopes-through-the-envelope-machine bee. If people of all levels work together, and if you have some decent snacks, then you duplicate what the Puritans did: combine work and play, making work playful and play useful.

That's what retreats do, when work groups go off someplace and talk together about the job, making plans for the next year. Retreats work best when the official agenda covers no more than half the time allotted. The rest of the retreat should involve earnest goofing around, preferably as a whole group. A hike, a game, readings, anything that the skeptics won't shoot down as utterly hokey, qualifies as useful goofing.

In almost every workplace there once was a device that pulled people together, encouraged short, informal conversation, and injected a bit of playtime and rest into the workday. It became a part of office lore and tradition. It was called the watercooler. Now that water is sold in little bottles, people don't hang around coolers anymore. Many supervisors would consider that a good thing, yet they agonize over office morale. They hire consultants, hold touchy-feely encounter meetings, admonish employees over battles, fight turf battles themselves. Is *that* efficient? Maybe some of them should try a little playtime, finding substitutes for the watercooler. One of the best is the coloring poster. In some central location, put up a large black-and-white picture and some markers in various colors. This could be a good place for regular meetings. Instead of sitting around a table, take turns coloring. It's interesting how a bit of kindergarten can

Playful Work

✦ Goldbeater Ephraim Bull spent more time gardening than goldbeating, especially after he had moved from his native Boston to Concord, Massachusetts. He spent years in an unsuccessful attempt to cultivate a grape that would ripen in the short New England summer. Then he spent sixteen more years working on a single promising local vine. In 1840 he achieved success: the Concord grape, which ripened a full two weeks earlier than any other. He spent another five years testing the variety before showing his find to the Massachusetts Horticultural Society. It was an instant success, but Mr. Bull himself died poor. He is buried in Concord's Sleepy Hollow Cemetery with Henry David Thoreau, Bronson Alcott, Ralph Waldo Emerson, and Nathaniel Hawthorne. Mr. Bull's headstone reads: "He sowed—others reaped."

✦ Quick, who invented the steamboat? No, it wasn't Robert Fulton. It was Samuel Morey of Orford, New Hampshire. Morey patented twenty-one inventions, including a steam-driven roasting spit and a windmill water pump. In 1792 he could be seen tooling up and down the Connecticut River in his self-propelled boat. He patented it in 1795 and piloted it from Hartford, Connecticut, to New York at a rate of more than five miles an hour. He would have launched the first steamboat line had his chief financial backer not gone bankrupt. Instead, Fulton and his people won the money and glory by infringing on Morey's patents. Unshaken, Morey happily continued sailing his invention in Fairlee Pond (now Lake Morey) in Vermont, right up until the day the boat sank. It lies there still.

Moral: The greatest hobbies are a playful version of a person's calling.

put things in perspective. A lot can get said over some detailed work with a marker. Blocks can serve the same purpose, or those soothing little executive toys that people put on their desks.

Do these things seem childish, trivial, and demeaning? Then they should fit right in with most office squabbles.

It's funny how much time and money we spend trying to act like grown-ups when kids often demonstrate the most efficient ways to work. Have you noticed how much of simple living is playful?

CHAPTER 12

Improving the Moment

On well-disciplined pleasure

I T MAY SEEM STRANGE to talk about play in the middle of a book about Yankees and simple living. Did the early New Englanders play? Did the *Puritans* play? As a matter of fact they did, though admittedly the first Yankees were no barrel of laughs. The Puritans said it was okay to enjoy something so long as its purpose was not pure enjoyment. "The wine is from God, the Drunkard is from the Devil," preached Increase Mather. The point, our forebears believed, was not to pass time but to "improve it."

One of the wisest ways to improve your time is to devote some of it to play—rightly understood, of course. For the sake of this discussion we'll use a pretty broad definition. Play is the time we take to balance our routines, to rest, and to prepare ourselves for the next stage in our lives. To play properly is not to waste time but to improve the moment.

Thus Explaining Why There Were So Few Puritan Comedy Clubs

THE FIRST BOOK ON HUMOR published in America, titled *The Government and Improvement of Mirth According to the Laws of Christianity*, came out in Boston in 1707. The author, Benjamin Colman, approved of jokes and noted that even the Bible allowed them. But being a good Puritan, Colman condemned too much of a good thing. "The measure of mirth may be prodigal and intemperate," he said. "There is a mean to be kept in all things. No excess is innocent. Mirth may be immoderate in the degree of it. Excessive *loud* it sometimes is, and sometimes excessive *long*."

Moral: The Puritans had few punch lines but a good point. Too much of anything isn't fun.

REST NOTES

EVERY SIMPLIFIER KNOWS that too much of a good thing is bad. If any one part of your life starts taking over the others, you need to balance the parts.

You can see evidence of imbalance in the health clubs of downtown Boston and in nearly every other major American city, where a battle takes place during lunch hour. Groups of men confront one another with frightening intensity. Injuries are common. These aren't street gangs; they are lawyers "playing" basketball. Their idea of a break from anger and aggression billed hourly is to do the same things on a different court. Many such ambitious people work so hard that they don't know how to play at all.

They brag that they are workaholics, noble sufferers of America's most attractive disease. But how well do workaholics work their lives?

Many people have forgotten a skill they had mastered in infancy, the ability to rest.

The historical characters who went farthest in life knew when to put on the brakes. You can experiment in literal braking. If you drive fast to work, see what happens if you leave early one morning and take the slow lane. Do you feel more relaxed? You're putting on the brakes. Here are some other habits of braking:

And He Can Do It with His Eyes Closed

H E THAT CAN TAKE REST is greater than he that can take cities.

—POOR RICHARD

Count yourself down. In Chapter 7 we mention a seconds-counting exercise that helps you measure your pace in life. A similar exercise works to slow you down. Count to ten by saying "one one thousand, two one thousand," and so on. Now count the same way while looking at the second hand on your clock or watch. If you find that you were originally counting faster than the seconds, set aside a few minutes in your daily schedule to slow yourself down to real time.

Take your pulse. Sometimes you can get your heart rate down just by tracking it. Measure your pulse in twenty-second intervals, making a little game of slowing the beats over three intervals. (It helps to be away from the phone and from curious coworkers.) An alternative is to buy or borrow a watch that measures your pulse; most sporting goods stores carry wrist monitors that also tell time. You'll learn what increases your rate and what makes it slow down. Does a coworker send it soaring? Do the two of you have problems that you need to work out? Or a budding romance maybe?

Before leaving for work in the morning, sit. Just sit for two minutes doing nothing. It's amazing how the frenetic pace doesn't seem so important while you sit there, if you can discipline yourself just to sit.

When you stop at a red light, practice relaxing. Let your shoulders get heavy. Breathe deeply, letting your stomach go in and out. Grip the steering wheel tightly, and then let go. Relax your face into a smile. Turn a beaming look of love for humanity on to the people in the next lane. Watch them grip their steering wheels more tightly.

Plan some breaks. If you keep a daily schedule, build in breaks, if only for a couple minutes at a time. Close your eyes. Put your head down. Breathe deeply and then shallowly and slowly. See if you can't slow your heart rate.

Catch a "Z" or two. There are few better ways to slow you down than naps. If you have a place at work where you can close the door and put your feet up, you can turn napping into the shortest vacation ever invented. Of course too much daytime snoozing interferes with nighttime sleep, and that defeats the purpose of a nap. If you find yourself dropping off into a deep sleep the moment you lie down during the day, you probably aren't getting enough at night. But a catnap of fifteen or twenty minutes, with closed eyes or light dozing,

---

At Least Reagan Slept in Private

DANIEL WEBSTER, in his older years, often liked a nap after lunch. He slept on a bench in Lafayette Square, across the street from the White House. "I have some talent for sleeping," he once bragged.

Moral: For lifelong energy, you have to know when to rest.

can reset your internal clock and keep it from racing. A nap can give you perspective on your day, the way a good vacation lends perspective to your life.

Naps get bad press in this country. Some critics blamed the Depression on Calvin Coolidge's snoozing. When people heard that Ronald Reagan napped, they declared him old, decrepit, and lazy. If he was any of these things, though, napping was not a symptom. It helped give him that famous calm demeanor. We all could look a lot worse.

THE PERFECT VACATION

MOST PEOPLE TRULY REST only once or twice a year, when they're on vacation. You often hear reasons why two weeks should be the minimum time off: "You need the first week just to relax. The second week is when you really start to enjoy yourself." This vacation axiom is usually true. You know you're getting into vacation mode when work seems distant and unimportant and you spend much of your time anticipating the next meal. It takes some skill to do vacation right. The goal should be to go back to work willingly, refreshed and restored and with a new perspective on what counts most in your life.

And how often does *that* happen to you?

The problem is that you probably live with other people, each with a different notion of what constitutes a proper vacation. You want nothing more than a rustic little cabin by a lake. Your spouse wants a city hotel room and a guide to every museum. Your kids want to spend vacation waiting in line for gut-spilling amusement rides. Unless you're the rare family that achieves vacation unanimity, or you can take separate vacations without regard for rumors of marital difficulty, it might be a struggle to get the battery-charging benefits of time off.

Moments Improved

✦ At forty-six, when P. T. Barnum was bankrupt and his wife was ill, he took a vacation on Long Island, staying at the house of a farmer. During a walk on the beach his family came across a twelve-foot whale that had washed up onshore. Barnum shipped it to a museum he had once owned in New York. The animal was exhibited in a large refrigerator, and the venture made a profit. The museum managers gave him enough of the proceeds to pay for the entire four months of vacation.

✦ In 1860 Milton Bradley's Springfield, Massachusetts, printing business was failing. One night a friend tried to cheer him up by playing him in an old English board game. Bradley got inspired to invent a game he could make with his own lithograph. The result was the Checkered Game of Life and a gaming dynasty. Players advanced on a checkerboard, using a spinner (dice and cards smacked of immoral gambling). The object was to reach "Happy Old Age" through clean living, avoiding "Ruin," "Disgrace," and "Suicide." It was the perfect game for a society still heavily influenced by Puritanism. Bradley sold forty thousand copies within a year. In 1960 the Milton Bradley Company put out an anniversary edition of the game. Its new goal: to become a millionaire.

✦ Depressed and tired, Horace Greeley left his office at the New York *Tribune* to take his first vacation in almost two decades. He "relaxed" by sailing to Europe and sending back dispatches about life in England, Scotland, Ireland, France, Italy, Switzerland, and the Rhineland.

Moral: People who vacation the way they work are having the wrong vacation or their calling is so pronounced that they don't need the break.

But throughout this book you have asked yourself how to accomplish the seemingly impossible. How can you live like a millionaire without the money? How can you "retire" while still working? You know that achieving these goals is not easy. They take discipline and imagination as well as the ability to make decisions. So you are mentally prepared for one of the toughest questions of all: How can you gain the benefits of vacation without going on vacation?

He'd Be Impossible on a Cruise

WE COMBAT OBSTACLES in order to get repose and, when got, the repose is insupportable.

—HENRY ADAMS

Well, okay, *go* on vacation, especially if you've already promised your family a trip to Cape Cod or Disney World. But even the ideal vacation comes only once or twice a year. Its benefits wear off, sometimes as soon as you return to the work that has piled up while you were away. The greatest single gift you can take away from vacation is a set of skills to apply to the rest of the year. Can you build enough relaxation into ordinary life to make vacations more of a pleasant change in routine and less of an emergency procedure? One way may be to take frequent small "vacations" lasting as little as a few hours.

THE THREE-HOUR VACATION

As WE MENTIONED in the "Helpmeets" chapter, there is no better way to atone for past thoughtlessness than a well-planned evening for your spouse. Fill a room in your house with flowers and votive candles. Ask friends to keep the kids for Saturday night. Order the best takeout dinner you can find, or cook up something in advance. Draw a bath with oil. Tell your lover to show up at a precise time. Have a glass of champagne by the tub. Lay out her clothing for the evening, and tell her to show up an hour later in the room you have arranged. Once there, dance to music on a borrowed boom box. The next morning make her breakfast. Have a gift waiting on her plate.

With a little imagination you can achieve some of the effect of a vacation without going away or taking two weeks off. You don't have to exclude the kids either. One enchanted winter evening rent the movie *South Pacific,* and turn up the heat in the room where the TV is. Wear bathing suits, and eat pineapple and takeout Chinese. Put little paper umbrellas in your drinks. Give beach toys to each kid.

One advantage that the three-hour vacation has over the regular kind is that expectations tend to be much lower, and you know how we feel about lowered expectations. If you give presents on top of the partying, you turn the occasion into an unexpected celebration and add a little perspective to all the other evenings.

A few hours are no substitute for a real vacation. But if you're like an increasing number of Americans, you find it difficult to take as much time off as you want. Instead of a long vacation once or twice a year, you take more frequent short holidays, built around long weekends.

Cotton Mather, Fun Guy

⇒►◆◄⇐

"LAUDABLE RECREATIONS may be used now and then," Cotton Mather allowed. "But, I beseech you, Let those Recreations be used for Sauce, but not for Meat."

THE THREE-DAY VACATION

I F YOU HAD A WHOLE MONTH OFF, you wouldn't have to make many decisions. You could fit almost everything in: a trip to the beach, visits to relatives, household repairs, naps, catch-up reading. A well-done long weekend, on the other hand, requires as much planning and self-control as does wealth without money. You have to set goals and targets for the proper long weekend. Here are three standard goals:

1. The weekend should give you some perspective on your life, making you less anxious about work.

2. It should relax you. A related target is to find yourself not cussing a red light on your way back to work.

3. It should give you benefits that are scarce in your ordinary life, such as intellectual stimulation, fresh air and exercise, time out from duties and chores, sleep, or guilt-free luxury.

If it is hard to meet all three goals in one weekend, take several long weekends in a year, focusing on one or two goals per weekend. To get what you want out of the three days, you might consider devoting the time to a single theme. Some examples:

The Romantic Weekend. A bed-and-breakfast, a little too much wine, and thou. Plan it right, and you don't have to leave home. Your kids may object to this, so it helps to have a children's weekend to make up for it later.

The Intellectual Weekend. Spend the time researching or just reading about a single topic, something that has always sparked your curiosity. Study a painting in your art museum; read about the artist, examine the influences, and talk to a curator about how the painting inspired other paintings. You can organize a whole weekend around a play or musical performance. Do you have tickets to a rock concert? Hold a seminar with a few friends, getting someone knowledgeable to play the band's albums and the music that influenced them.

The Couch Potato Weekend. Stock up on convenience food. Put a fresh battery in the remote control. Rent a stack of movies; hunt up the TV listings. Avoid films that smack of art or good taste. Buy trashy magazines, bubble bath, snacks. Stay up late; sleep late; ditch the phone; don't leave home. You should go back to work happy to get out of the house, having had a refreshing excess of a good thing.

The Cook's Tour. Make a map of the food you and your family most want to eat in the course of three days. Plan the entire long weekend around food festivals, restaurants, delis, coffee shops, and bakeries. Spend the following week eating raw vegetables and cereal for dinner. Or plan a follow-up weekend that we call:

The Self-Made Spa. If you belong to a health club, schedule two hours a day in it, interspersed with vigorous walks and long naps. (In some clubs you can bring the kids along cheaply.) If you exercise at home, borrow some fitness videos. Before the weekend begins, fix healthful meals that you can easily whip together or heat in your microwave. Give each other massages. Go to bed early, get up early.

Shunpiking. There are two ways to shunpike, or drive back roads and explore new territory: planned and unplanned. Planning a several-day driving trip ensures rooms in motels or spots in campgrounds and helps avoid arguments about where to go next. On the other hand, the unplanned trip lets you be spontaneous. An inexpensive compromise is the use of your home or a friend's house as a base. Explore during the day, and come back at night. Hit every diner within a forty-mile radius, or go from yard sale to yard sale or historic site to historic site, or combine all those themes, stopping at whatever seems interesting.

Overnight Tenting. There are few better ways to get a change of perspective than camping. A vacation from routine like nothing else, it makes you glad to go back to work, where already brewed coffee is just sitting there. If you have small children, you should gain some camping experience on your own before attempting an ambitious trip. Shop for local hiking guides that show trails with shelters. The Appalachian Trail, stretching twenty-two hundred miles from Georgia to Maine, is the most elaborate, with lean-tos every five to ten miles.

The Family Day Hike. Before you try an overnight, first master the daylong family hike. There is no simpler way to spend your family time— or more difficult, if you do it unwisely. Bring water (your kids will actually drink it if it's in a cool-looking plastic canteen), and pack lunch. Make sure you have a destination: a mountaintop, a stream, a pond, a meadow, a hawk's nest, an overlook, a rope swing, even an old stone wall or an abandoned piece of farm equipment. It's best to have a bunch of destinations, landmarks along the route that help measure progress. Try to invite friends for your kids; they hike better with their peers. Bring a collecting bag for interesting stones, pieces of bark, leaves you want to identify later, flowers you can press between the pages of a book, the scat if you don't watch your kids closely. Prepare diligently, avoid unrealistic expectations, and you just may have an entire family enjoying itself in the woods. Keep in mind that you may not all be enjoying the same things, though.

STAKING OUT FUN TIME

A FTER YOU TAKE CARE of all your obligations—work, community meetings, kids' sports and lessons—who has time to hike or to leave on long weekends? To reserve time for play, put it on the calendar before anything else gets scheduled.

If this notion sounds alien, consider the fact that you already book time off; your calendar comes with dates for major holidays. You just need to add some. Book the longer vacations. Then look for Fridays and Mondays that are free for the whole family. Lastly, mark two-day weekends that you want to reserve for particular activities. It's a good idea to plan a season at least a month before it starts, so that the dates don't get preempted. Plan summer, for example, by the end of April. If you have to book hotels or resorts, you should schedule even sooner.

Hold a meeting with the family to plan the next season. What does each member most want to do during those three months? One kid wants to go to a drive-in movie at least twice. The other wants to climb at least two mountains. Your spouse wants a two-day canoe trip, and you want a shopping trip at a big mall two hours south. If you're the listing sort, write down all the activities for each person. Eliminate anything that's impractical or prohibitively expensive. Calculate how much time you need to accomplish everything. Eliminate low-priority items. Then set aside the necessary weekends, evenings, or days off. Mark them on the calendar so you can turn down any intruding obligations. That way you keep the complications from overwhelming the simpler things.

Listing can help for those periods when it's hard to know what to do, such as mud season. Museum going, bowling, shopping trips, a short-term membership at an indoor swimming pool: Anything qualifies if it lets you take advantage of the time of year instead of suffering from it.

Such times require the greatest diligence and imagination to stay in physical shape. Your exercise options tend to shut down in miserable weather either because you can't get outside or because you just don't feel like driving through sleet and wind to the Y to go swimming. You want to curl up and sleep through the season.

Well, who doesn't? Hibernating is one option during the dark time of year. But there are others, as the next chapter shows.

CHAPTER 13

The Soul's Vessel

The body, and how to control it

THERE WAS A TIME when people didn't think very much about their bodies unless they were sick. The Puritans believed that illness was a physical manifestation of sinfulness. Most doctors in early New England were ministers skilled in treating moral disease. People who kept themselves free of illness often grew impressively plump. This was a sign that God favored them with physical prosperity. To be plump was to be good-looking.

These days the opposite is true. If you want to be admired, you should combine driving greed with agonizing self-restraint. It is hard to imagine a more complicated way to live.

The splendid physiques you see in movies cost a lot, requiring dietitians, personal trainers, home weight-training equipment, and maybe a little surgical magic. And they demand time that people with steady jobs just

206

don't have. If you're rich in hours and dollars, you, too, can have a Hollywood body along with all the other millionaire goodies.

What? You're not rich? Well, then, congratulations. You have lowered expectations about your body. Who expects your normal citizen to have an eye-popping chest and abs of steel?

Fashion can skew our expectations. Sexy billboards that hawk underwear may make our contentment with our merely utilitarian bodies seem as if we're settling for less. The wealthy don't have to choose between fitness and their jobs and families. They can exercise at home, vacation in spas, and hire people to cook healthful meals. But as we have seen, you don't have to be a millionaire to be happy with your possessions. You just have to make decisions and then follow through with them. The same goes for your body. It may have seen better days, but you couldn't live without it.

A Fisher of Souls

⟹➤●◄⟸

IN THE EARLY 1700s a minister named Joseph Seccombe of Kingston, New Hampshire, wrote the first American book ever published on sport. An avid fisherman, the Reverend Seccombe railed against restrictions on outdoor pleasures as "Bigottry and Superstition." Besides, he said, a bit of brisk fun is good for you. "Recreation and Exercise are necessary for the better Support of the Body," he wrote. "And the Soul, during her Residence in the Flesh, must have Suspensions from her more abstracted and serious Pursuits."

Moral: Reverend Seccombe understood what many health faddists miss: A truly simple health plan is good for the soul.

BODY AND SOUL

ACTUALLY MANY EARLY NEW ENGLANDERS thought you *could* live without your body. To them it was just a vessel to hold the immortal soul. If you value the container more than the contents, they believed, you commit the sin of vanity, with alarming consequences for your soul. Philosophers in Europe and America once kept human skulls on their desks to remind them that their souls were more important than their bodies over the long haul. Talk about your ultimate health plan. It would make an interesting exercise video: a Puritan divine barking, "Give me ten searching looks to heaven! Eyes up, everybody! Don't forget to breathe!"

Okay, that's a ridiculous image. But we've seen exercise videos that don't come off much better.

If you think of your body as an important possession, but still just as a

---

Dying Art

IN THE EIGHTEENTH CENTURY the Andover Theological Seminary in Massachusetts required students to make coffins. The work reminded the students of their fleeting life on earth while earning good money for the seminary.

It's just like a Yankee to combine a heavenly lesson with an earthly profit.

Moral: Avoid the sin of vanity—of getting obsessed about your body— and you acquire an important attribute of the simple life.

possession, you can begin to separate your mortal cravings from those things you desire as a person. There are three basic goals to caring for this body of yours:

1. Good health. Illness or debility can vastly complicate life.

2. The ability to carry out the physical activities you want to do: climb stairs without gasping, play baseball with kids, go on a long bike ride, carry a pack.

3. Adequate personal appearance. You may not want to be repellent to the opposite sex or to yourself.

Of these three categories, looks seem the least important, yet we spend fortunes in time and money to take care of appearance first. If you had nothing to worry about but your body, a career of diet and exercise would be simple living. But your template for improving yourself physically should not be a hard body. It should be your *own* body, at its best.

Back in Chapter 4 we talked about the reasons why nearly all dieters fail and why a few succeed. Those who lose weight permanently don't try to become other people; instead they decide to *restore* themselves to their true health and appearance. Picture yourself in your mind. What do you look like? That picture may not be entirely accurate. It could be a bit out-of-date. People over the age of thirty tend to think of themselves as younger than they actually are. A graduate of Middlebury College once attended the wrong reunion. He showed up during alumni week and hung out with a group that, though strangely unfamiliar, looked his age. He had a great time until someone asked him his class and directed him to the other end of campus. There he found a group of balding, paunchy, middle-aged alumni. The worst part was he recognized them as his classmates. He left early.

Don't pity that guy; if your image of yourself is better than what you see in the mirror, you have the makings of a good diet and exercise plan.

Great Moments in Health

+ Sam Adams's newspaper, the Boston *Advertiser,* was too radical for most Bostonians. But people read the paper anyway because of its great practical advice. One of its more talked-about hints: changing babies' clothing regularly, despite the popular notion that clean linen might "rob Children of the nourishing juices."

+ In the fall of 1956 logger Barney Roberg was working alone in the woods near Patten, Maine, when a white pine tree he was cutting kicked back off the stump and pinned him, bleeding, to another tree. It was impossible to use his chain saw to cut the tree in such a way as to free himself. So he cut his leg off. Then he tied a tourniquet around the stump and crawled two miles to his jeep. Managing somehow to operate the gas and clutch pedals with only one foot, he drove himself out of the woods and found assistance. Eight weeks later he was back at work, driving a bulldozer. Roberg later recalled that the doctor in the hospital said the only chance he had for survival was to allow the removal of the rest of his leg above the knee. "Listen here, Doc," Roberg replied, "I done all the cutting on that leg that's going to be done. I got it trimmed up just the way I want it. Now you leave it alone."

+ The great eighteenth-century Harvard scientist Edward Augustus Holyoke warned against drinking "cold water or other weak small Liquids" after exercise without first downing a glass of rum. He ate lots of fruit, smoked two pipes a day, and on his hundredth birthday walked to a dinner given in his honor.

Moral: Good health includes a healthy dose of self-help.

YOU VERSUS YOUR CRAVINGS

THE BODY YOU SEE IN THE MIRROR is the result of genes, time, and habits. As you get farther from the age of twenty-five, either your habits must change or your body will. You can either decide not to mind or do something about it. That means changing your habits.

Option One: not minding. This may be the right choice for you. Does your lover seem happy with the way you are? Do you enjoy sports or walking or gardening without feeling crippled? Does your doctor seem unalarmed during a checkup? If health, abilities, and appearance are in good working order, then it just might not be worth changing your body. Your habits may be fine as they are, so why go to the trouble? The trick to simple living is not just to develop the right goals. First you have to know when to be satisfied.

Option Two: changing your habits. If your body is out of whack in any of the three categories, then you can exercise this option.

Before you start fixing, though, you need to know what's broke. If you are overweight, for example, you still need to know *how* you are overweight. Does a chart in a magazine say you weigh too much for your height? Don't believe it until you talk to a doctor. Without some knowledge of your medical history and genetic heritage, it's hard to say you weigh too much for good health unless you're truly obese, meaning 20 percent heavier than the charts say you should be. If you happen not to look like an underwear model, that doesn't mean you're unhealthy. Skinny isn't necessarily fit.

Are you disgusted with the way you look? Your appearance may not be the problem; talk to a medical professional or a member of the clergy about your feelings. No diet plan will cure you of a psychological or spiritual ailment.

Do you look like a stranger in the mirror? If you're convinced your weight is the reason, it still might be a good idea to talk to a close friend who can give you an honest assessment. Maybe you *do* weigh more than you should.

If you already have reasonable habits—if you don't overeat, if less than 20 percent of your diet is from fat, if you get half an hour's continual exercise at least three times a week and avoid consuming much alcohol—then chances are that your body is close to its natural state. The most successful diet plans, remember, are those that aim at bringing the body to this state. Call it your fate, and remember our oft-repeated moral that a well-chosen goal looks a lot like fate. (The obverse of this principle is

---

Couldn't He Just Settle for Makeup?

NATHANIEL HAWTHORNE wrote a short story, "The Birthmark," about a disastrous makeover. A great scientist marries a beautiful woman who is nearly flawless except for a tiny mark on her cheek. The doctor becomes obsessed with the spot, the only thing standing between the woman and perfection. He experiments on her night and day and finally creates a potion to get rid of the mark. But just as the spot disappears, the woman dies. Probably the scariest dermatology story ever written.

Moral: Although he probably didn't mean to, Hawthorne has written a cautionary tale for modern Americans who can't be satisfied with the bodies they (or their spouses) have.

that your fate, including your body's natural state, makes a good goal.) You could improve your body, of course. Cut the fat even more; avoid alcohol altogether; exercise longer, more vigorously, and more often. Your body could become an interesting hobby, a continuing physical experiment. Some people work on their cars or their gardens. You work on your body.

But if you feel ashamed because you don't follow these superhabits, you might work first on your shame, not on the habits. The first habits to change are those that cause your body to complicate your life. Dramatic diets and excessive workouts can be just as complicating as eating like a pig and living like a sloth.

While we're at it, though, let's get to the eating-like-a-pig part.

In a bit we'll talk more about goals and targets that can help you establish good habits and eliminate the bad ones. But first, let's list some larger principles. If you are what you eat, then a principled eater is . . . well, let's not get carried away. You may be surprised to find that much of the list is not very painful. Why should eating (or not eating) be a form of punishment? Excessive dieting does not simplify your life any more than excessive eating does.

In fact, as you'll see, we don't believe in dieting at all.

SIMPLE EATING PRINCIPLES
(A Baker's Dozen)

1. Don't diet. In the chapter "Weaning the Affections," we talked about budgeting and dieting being the same thing. The problem with both is that they tend to create goals that are too short and difficult. They aren't tied to lifetime habits. It is possible for a person who says, "I am on a diet," to lose some weight. But all the lost poundage usually comes back, and then some. There are two important reasons for the long-term failure of diets. One is that the very expression "I am on a diet" implies that it's temporary. If you're "on" a diet, then you probably intend to go "off" it at some point. You're fighting your body's natural tendency to stick to habits.

This leads to the second reason a diet almost always fails over the long run: Your body gets used to it. If you eat dramatically less, you might lose weight rapidly. But your system quickly adjusts to the new intake, using each calorie more efficiently. When you go off your diet, your body dutifully harbors the extra food as fat, at a greater rate than it did before you began your weight loss program. In other words, the less you eat, the better your body gets at converting calories to fat. It's a very fast learner, your body.

If you want to become a slimmer person, don't set short-term dietary goals. Establish permanent habits, and gradually reduce the amount you eat. Give your body time to get used to being thinner, and then you and it will be allies, not enemies.

2. Don't give up anything. Unless your doctor forbids certain foods, avoid painful taboos. Don't forswear ice cream, steak, french fries, or oysters. If you try to give them up entirely, you will feel like a failure when you eat them. Just don't consume as much. Eat smaller portions less often. Has it been weeks since you ate a steak in a restaurant? Go ahead and order the steak. But don't get the kind that fills up a large plate, or if you do, cut it in half and immediately ask for a doggie bag. An occasional ice-cream cone isn't bad for you. But order one scoop; two aren't twice as enjoyable. And don't make going out for ice cream a habit. That ruins it as a treat.

3. Don't just eat "lite." Many people attempt to lose weight by relying on processed foods with reduced fat and calories. There is nothing inherently wrong with these foods, but studies show that consumers who buy them tend to eat more of these foods than they would if the fat were left

The First Fad Diet Ever

TALK ABOUT DIGESTING THINGS to their essence. New Hampshirite Horace Fletcher elevated chewing to a virtue in two best-selling books. A painter, journalist, and shipping magnate, Fletcher flunked a medical exam for life insurance in 1895. Determined to lose fifty pounds and to cure his chronic indigestion, he discovered the mealtime secret to happiness and well-being: chewing every mouthful until the food "swallows itself." He described this principle in his books, *Menticulture, or The A-B-C of True Living* and *Happiness as Found in Forethought Minus Fear-thought*. "To fletcherize" became an expression known to every well-masticating household. Among his most famous adherents was the ruminative novelist Henry James.

The cure worked for Fletcher himself as well—he celebrated his fiftieth birthday by riding almost two hundred miles on a bicycle—but it didn't work perfectly. He died at the age of sixty of bronchitis.

If you're trying to limit the amount you eat, consider following the esophageal ethic of Horace Fletcher, who chewed one hundred times before every swallow. At the very least you will eat less between meals. You won't have time.

Moral: Don't fall for diets. Fall into habits.

in. The result: larger portions of less-satisfying food, no savings in calories, no lost weight.

It's good to cut some fat out of your diet. Researchers now say that a 20 percent fat content is healthy; the average for Americans is twice that amount. But if you cut out the fat without also reducing the *amount* you eat, you may not be helping yourself. Instead of limiting what you eat, limit how much. You eventually should find yourself feeling full with less food. Your body adjusts more easily to smaller amounts of food than to limitations on the types of foods you eat. Eat as varied a diet as you can, limit the fat-laden dishes to occasional treats, and eat less overall. You'll get slimmer and avoid self-pity.

4. Plan to eat in excess. Now and then you just have to cut loose. That's what this principle is for. As you know by now, a central concept in simple living is to do nothing to excess, including the excessive avoidance of excess. An overly restrictive life can be complicated and doomed to failure. Don't attempt to eliminate all your vices. Corral them instead. Limit ice cream to the weekend, for example. (That's a good system for alcohol as well. Don't have more than two drinks in a day, and drink only on Friday and Saturday nights.)

Another technique is to binge on the holidays. Don't stint on the gravy and pie on Thanksgiving. Pig out at New Year's. Eat all you want on your birthday, guilt-free. What's the sin in celebrating? The Puritans did it like gangbusters. But don't just binge; *use* the bingeing as a way to eliminate self-pity. Have you chosen to cut way back on pie? Give yourself a pie-eating time to look forward to. Treat it as a kind of food vacation, when you let your dietary hair down. The rest of the time you have to get real. So what if you gain a pound or two over the holidays? You planned to all along.

Nearly everyone strays from good eating. But you don't have to lose control; just *plan* to stray, and use your eating holidays to keep from straying the rest of the time.

5. Eat *really* fast food. Not only are most fast-food meals terrible for you, but they're not always that fast. You have to drive to the restaurant, wait in line, give your order, pay, discover that your order is incomplete, go back and try again. Sure, it's still probably faster than if you went out for a sit-down meal with table service. But if you tend to go out for lunch at work, consider this alternative: Pack a lunch of fruit, a hunk of good unsliced bread, and a can of fruit juice. You may have to peel an orange or banana, but that's it. You don't have to wait in line, heat anything up, or even spend much time packing in the morning.

> ## Chocolate Being an Exception
>
> —————•»●«•—————
>
> Eat to live, and not live to eat.
> —POOR RICHARD

6. Snack between meals. If this principle seems surprising, consider that *when* you eat isn't as important as *what* you eat and how much. Your body lays on less fat if it's never too hungry or too glutted. If you eat some fruit now and then—especially around three o'clock in the afternoon, when your body's blood sugar tends to be at its lowest level and energy may be flagging—you might eat less at mealtime, and there may be less temptation to eat chips or candy for an energy boost.

7. Cook in bulk. Create your own fast food and snacks by preparing them once or twice a week. Cook a large amount of pasta shells or macaroni, for example, and keep it in the fridge. Buy different sauces to go with it, along with cottage cheese and oil and vegetables for pasta salad. Keep a large bowl full of as many different kinds of fruit as you can find in season. Save small paper bags when you go shopping, and reuse them as lunch bags. Buy dried fruit for snacks at work.

8. Eat a Puritan dinner. If you can swing it, make midday your big mealtime, as our forebears did. Pack some hot soup or stew in a thermos with lunch. Then eat light for supper: salad, fruit, milk and cereal if you like, or a baked potato hot out of the microwave. You're less likely to put on weight if you don't go to bed full. Besides, a light supper is easier to prepare after a day of work.

9. Give thanks for your food. Why is saying grace a good eating habit? Besides being one of the most common ways for families to worship on a daily basis, a mealtime blessing makes you more conscious of what you're eating. Consider naming the food as you give thanks for it. Don't just consume; partake. If your eating habits are bad, one reason could be that they are unconscious; you take food for granted. A little ceremony before you eat could make you more aware of eating.

10. Eat slowly. Follow Horace Fletcher's advice (see the sidebar on page 215), and chew each bite. Establish chewing as a habit, and you may not have time to eat as much as you used to.

11. Eat until you're not hungry. Our worst dietary practices have to do with extremes. We eat beyond hunger, then periodically starve ourselves with diet plans. Instead we should learn to let our bodies tell us when to stop eating.

Most babies know this art better than adults do. Breast-feeding infants take in exactly what they need. They have the simplest diets of all: no complicated choices, extremely fast food (a few screams, and boom! there it is), and no anorexic models to compare themselves with.

We adult humans can adapt this same principle—or "infant formula," if you will. Eat when you're hungry. Stop eating when you're not hungry. If you stick mostly to the foods that are good for you, avoiding too much fat and sugar, then your body will take what it needs and will tell you when to stop. The long-term result, if you exercise properly, will be the weight you're supposed to be.

12. Eat for after the meal. Conduct a little cost-benefit analysis before you eat something. Will you be glad you ate this food an hour from now? A day from now?

You don't have to regret eating a candy bar. If you're sure you will enjoy it, go ahead and eat it. But if fat and calories will outweigh the pleasure an hour after you've swallowed it, the candy bar may not seem worth it. The pleasure should outweigh the pain, including the painful regrets.

13. Treat yourself; don't reward yourself. When you eat something that isn't good for your body, do it for the pleasure, not as a reward for some good deed you did. If you use junk food as a bribe, you risk inflation, giving yourself bigger rewards for less effort. You want an ice-cream cone? Go ahead, as long as the pleasure outweighs the pain. Don't do it because you've gone for a run. Exercise, like eating, should be done for its own rewards.

CHAIRMAN MAO'S REVOLUTIONARY WEIGHT LOSS PLAN

YOU MAY FIND DIETING far removed from the subject of the Chinese Revolution. True, Mao Zedong doesn't seem to have worried much about overeating. He lived in a country where the point was to get enough to eat, not how to burn it off again. (In fact, he is accused of fomenting mass starvation.)

Nonetheless, you can apply Mao's strategic wisdom to various aspects of your own life. When Henry Kissinger was a Harvard professor, he admired the Chinese Communists for this principle: **Once you set a goal, stick to the goal, not necessarily to the details of the plan.** Mao went into each battle expecting to win. When he lost, which happened pretty often, he didn't conclude that the plan was terrible; he just recognized that the battle was.

Like every great military leader, Mao knew the difference between strategy and tactics. Strategy is the plan that takes you to your goal; tactics are what you do to carry out the strategy. Despite tactical setbacks, a great strategy often wins wars.

You can see why Kissinger admired his enemy. But Kissinger is a notoriously unsuccessful dieter. When he was secretary of state, he had three hundred suits to match his wildly fluctuating weight. Maybe Kissinger should have used Mao's wisdom at mealtime. A good strategy for weight control is to eat less junk food and to begin exercising. Some tactics would include cutting out the candy bar you have during coffee break and doing twenty sit-ups before breakfast every morning.

Three days into your weight loss plan you find yourself pumping quarters into the office candy machine. Has your diet failed? Mao wouldn't think so. He would have seen that wayward candy bar as a battlefield setback and might have recommended one of several alternatives:

- ✦ Eat a bit less over the next week than you initially intended.
- ✦ Expect to lose weight a little more slowly than you planned.
- ✦ Change the goal to allow a little more weight than originally planned. (Actually Mao wasn't big on changing goals, but we're no revolutionaries.)

There's only one downside to the Mao weight loss plan. The Chairman didn't see his revolution succeed until decades after he started. You may wish to see results a bit more quickly than that. Still, you get the point. The Mao technique works on anything where you need to set goals and stick to them.

Have you noticed how similar the Communist Chinese were to the early Puritans? An occasional sin or retreat doesn't prove you won't get to heaven—or to a workers' paradise. When you believe that a goal is your fate, straying becomes nothing more than a slight detour.

EXERCISE OPTIONS

Iᶠ ʏᴏᴜ ᴛʜɪɴᴋ ʏᴏᴜʀ ʙᴏᴅʏ'ꜱ ɴᴀᴛᴜʀᴀʟ ꜱᴛᴀᴛᴇ is skinnier than its current state, then the most efficient way to reform is to eat better, eat less, and combine these habits with exercise. Exercise is overrated as a sole means of losing weight. One candy bar can contain more than eight hundred calories, about two hours' worth of intense workout. It takes less time to avoid eating a candy bar than it does to work off the eight hundred calories. That's one reason why so much household exercise equipment lies around unused. People work out for a couple of weeks, get frustrated that they're not losing weight, and give up. An exercise routine can actually make you heavier; muscles are denser than fat, and the bathroom scale may not give you a cheerful report even when you're fitter.

If you're thinking about exercising more, go back to the three original body goals: health, physical abilities, and appearance. "Weighing less" is too restrictive a target. Stick to the lifetime bodily goals, use three- or six-month targets to measure progress, and you may actually hit on some exercise that doesn't feel like torture.

In Chapter 4 we talked about setting multiple targets, being happy when we met some of them, and using the information if we didn't meet any of them. Three broad categories to use for exercise targets are aerobic capacity, strength, and flexibility.

Aerobic capacity is the ability of your heart and lungs to deliver oxygen throughout your body. If you can run up several flights of stairs without getting winded, then you're in good aerobic shape. If you find yourself gasping when you walk to your car, your body isn't efficient with the oxygen you're breathing.

Strength is your muscles' ability to work the way you want them to.

As people age, they tend to lose strength faster than they lose aerobic fitness. But it takes less time to regain strength than it does to improve aerobic capacity.

Flexibility is something else you often lose with age. Can you touch the floor with both your palms while bending your knees only slightly? Then you're very flexible. Do you have trouble tying your shoes? Then you're not. Women tend to stay limber later in life than men do, but even guys can gain flexibility through regular stretching.

What does all this have to do with getting skinny? Very little, unless you combine exercise with healthful eating. By toning up various muscle groups, however, you can also make parts of your body look less flabby. You may not weigh less, but you look better.

ACCIDENTAL EXERCISE

THERE WAS A TIME when people got all the exercise they wanted, and then some, during the working day. People got paid to exercise; they walked behind plows, or carried bales of hay, or strained to pull horses out of the mud. Nowadays the couch potato is our national vegetable. Thanks to suburban developments, elevators, cars, "service" jobs, and household laborsaving devices, we don't walk, pull, or push, or lift, or climb, or even get out of chairs as much as we used to. We are an increasingly unfit nation.

Your life doesn't have to be that way. Before you sign up for another aerobics class or buy the latest-model treadmill, consider some ways you can pick up exercise here and there in your normal day:

Park far. Want to save time when you park your car at crowded places?

Uncle Tom's Aerobic Plan

H ARRIET BEECHER STOWE walked twice a day for a total of five to seven miles. "If I am not feeling well, I can usually walk it off," she said. "Or, if not, I sleep it off, going to bed by eight o'clock."

Moral: Exercise and health are a better match than exercise and appearance. Mrs. Stowe is not remembered for her beauty, but she had the stamina to write some of her century's most important literature.

Don't agonize over finding a spot up close. Park a distance away and walk.

Take the stairs. Eschew the elevator whenever possible, at work, in shopping malls, at the airport, in hotels. The stairs are often faster. If the doctor says your heart is fine, begin by climbing slowly, one step at a time. After a few weeks of stair climbing, vary the routine: Take two steps occasionally, or jog some flights. Do you perspire a little? People probably won't notice. Fix yourself up in a bathroom.

Ditch the kitchen gadgets. Give away or sell electric devices. Start with the electric can opener; the manual kind is great for strengthening your grip and your wrists. Ditto for eggbeaters. Try food processing with a knife and a grater. You save money on the equipment and repairs; you save shelf space; you may even save time, since many electric kitchen tools are harder to clean than the human-powered kind; most of all, you gain upper-body strength. (A washboard instead of a washing machine would be even better, but we don't want to push things.)

Carry your own luggage. Airports are rumbling with the sound of suitcases that have casters built into them so they can be dragged like pull toys. They're clever inventions but bad exercise equipment. If you want to save your back and get fit, acquire a frameless backpack. Sporting goods stores and catalogs sell them in all sizes. Most fit in airplane overhead luggage compartments. You can carry packs hands-free, with little strain on back and shoulders. Packs don't wrinkle clothing as much as you think, and fitness research has shown that walkers get considerably more exercise with a weight on their backs.

Run your own errands. Do you have a memo for an officemate? Dash it over yourself. Instead of sending an E-mail message to someone on the next floor, pop up and talk personally. If the boss allows it, look for any excuse to get out of your chair.

Change your commute. Do you take the bus to work? Walk an extra stop or two. Do you live within several miles of your job? Try walking, running, or riding a bike. (It helps if there's a shower or at least a place to change.) If you blend exercise with commuting, you make the self-discipline part easier; it's just part of the commute.

CROSS TRAINING

S UPPOSE YOU WALKED to and from the bus stop five times a week, took the stairs instead of the elevator up three flights to your office, and went bicycling or hiking with your kids on the weekend. You would be in better shape than most Americans, fewer than half of whom get any regular exercise. You would also be practicing a technique recommended by top fitness experts, cross training. The term simply means doing more than one kind of exercise regularly. If you went jogging every weekday, your legs would probably start feeling tired by Friday. But if you swam twice a week and jogged three times a week, you'd have more energy for both. This imitates what people were bred to do naturally, a variety of things. Our Cro-

A Smoker Is Reborn Every Minute

---⇒●⇐---

THE FOUNDATION OF SUCCESS IN LIFE is good health; that is the substratum of fortune; it is also the basis of happiness.
—P. T. BARNUM, who smoked ten cigars a day before he quit cold turkey

---

Magnon ancestors ran away from enemies, walked in search of food, and carried wood. They were cross trainers.

Our hunter-gatherer ancestors practiced another form of exercise whose benefits have only recently been discovered: long slow distance, or LSD. Studies of middle-aged athletes show that a weekly low-key, long-lasting activity caused their weight to drop significantly. A slow jog lasting three or four hours (they were athletes, remember) taught their bodies to convert fat into fuel. Instead of just burning sugars, the way we usually do when we exercise, the LSD athletes burned up fat—even during their shorter, more intense exercises. There is every reason to believe that you can teach your body the same trick by going on a weekly hike. A mountain a week could provide the fat-burning lesson your body needs. If you live in flat terrain, wear a pack and try to maintain a brisk walking pace.

LSD is no substitute for other exercise. To be in your best shape, you should do some sort of activity for twenty minutes or more, three or four times a week. Nor is LSD alone the best way to lose weight. But the combination of good eating, a hike a week, and two or three other forms of exercise during the workweek could take you reasonably far toward the three goals of health, prowess, and looks.

"Reasonably?" you say. "What's so reasonable about exercising six or seven hours a week and eating like a saint?"

Naked Ambition

———→►●◄←———

JOHN QUINCY ADAMS took an occasional morning swim in the Potomac when he was president. Once he swamped his boat and lost most of his clothes. He walked back to the White House half naked and embarrassed.

Moral: Dignity should never get in the way of fitness. Remember Adams the next time you feel self-conscious about exercise.

If it doesn't sound reasonable, it probably isn't for you. Not yet. The best way to get in shape is to take your time.

PHYSICAL TARGETS

DECIDE TO GET IN SHAPE FOR THE NEXT DECADE, not the next week. Set modest three- or six-month targets to measure your progress. As you meet the targets, gradually up the ante.

Let's set a few sample goals and put some targets with them. In the health category we want to stay uninjured. Our abilities goal is to get out of bed in the morning without groaning and to be a hiker unusually late in life. For appearance, we want to weigh about ten pounds less than we do now and to keep that weight off forever. We also want people to think we're ten years younger than we actually are. Or maybe twenty years younger, by the time we're, say, ninety.

Those are the goals. Now for the targets and the training to go with them. It's time for a table.

TARGETS

	HEALTH	ABILITIES	APPEARANCE
Three-month targets	Stay uninjured. Go three months without a cold.	Walk from bed to bathroom in the morning without staggering. Run/walk two miles. Hike four miles of an easy trail.	Lose two pounds. Fit in pants bought last year.
Six-month targets	Stay uninjured. Go six months with just one cold.	Walk easily to the bathroom in the morning. Run two miles. Hike four miles of a hilly trail.	Lose three pounds. Fit in suit bought three years ago.
One-year targets	Stay uninjured. Go one year with just two colds, no more serious illness.	Get up in the morning without feeling uncomfortably stiff. Run four miles. Hike up three-thousand-foot mountain without difficulty.	Lose five pounds. Fit in suit bought five years ago.

Setting cold prevention as a target may seem like tempting fate, but there is evidence that sustained periods of fresh air and raised body temperature really can fight colds. A strong body is less susceptible to diseases in general. At any rate, if you come down with more than two colds in a year, you can look for encouragement to other targets.

Notice that training and targets get a bit blurred in the "Abilities" column. The more exercise you get, the more you're capable of doing. This is part of the ratcheting-up phenomenon we talk about in previous chapters. A four-mile run may seem impossible at first, routine after a year or so. Let's look at a sample exercise plan, keyed to the table above. It's just a sample, mind you; a real plan should have your physician's approval and would have to be geared to your own age, abilities, goals, and schedule. Consider the table below a template for your own plan.

TRAINING

MONTHS 1–3

Aerobic Fitness   Brisk two-mile walk during lunch hour twice a week.
Take stairs instead of elevator at work.
Short weekend hikes with family in state park at least once a month.
Two-mile walk/jog after work once a week.

Flexibility   Each Sunday morning, do stretching exercises with a videotape.
Before bed every night, bend over (with knees slightly bent) and try to touch toes.
Try to remember to do a bit of stretching at work.

Strength   Borrow a video from the library on calisthenics. Learn proper sit-up (or other stomach exercise) and safe push-up techniques.
Install a chin-up bar in bathroom doorframe. Every night (with help of a chair if necessary), try to do one pull-up.

Months 4–6

Aerobic Fitness   Brisk two-mile walk during lunch hour twice a week.

Take stairs instead of elevator at work.

Weekend hikes with family in state park at least once a month. Talk them into hillier terrain.

Two-mile jog once a week after work or on weekend.

Flexibility   Do shortened version of Sunday stretching routine for ten minutes after getting out of bed every weekday morning.

Continue full stretch every Sunday.

Light stretch before bed every evening.

Try to remember to do periodic stretching at work.

Strength   Every weekday morning, combine stretching with ten sit-ups or stomach crunches and ten push-ups.

Every weekday after work, do one pull-up. Try to work up to two pull-ups.

Months 7–12

Aerobic Fitness   Brisk two-mile walk on lunch hour twice a week.

Take stairs instead of elevator at work.

Talk family into climbing a few peaks.

Gradually increase weekly run from two to four miles.

Flexibility   Get up fifteen minutes early each weekday to do stretching and strength routine.

Continue full stretch every Sunday.

Light stretch before bed every evening.

Try to remember to do periodic stretching at work.

Strength   Build up to twenty sit-ups and twenty push-ups each weekday morning.

Build up to four pull-ups and three chin-ups every weekday evening.

The one-year routines above may look positively crazy, especially if you've never done regular exercise. Does it seem like a lot of time? Do the exercises seem impossible? Then don't look at the "Months 7–12" section. Look at the section for the first three months. Devote just one hour of your workweek to exercise during this period. On the weekends make sure you do something fun that lasts at least an hour—biking, hiking, skiing, swimming—anything that gets you outside and breathing. (Or inside and breathing if the weather stinks.) After a few months up the ante. You'll probably be capable of greater athletic feats. Add a short morning exercise routine. After a while this shouldn't seem the torture it looks at first. If you turn down the heat at night, a little early-morning exercise warms you up better than a shower, and it has the advantage of speeding your metabolism, allowing your body to burn more calories during the day.

By combining the right exercise and eating and by setting modest targets that gradually increase, you might surprise yourself by actually meeting some of those targets. If you meet all of them, you may have set your targets a bit low. A little failure is good for the soul.

Phil Jensen's Daily Constitutional

A T SEVENTY-FOUR, Phil Jensen of Berlin, New Hampshire, climbs Mount Washington every day. He trots up the Northeast's tallest peak (6,288 feet) in ninety minutes—half the time of a normal fit person.

Moral: A high goal to one person can seem routine to another. One is resolution; the other, habit.

THE GOAL OF A NEW MACHINE

IF YOU'RE THINKING OF BUYING EXERCISE EQUIPMENT, look in your newspaper's classified listings for used stuff. Few people stick to their home equipment more than several months. To make sure you use your machinery over the long run, don't buy it until you already do at least two kinds of exercise routinely, such as running and aerobics class. Plan to use the home machine when the weather is bad or you can't get to the gym. Don't make the equipment your sole means of training; use it for cross training. The best machine employs most or all of your large-muscle groups so that you can get maximum aerobic benefit with minimal strain. A popular kind imitates cross-country skiing. It doesn't hurt your back, and it is a more rigorous workout than it feels—a high ratio of gain to pain. A rowing machine offers a similar benefit, but it can be hard on bad backs. If you travel a lot, consider packing one of the most efficient aerobic devices ever invented, a jump rope.

If your equipment doesn't come with a manual, find an explanatory book or video. Start slowly, concentrating on proper form to avoid injury. Spend ten minutes on the machine your first several times, then twenty minutes of slow movement. Increase your speed over the months until you're going as fast as you like. Then increase your time to half an hour or more.

TRAINING FOR EVENTS

SUPPOSE YOU'VE HAD a successful year of losing weight, getting stronger, and feeling younger. Your spouse looks at you with lust. Friends gossip about you. Your closet becomes a treasure chest of once-unwearable clothing. You're now ready for the big time. Like any good athlete, you can use a little competition.

You don't need other people to compete; your own targets make for good sport. All you need is an event to train for. You can make it up if necessary. "I'm in training," you can say to yourself proudly. This sounds much nobler than "I'm on a diet" or "I'm learning to jog." There is the danger that a big event can work like a diet, making you overly smug if you meet a goal. To avoid that trap, plan an event at least once a year, to give you a regular training season.

If you've never competed athletically as an adult, select an activity you'd most want to train for, such as a run, or a swim, or a mountain climb. It should seem pretty hard but doable. Get your doctor's okay first. Here are a few sample events, both organized and personal.

The two-mile Thanksgiving "turkey trot." This is a common event, often sponsored by local recreation departments or chambers of commerce. If you run four miles comfortably, this race is right for you. Establish multiple targets—for example, to complete the race in less than fifteen minutes, finish better than the bottom third of your age-group, pass at least ten people, and not feel terrible at the end. Decide to be satisfied if you meet two out of the four targets.

Begin training for the race three months ahead of time. Cut way back on alcohol. Eat like someone in training, avoiding fats and refined sugar. If you can run the racecourse, time yourself on it once in a while. Mark out a mile's road running with your car odometer. Try to set a regular pace, such as eight minutes to the mile. Increase the amount of stretching you do in the morning. Vary your workouts, running a slow and easy four miles now and then and an occasional fast two miles. One week before the race, taper your training routine, easing up on the speed and mileage so you'll be fresh on race day.

The tough mountain climb. Look in regional guidebooks for a challenging peak that you could do safely in a day. If you can comfortably climb two thousand feet in several hours, look for a hike that takes you up three thousand feet. This is not a competitive event in the sense of beating your hiking partners up the mountain; it's a more personal challenge.

Train for the event three months in advance by making sure you have properly broken-in boots or shoes with good ankle support, along with clothing that will keep you warm and dry in dramatically changing weather. Increase your aerobic exercise. Build up your legs by jogging upstairs at home or work. Establish a plan for running a certain number of flights each week. If you have the time and money, find a health club with stair-climbing machines. These impressive (and expensive) inventions let you set and measure your own pace, and they're better for the knees than regular stairs. On the weekends practice on easy mountains if you can get to them.

The big game. Is there a neighborhood basketball court where young jocks hang out? Work up to inviting yourself into a game. Or enter a health club tennis tournament or some other low-key competition in your best sport. It may not be a big deal to the people you play, but it is to you; you've trained for the competition. Practice your sport at least twice a week for three months before competing. Get into shape by setting targets for fitness, flexibility, and strength. Taper off the week before the event by easing up on the aerobics and the practice and by increasing the amount of stretching.

The family Olympics. Set aside a Saturday or Sunday three months in advance, and ask each family member to name an athletic feat. To avoid strains on family ties, establish a different feat for each member. One might attempt to do thirty push-ups, another to run two miles in fourteen minutes, still another to dance the twist through an entire Chubby Checkers recording.

Train for the event, setting interim targets. Consider posting a chart in the kitchen to show progress.

Devote part of the big day to each event, geared around each member. Reward a blue ribbon to anyone who accomplishes a stated feat. Give a red ribbon for an effort that comes within 20 percent of the goal, a yellow ribbon for a noble try. Or you could give out little gifts, such as small framed pictures (snapshots or children's drawings) of the athletes in action.

Don't feel obligated to up the athletic ante in these ways until you have already met your initial targets; a year's exercise is a good minimum. But after a while you may challenge yourself almost automatically. As you certainly know by now, we call that ratcheting up.

CHAPTER 14

Low Fruit

In which the reader decides what to do and when

Y OU MAY HAVE MANAGED to get through this book without having set a single goal, gained one good habit, or found a clue to
your calling. Thoughts about discipline and the future can be
daunting, and you may be wondering where to begin. That is
what this chapter is for: to help you start simplifying.

If you were an early New Englander, you would know exactly where
to begin. Your minister and your neighbors would have been helpfully in-
forming you of your faults all your life. As for your calling, you probably
inherited it, or else your father announced it when you were old enough for
education or apprenticeship. Habits arose from family life and your calling. If you were literate, you might have kept a diary to assist your family
and neighbors in pointing out your sins. You would have applied yourself
to correcting them, decrying your worthlessness while noting with inward

satisfaction that you were basically not such an evil person.

These days we don't particularly appreciate attempts to point out our faults, we might object to having our fathers announce our careers, and our habits might be in serious need of correction. So unlike a Puritan, we can't expect to launch ourselves into self-improvement programs and un-complicate our lives right off the bat. It takes time and a couple of valuable principles, to wit:

Discover your destination; then take the easiest route. A good plan should be a relief, not a burden. In this chapter we suggest a yearlong schedule for uncovering your calling and then choosing ways to fulfill it.

Pick the low fruit first. Set out to improve what's easiest to improve. Eliminate the complications that are most happily abandoned.

A SIMPLIFYING YEAR

I F YOUR LIFE IS AN ABSOLUTE WRECK, you need something more than this book. If it is not a total mess, don't panic about improving it. Take your time. Go over the parts of the book that mean something to you. Do the exercises in Chapter 3 that interest you. Then let your thoughts percolate for at least a month. After that, set a date on your calendar for beginning your year of simplifying. Don't start during vacation; save vacation for vacation. On the other hand, your year shouldn't begin at an especially busy time. If you like to walk while you think, begin your simplifying year during the season when walking is best for you. A Saturday or Sunday makes a good starting day.

Try to mark the date on your calendar long in advance. Congratulate yourself for having accomplished a couple of simplifying tasks: reading this book and establishing a beginning simplifying date. If you have been thinking about your purpose in life and about what makes you happy, congratulate yourself again. You still have plenty of time to nail down your calling once your year begins.

Don't get nervous about that starting date. It should be the beginning not of tough times but of useful thinking. You don't have to make a big announcement about it either unless you're into announcements. Just look forward to a time when you will think about yourself.

First month: find your calling. If you haven't satisfied yourself with the exercises in Chapter 3, do them on the first weekend of your simplifying year. Think back on your childhood, and work your way up to the present. In what ways are you different from the person you consider your true self? How much trouble would it take to eliminate the obstacles in the way of that "fate"?

You can do an additional exercise that New Englanders of the nineteenth century adored: Write your own obituary. How would you want your life summed up? "Movie Buff Suffers Fatal Stroke in Mansion Built by Successful, Adoring Children"? "Nonagenarian a Casualty of Bungee Accident"? Well, let's be serious about this. What can you realistically hope for in a summation? What accomplishments, private and public, would you most want listed? What lasting effect, however small, would you want to have on the world? Your obituary can't say everything about you, but if you write it yourself, it can help describe what your life means to you.

In a similar exercise, try describing your ideal death scene. Victorian New Englanders went nuts over such morbid stuff. Do you picture your death as heroic, as a quiet summation, as a family event? Imagine the circumstances beyond the scene itself. Are you leaving a good estate to loved ones, a life with few regrets? How can you arrange for the estate? What regrets need avoiding?

If only you really could read the ending, like flipping through to the last

The Paperback Rights
Would Be Disputed, Though

B ENJAMIN FRANKLIN was only twenty-two when he wrote his famous epitaph, which never actually found its way onto his tombstone:

The Body of
B Franklin Printer,
(Like the Cover of an old Book
Its Contents torn out
And stript of its Lettering & Gilding)
Lies here, Food for Worms,
But the Work shall not be lost;
For it will, (as he believ'd) appear once more,
In a new and more elegant Edition
Revised and corrected,
By the Author.

Moral: Some people believe in self-improvement even after death.

page of a mystery novel. But you don't really want to do that anyway, do you? Besides, you're helping to write the book. Naturally you will want to imagine the happiest possible ending. How would you sum up a simple, happy life? Employ the first six chapters in this book. What burdens of fashion or unnecessary duty can you jettison to lighten your life? What obstacles to your fate can you most easily eliminate? What new habits do you need?

Nice Endings

Clara Barton's last words: "Let me go! Let me go!"

Daniel Webster's last words: "I still live." (It was engraved on popular Sheffield razors.)

John Adams's last words: "Thomas Jefferson survives."

Harriet Beecher Stowe's last words: "I love you."

The last words of William Brattle, Loyalist general during the Revolution and famous epicure: "Set the plate by for dinner."

P. T. Barnum didn't need last words. When he took to his deathbed in 1891, the New York *Evening Sun* ran his obituary early so he could read it before he died.

Moral: The end of a well-founded calling can be immortality.

The exercises should offer faint hints that get stronger as you go, until you can clearly hear what you have set out to hear, which is your calling.

Second month: goal setting. Your goals should arise directly from your ideal fate. If only one goal compels you, fine. If you come up with several, so much the better. You do not want to complicate your life with an excess of goals, but if you set three, or four at the most, they can complement each other. Pride in one accomplishment prepares you for another. Any goal that gains you time, energy, or home comfort can make other goals seem doable. Talk to your family about how your aspirations might affect them. Set goals for yourself, not for others. Few people are less bearable than those with exciting plans for improving their friends and loved ones. That is one Puritan trait you may not want to emulate.

In considering goals for yourself, review Chapters 8 through 13, and establish some broad categories. Here are some samples :

Simplify relations with my partner.
Simplify relations with my community and friends.
Simplify relations with my kids.
Become happy with what I own.
Become happy with my work.
Enjoy my free time more.
Become happy with my body.

Which is most important to you? Which is most out of sync with your calling? Now get more specific: What in these categories most needs fixing? With your partner, your goal might be to spend more quiet time; with your friends, social time; with your kids, quantity time. To become happy with what you own, you might consider two or three goals: shedding some possessions, finding the means to acquire others. In the free time category, you might be saying to yourself, "What free time?" In that case the goal could be to acquire some. For the body category, you can decide what is your real, fated physique and set goals that prove it. They might include losing weight, becoming a good walker, feeling less stiff in the morning, or attaining serious athletic prowess. Don't attach specific numbers to any of your goals. That's what targets are for, as we described them in Chapter 4.

The next step is to set your satisfaction levels. How little of your goal can you meet and still feel happy about it? How much effort would it realistically take to reach that state? Is the effort worth it? In other words, is your life simpler if you work toward your goal or if you skip the whole thing? If you wish you were skinnier, for example, the question is whether your plumpness is messing up your life enough to make it worth your while to change your eating habits and start some serious exercise. If you're considering a goal to change jobs, would the hunt disrupt your family life? Or would it be simpler to stay where you are and declare yourself satisfied?

Third through sixth month: experimenting. Once your goals are set, you will want to establish targets to measure success. But first you must establish a baseline of measurement. Spend several months doing research on your goal: what you think it will take to achieve it; the size and scope of the obstacles in your way; the habits and skills you need. On some goals, plot samples come in handy. Here are various ways you can measure yourself, culled from the other chapters in this book and matched with goal categories:

> ## Persistence Equals IQ
>
> "**G**ENIUS IS INFINITE patience," said Michelangelo. This was one of Louisa May Alcott's favorite quotations.

GOAL CATEGORY	MEASUREMENTS
Possessions (Chapter 10)	Moot move
	Household plot sample
Work (Chapter 11)	Research education needed for a job
	Background research on employers
Rest (Chapter 12)	Counting seconds with and without watch
	Analyzing vacations you've taken
Body (Chapter 13)	Consulting a doctor about fitness routines
	Week's diet plot sample

You can "measure" where you stand with spouse and children as well. Examine the times you or your kids have become angry. Think of how you handled an argument with your partner. How could you have done better? Your behavior is your baseline. How you wish you behaved can be a target.

This period can also give you a chance to scope out potential mentors, as we discussed in Chapter 8. Is there someone who seems especially accomplished in a category you want to improve? Talk to the person. Ask for advice. Get her to share the ways she screwed up as well as her successes. Besides being educational, the failure of a superior is reassuring to the rest of us. If you don't feel comfortable talking to your chosen mentor, watch him or her from afar.

Seventh through ninth month: habituating and sloughing. This is the crucial simplifying period, when you begin to get rid of complications and obstacles. During these three months you work on time and habits.

+ Look at Chapter 6 for ways to find pockets of time. You can free up hours for your goals or see the extra time as a goal in itself.
+ Get rid of social obligations that don't satisfy you and have little to do with your calling. See our advice on learning to say no.
+ Decide how much time you want to carve from your television habits.
+ If you can get yourself up at five every morning, you have something in common with history's most admirable New Englanders. Consider following our plan for changing your wake-up time in the fall.
+ Examine your commuting time, and see if some of it can't be spent on your goals.

Next, set habits specific to the individual goals. Begin sloughing off the ones you don't want, and acquire those most useful for meeting your targets. Remember, start with what's easiest, do what most readily becomes automatic. See the individual chapters for suggested habits.

One obstacle to toss aside is unrealistic expectations. Ditch the hopes of becoming a millionaire; establish habits that let you live like one. Forget looking like a bodybuilder (unless that's a specific, realistic goal you have set). Instead, set habits of mind and body that allow you to be satisfied with your truest physique.

Tenth through twelfth month: measuring and ratcheting. This is the time to repeat the measurements you made before you established

---

Henry Adams Knew When to Hold 'Em

HENRY ADAMS GAVE SOME INGENIOUS ADVICE on fate in his autobiography, *The Education of Henry Adams.* "Whether life was an honest game of chance, or whether the cards were marked and forced," he wrote about himself, "he could not refuse to play his excellent hand. He could never make the usual plea of irresponsibility. He accepted the situation as though he had been a party to it, and under the same circumstances would do it again, the more readily for knowing the exact values. To his life as a whole he was a consenting, contracting party and partner from the moment he was born to the moment he died."

Moral: In joining your fate, you are a consenting adult. This may not be completely true, but it is a good attitude.

A Sample Year of Simplifying

HERE IS WHAT A PLAN for a year of simplifying might look like for a woman with husband, career, and children:

May. Simplifying year begins. I reread the first several chapters of this book. I write my obituary and a description of my much-mourned death. I describe my calling: to be an accomplished outdoorswoman, a skilled professional, and a good wife and mother. I spend the month testing it. Is this really my destiny?

June. I set goals: to keep up with my husband in hiking the Presidential Range in New Hampshire; to learn to paddle a canoe in mild whitewater; to improve the time we spend together as a family; to quit my job and become an independent consultant working out of my home.

July–September. I hike two small peaks with a backpack, timing myself by the mile to establish a baseline for progress. I call my friend, an experienced outdoorswoman, for advice on gear. I research canoeing clinics. I discuss with family how many times a week we could realistically have dinner together. I do a plot sample of household income and expenses. I say yes to helping with Green-Up Day, no to a second term as a library trustee.

October–December. I begin getting up at 5:00 A.M. I do a morning exercise routine. I make preparations for dinner. I spend an hour each morning working on consulting assignments. I limit television to an hour each evening.

January. I go on a New Year's walk with husband. I rethink goals. I do another household plot sample. I use the neighborhood health club's annual open house to test my fitness on a stair-climbing machine. I reset new targets for March. I plan year's vacations, goals for family play time.

February. I keep it up!

March. I do the first mountain climb of the season. I attend a weekend canoe clinic in an indoor pool. As part of spring cleaning, I do a moot move. I plan a financial retreat with husband. Main topic: Can we shift some of children's college savings into expenses so I can quit my job?

April. I do an easy whitewater paddle with husband.

May. I celebrate successes. I plan moments of excess. I set higher targets. I rethink goals.

your first targets. Account for what worked and what didn't. Where you have succeeded, ratchet up by setting new targets. Where you have failed, lower your expectations.

At the end of the year congratulate yourself on the ways you have simplified your life. You should have a sense of control you never had before. You are pursuing your calling.

We hear much talk about "self-esteem," a term that would have made our predecessors in New England nervous. To esteem yourself smacks of pride, one of the worst of sins. To think too much of yourself could be proof that you aren't one of the elect after all and so have no reason for self-esteem in the first place.

And yet (with the Puritans there always was an "and yet"), as unworthy as the early believers seemed in the eyes of their God, they appeared just a bit more worthy than all the other sinners. Underneath the vaunted humility of the Puritan saints was the conviction that they were among God's chosen people. Over the generations this attitude sometimes lapsed into smugness and real snobbery. But there is a lesson for all of us in the Puritans' inner sense of worth: We can quietly hold the feeling that we are capable of setting somewhat higher standards for ourselves than may be expected of us. If you actually believe in improving yourself, in making decisions that simplify your life, you already stand apart from most people. If you act on those decisions and set goals and accompanying habits, you probably can expect to improve. The more you improve, the more you will discover the faults and complications that need fixing. But you might also begin to see yourself as chosen for a noble calling, which is your life.

You may never have lived in New England, but if you have found your calling, you have found simplicity. You are now the Yankee-est of Yankees.

Index

n that right." You would not receive a
rumor about your friend because you
your friend's usual behavior. You have
d and talked with that person enough
ow what he or she is likely to do or
do. If someone asked you how your
would feel about a certain matter,
vould know or could at least make a
guess.

must know God's character just as
s we know our friend's character. If
ne said God told her something that
against His Word, you shouldn't have
nk about it. By instinct you should
"That doesn't sound like God to me.
uldn't say that."

grow acquainted with God when we
time in prayer conversing with Him,
e with us. We know when He is on
ene. We learn how He communicates
s: through His Word, by His Spirit,
gh dreams and visions, or by the
ming words of others who walk in the
and give sound counsel.

it shall come to pass afterward, *that I*
our out my spirit upon all flesh; and
sons and your daughters shall proph-
your old men shall dream *dreams,*

meditating, and rehearsing His words.

True worshipers recognize God's voice
and that of His messengers. Think about it.
You can easily recognize the voices of those
you know well. Even if they try to disguise
it you would be quick to say, "Oh, so-and-
so, I know that's you!" Your close friends
don't have to announce who they are when
they call you on the phone because you have
spent so much time together that you
recognize the tiniest inflection of their
voices.

HEAR WHAT THE SPIRIT SAYS

What about people who commit terrible
crimes and swear God told them to do it?
Obviously they got their wires crossed! So
how *does* one know when the Spirit of God
is speaking to them? Simple. God never
goes against His Word. He will never suggest or command something that doesn't
line up with His written Word. Some might
wonder about the instance when God told
Abraham to sacrifice Isaac, but two important points apply to this case: First of all,
God's Word was not yet documented. Second, God did not allow Abraham to complete the mission, thus being consistent with
His Word even before it was written. He
supplied a ram in the bush to be the sacrifice

He had requested. God's command was simply a test for Abraham. Would he be willing to give to God what was dearest to Him? The answer was yes.

Since then, the Word has been preserved for our benefit so that on days when the noise of the world drowns out the voice of God or robs us of our ability to discern the leading of His Holy Spirit, we have a written mandate that renders us without excuse. This is why it is so important to know the Scriptures through and through, not in part but the whole.

Study to shew thyself *approved* unto God, a workman that needeth not to be ashamed, rightly dividing the word of truth.
(2 Timothy 2:15, KJV)

The *sum* of Thy word is truth,
And every one of Thy righteous
   ordinances is everlasting.
                    (Psalm 119:160, NASB)

Taking bits and pieces of God's Word out of the context of its entirety is dangerous. If you overhear a portion of a conversation, you are at risk of misunderstanding the overall content. This is why we must not dissect the Word of God without having a

solid understanding of the
urge people to find a versi
that is easy for them to co
then to read it all the way
novel before studying it to
book by book. This way you
picture of God's heart and
consistent in His views. Cor
belief, the Bible does not
God is not a schizophreni
feeling this way, the next d
flip on us. No. He sticks t
disciple James said that Go
He doesn't change like s
(James 1:17). He is not mo
true to Himself, to His Wo
His Word because He *is* the
my friend, is that!

But let's get back to re
voice. Knowing His mind a
His Word is crucial. What
true about people makes a
in how you receive news
them. If someone deliver
you from your best friend
of that message was comp
or her nature, the first thi
is, "That doesn't sound
don't believe my friend s
double-check. You couldi

your young men shall see visions. (Joel 2:28, KJV)

Sometimes, after you've shared your heart with the Lord and are waiting quietly in His presence for His response, He will impress a portion of Scripture on your mind for you to read that will be a word of instruction or comfort to you. Or by His Spirit He will communicate to your spirit and you will have a sense of deep knowing, a conclusion, and a peace about the subject you have laid before Him. Sometimes He sends someone to you who has the answer you seek. And sometimes He will speak to you in dreams and grant an interpretation, as he did with Joseph in the book of Genesis and Daniel in the book of Daniel.

What made Joseph so sure he had a word from God when he dreamed his dream? What made Joseph and Daniel so precise in their interpretations of other men's dreams? First, there was no mystery to the meaning of the dreams that God sent. I believe we have bad dreams, "pizza dreams," good dreams, and God dreams. Some dreams leave us shaken, worried, or exhausted. These are not from God. Even when He sends dreams to warn us, we have a sense of knowing that God has a solution already planned. He just wants you to be alert and aware of what is going on. When God deals with unbelievers or the disobedient, their dreams may be filled with news of coming judgment, as in the case of King Nebuchadnezzar and the baker in prison with Joseph. Sometimes the things foretold could be averted, sometimes not. So much for bad dreams. Good dreams just make us feel, well, good! They titillate our personal desires. But God dreams make an impact. They leave an impression on our spirits. We awake with a deeper understanding, a sense of purpose, or greater awareness of things to come.

> And he said, Hear now my words: If there be a prophet among you, *I* the LORD will make myself known unto him in a vision, *and* will speak unto him in a dream. (Numbers 12:6, KJV)

> Now a thing was secretly brought to me, and mine ear received a little thereof. In thoughts from the visions of the night, when deep sleep falleth on men . . . (Job 4:12–13, KJV)

I heard a preacher once say that God uses dreams to speak to those whose attention

He cannot get during the day. But Scripture teaches that nighttime is when God whispers secrets to us, things for us to ponder in our heart, as Mary did. But more on that later. Being in touch with God constantly, even as we go on our way throughout the day, keeps us in tune to His voice whether we are asleep or awake. We should constantly apply ourselves to this communion with Him.

NIGHT SESSIONS

When I was still quite young in the Lord, I went on a seven-day fast to seek His direction for my life. During this time I had a dream. I couldn't shake it when I woke up. I pondered it, I shared it with my spiritual mentor, but I could not come to an understanding of what it meant. Even so, I knew that it was a message from the Lord to me.

The following Sunday a visiting minister spoke at my church. My mind drifted over my dream until the words of the sermon snatched me out of my musings. The minister was recounting a story that matched exactly what I had dreamed! He was using the story to make a point. As he continued his lesson, an understanding of what God had been saying to me became strikingly clear. He was encouraging me to overcome fear, something I was really struggling with at the time. I sat there weeping, so awed by the thought that I was important enough to God that He would send someone to speak words into my life in order to set me free. And God wants to be able to speak to all of us in a unique way that will get our attention and bless us.

Unfortunately, even the most spiritually sensitive person can become dull in the spirit and miss the voice of the Lord if he or she has become bogged down in selfish desires and ambitions. Our own agenda quite often crowds out the voice of the Lord. Consider Balaam, who was called by Balak, king of Moab, to come and curse the children of Israel (Numbers 22). The Lord told him not to go. But then the same ambassadors returned and offered Balaam a hefty reward for carrying out their request. For some reason Balaam thought this should change God's mind! This irritated God. He released Balaam to go, but not without a severe warning along the way. As Balaam made his way to meet the king of Moab, God sent an angel with a flaming sword to block his path. By now Balaam's sights were so set on the money, he didn't see the angel. But his donkey did.

After three temper tantrums and much

abuse to the animal, which was trying to avoid its undoing at the hands of the angel, Balaam heard his donkey point out what he had failed to see. (Personally, that's when I would have been out of there.) Balaam could hear a donkey speaking but couldn't see the angel — go figure! Now it's a shame when an animal with the reputation for being dumb has more sense than you do. But that is what selfish ambition will do. It will kill your discernment and make you short-sighted. In Balaam's case, because the lives of others were involved, God made sure Balaam got the message. The angel made it clear that Balaam would be in deep trouble if he insisted on proceeding against the Word of the Lord. Well, that ended that drama. Truly the fear of the Lord is the beginning of wisdom (Proverbs 9:10). Balaam showed up on the scene and blessed the Israelites instead. His rationale to the king of Moab? "How can I curse what God has blessed?" The end. By God.

Now I haven't heard of any donkeys talking lately, so what does it take for you to get God's message? He has promised to give us instruction whenever we desire it.

If any of you lacks *wisdom,* he should *ask* God, who gives generously to all without finding fault, and it will be given to him. (James 1:5)

Whether you turn to the right or to the left, your ears will hear a voice behind you, saying, "*This* is the *way; walk* in it." (Isaiah 30:21)

I will *instruct* you and teach you in the
   way you should go;
I will counsel you and watch over you.
(Psalm 32:8)

What incredible promises! God will not only give us instruction, He will give us advice! This type of exchange is birthed out of having a relationship with One who cares for you deeply. I think of Jesus on the Mount of Transfiguration, when God sent Moses and Elijah down to talk with Him. Don't you want to know what they talked about? I suspect they were talking about the intricacies of dealing with God's people. It was a time of encouragement and refreshment for Jesus. Peter, James, and John were there. They had climbed up the mountain with Jesus. Notice that not *all* of the disciples went. Only these three: John, who longed to know the heartbeat of Christ so deeply that he laid his head against Jesus' breast; Peter, who received the revelation of who Jesus truly was and built His church on the foundation of that understanding; and James, who was the first of the twelve disciples to die for his faith. These were the three who held key positions in the birthing of the early church.

DOING WHAT IT TAKES

Peter, James, and John, though they did not understand the big picture of Jesus' ministry in the beginning, were not content merely to follow Christ and see if He would help them achieve their personal agendas — personal miracles, freedom from the Romans, financial security, whatever. No, they wanted more. They were men on a mission. They were in search of the kingdom of God. If Jesus knew the way to get to God, they wanted to go there. They were willing to follow Him as far as necessary to reach their heavenly goal. True worshipers go the extra mile to see the Lord as He truly is, and their efforts are rewarded.

After six days Jesus took with him Peter, James and John the brother of James, and led them up a high mountain by themselves. There he was transfigured before them. His face shone like the sun, and his

97

clothes became as white as the light. Just then there appeared before them Moses and Elijah, talking with Jesus.

Peter said to Jesus, "Lord, it is good for us to be here. If you wish, I will put up three shelters — one for you, one for Moses and one for Elijah."

While he was still speaking, a bright cloud enveloped them, and a voice from the cloud said, "This is my Son, whom I love; with him I am well pleased. Listen to him!" (Matthew 17:1–5)

Are you willing to come apart from the rest? To climb to another level? We tend to like mountaintop experiences only when they don't require anything of us. We like to build memorials to good feelings, but generally we are not allowed to remain there. We go up to get instructions and are then sent back down to live out what we have received. In every case where people in the Bible met God on a mountain — Moses, Elijah, Jesus — they were instructed to go back down and use what they had received from Him. In this life, those who go down willingly always find their way up again. God either leaves markers for them to find their way or supernaturally lifts them there with His own hands.

Such mountaintop experiences are available for all who truly want to hear God, and there is a difference between listening and hearing. Everyone knows a bad listener. Bad listeners insult us with their inattention. Yet they will insist that they are listening. When questioned on whether they truly heard us, they cannot repeat what we have just said. But God has a way of determining whether we have truly heard what He has said.

> Anyone who listens to the word but does not do what it says is like a man who looks at his face in a mirror and, after looking at himself, goes away and immediately forgets what he looks like. But the man who looks intently into the perfect law that gives freedom, and continues to do this, not forgetting what he has heard, but doing it — he will be blessed in what he does. (James 1:23–25)

Remember the mountaintop experience of the disciples? They were ready to just stay there and grow comfortable hanging out with Moses and Elijah, but God had a different plan. I called you all the way up here so you could hear my instruction, He said, and here it is: Listen to My Son and do what He says. Get refreshed by what Moses and Elijah share. Bask here for a minute but do not build a monument to the experience. There is work to be done, and I need you to hear Me and obey. Then you will be blessed.

HEARING AIDS

Spiritual hearing problems have a lot to do with our proximity to God. The further away we are from the Lord, the harder it is to hear Him. The pursuit of worldly knowledge rather than godly wisdom also gets many of us in trouble. The knowledge of good and evil or worldly philosophies alone robs us of the blessed life God wants to give us. It robbed Eve and it robs us. It is called living a lie. We are no smarter for our acquisition of knowledge because we still lack understanding, and wisdom demands that knowledge and understanding both be present in order to meet God's requirements of us. Yet God promises to be generous toward us when handing out wisdom. Knowledge plus understanding is what He requires of Himself, and the servant is not greater than the master.

By wisdom the LORD laid the earth's
   foundations,

by understanding he set the heavens in
place;
by his knowledge the deeps were divided,
and the clouds let drop the dew.

(Proverbs 3:19–20)

Blessed is the man who finds wisdom,
the man who gains understanding.

(Proverbs 3:13)

The tricky part is that we have so much
besides wisdom to choose from. So many
other trees — worldly philosophies of self-
help, even some self-centered faith teach-
ings — hold fruit that looks delectable. It is
easy to remember our own spirits and forget
God, to forget our source of blessing and
mistakenly think that we are our own
source. Nothing could be further from the
truth.

> For although they knew God, they neither
> glorified him as God nor gave thanks to
> him, but their thinking became futile and
> their foolish hearts were darkened. Al-
> though they claimed to be wise, they
> became fools. . . . They exchanged the
> truth of God for a lie, and worshiped and
> served created things rather than the

Creator — who is forever praised. Amen.
(Romans 1:21–22,25)

Trust in the LORD with all your heart
    and lean not on your own
    understanding;
in all your ways acknowledge him,
    and he will make your paths straight.
Do not be wise in your own eyes;
    fear the LORD and shun evil.
This will bring health to your body
    and nourishment to your bones.

(Proverbs 3:5–8)

Open your ears, hear "thus sayeth the
Lord," and take heed. Mary did. She was
not startled by His word to her; rather, she
heard it and yielded to it. And she was
blessed.

THOUGHTS TO PONDER

- When was the last time you really
  heard from God?

- Do you readily recognize God's voice?
  How do you separate His instructions
  from your own longings?

- Do you welcome God's instruction

even if it is contrary to your desires?

- In general, how do you respond to God's voice?

- How do you demonstrate that you have heard from God?

5. Believing the Unbelievable
Developing a Workable Faith

And *blessed is she* that believed: for there shall be a *performance* of those things which were told her from the Lord.

Luke 1:45 (KJV)

I sat across from my two friends at a restaurant and smiled broadly. "So I hear you are getting married," I said to them. "Congratulations!"

My girlfriend looked quite surprised and exclaimed, "He told you that?!" She jabbed her boyfriend, my closest male friend, with her elbow. "I didn't believe him when he said it, so I didn't pay any attention to him. But since he has told you, I guess it's official!" I couldn't believe my ears. The girl didn't take her boyfriend seriously! It took my confirming his words for them to take root and kick her into action.

Later, as I mulled over the situation, I thought about the irony of it all. This woman had been waiting so long for the day when he would say he was ready to get married that when he finally and calmly made his announcement, she disregarded what he said. Her fear of disappointment had kept her from asking him whether he was truly serious. Therefore no plans had been made to finally secure her dream. Isn't that what we sometimes do to God when He whispers a long-awaited promise in our ear?

Dare we hope He really means what He says? Perhaps if we don't grasp His words too tightly, we won't be disappointed. Yet He warns us that unbelief impairs our ability to receive from Him.

In the same way, faith by itself, if it is not accompanied by action, is dead. . . .

You foolish man, do you want evidence that faith without deeds is useless? Was not our ancestor Abraham considered righteous for what he did when he offered his son Isaac on the altar? You see that his faith and his actions were working together, and his faith was made complete by what he did. And the scripture was fulfilled that says, "Abraham believed God, and it was credited to him as righteousness," and he was called God's friend. You see that a person is justified by what he does and not by faith alone. . . .

As the body without the spirit is dead, so faith without deeds is dead. (James 2:17, 20–24,26)

How can you call someone a friend if you do not trust him? It actually hurts God's feelings when we don't believe what He says.

And without *faith* it is *impossible* to *please* God, because anyone who comes to him must believe that he exists and that he rewards those who earnestly seek him. (Hebrews 11:6)

What does it take to please God? He simply wants us to trust and believe Him. Isn't that all we expect from our friends?

A friend of mine promised her daughter that she would make her a dress for a special occasion. The mother was so excited as she told me about the intricate design she was painstakingly working on to make the dress really special. Late in the night she would sit, sewing, anticipating the look of pleasure on her daughter's face when it would finally be finished. But because her daughter never saw her mother working on it, she kept questioning her mother about the dress. Was she really going to make it? When was she going to get started? Was she sure she would have it finished in time? On and on. My friend became so vexed at the lack of trust her daughter displayed that she finally exploded in frustration, "If you don't stop bugging me about that dress, I won't finish it!" She wanted to surprise her daughter. Her daughter's lack of faith in her took the joy out of the experience, and she grudgingly finished the dress without the special touches she had previously planned.

LOOKING HEAVENWARD

I think of Aaron, Moses' brother, left at the foot of the mountain while Moses went up to get a word from God for the people. Aaron didn't have enough conviction about the faithfulness of God to withstand the Israelites' unbelief. So he let them talk him into making an idol for them to worship. Meanwhile, back at the ranch (or should I say up on the mountaintop), God is making all kinds of elaborate plans for Aaron's life. Making him the head of the priesthood, outlining every detail down to what Aaron would wear! Aaron wasn't thinking about God, but God was thinking about him. How embarrassed do you think Aaron was when God's plans were brought to light in spite of Aaron's bad behavior? How disappointed do you think God was with Aaron's inability to trust Him for a blessing? How many times do you think you've been in Aaron's shoes? Well, that's another thing to make you go "hmm."

Sometimes I think we kill the joy of blessing for God. Two things happen: We grieve His spirit by constantly questioning His motives, or we become paralyzed by our unbelief. Either way, we fail to take the steps that are necessary if we are to take hold of what God has prepared for us. It's like receiving a check in the mail and failing to cash it because we aren't sure it is legitimate, and then going on our way complaining about not having any money. It's like not using a gift God has given us because we don't believe we can prosper by it. This is a biggie. Why don't we step out in the area of our giftings? Because our faith is misplaced. We have turned our faith toward ourselves rather than God. "I don't think I can do it," we say, and we are absolutely right. But *God* can. Through *you!* As my friend Sherri Rose Shepard says, "He is God; you are not." Now that ought to set you free.

Our faith must be turned heavenward at all times. The average person feels bound by the expectations of others. How often have you said to someone who was trying to talk you out of doing something you had promised to do, "But they're counting on me"? Well, God doesn't like to disappoint us either. Yet He constantly suffers disappointment over our lack of trust in Him. Mary delighted God's heart. He told her something that sounded absolutely impossible, and she believed Him!

She told Joseph, her fiancé, what was about to happen. She didn't say, "Well, I'll wait until my body feels different and I know a baby is in there" before affirming what God had told her. She knew God's voice. She believed Him and acted on what He told her. After letting Joseph know, she went to visit her cousin Elizabeth, where she received further confirmation of what had been told her by God. You see, I believe the purpose of faith is two-fold. It warms God's heart that we believe Him, but it also propels us into action. Faith takes the check to the bank and cashes it. A check is no good until it is cashed. You can walk around broke with a million-dollar check in your pocket. Your poverty ends when you believe the bank has the resources to fill the order written on the check and you take the steps that are necessary to receive those resources. What makes us leave our money in banks? What makes us so sure it will be there when we need it? The same thing that makes us get on a plane and take for granted that we will reach our destination and disembark safely. One little word: faith.

> Now *faith* is being sure of what we hope for and certain of what we do not see. (Hebrews 11:1)

We put so much trust in technology and the ability of man without considering the likelihood that those things will disappoint us. How much more should we put our trust in God, who is truly able and faithful to do what He says? How can we be sure of what we hope for? How can we be certain of what we do not see? Because of the source of the promise.

> *God* is not a man, that he should *lie*,
>   nor a son of man, that he should
>   change his mind.
> Does he speak and then not act?
> Does he promise and not fulfill?
>   (Numbers 23:19)

What hinders our faith? Could it be our preconceived notions of how God should or will act in a situation? Could it be our personal timetable of when we think that

He should come through? It amazes me how often we assume the way in which God will carry out His promise to us. We stand looking to the left, waiting to see Him come over the horizon. All the while He is coming from the right. But we cannot see him, so we decide He is not coming. At other times the clock on the mantel of our hearts chimes the hour, and in the deafening silence that follows we begin to undress and settle in for a night of weeping, concluding we've been stood up. Then He appears in the morning, bringing His joy with Him. When questioned as to why He didn't come the night before, He looks at us quizzically and answers, "You never asked me when I was coming, so I believed you would wait."

Up Close and Personal

Mary asked questions. She asked the angel how this most wonderful miracle of bearing God's Son was going to occur. Gabriel told her that the Holy Spirit would come upon her. The Son of God, the child she was to bear, would be conceived out of her intimacy with God Himself.

This is a "selah" moment — a time for us to stop and ponder. Everywhere in Scripture that a godly union led to conception the same words are used:

And Adam *knew* Eve his wife; and she conceived. (Genesis 4:1, KJV)

And Cain *knew* his wife; and she conceived. (Genesis 4:17, KJV)

And Adam *knew* his wife again; and she bare a son. (Genesis 4:25, KJV)

Elkanah *knew* Hannah his wife; and the LORD remembered her. (1 Samuel 1:19, KJV)

See the pattern? According to good old King James, the consummation of a godly union is always referred to as "knowing" the person. However, when the union was out of order — without love or covenant between the two — the King James translation makes a significant distinction, referring to the union with phrases such as "lay with" or "went in unto."

And he [Abraham] *went in unto* Hagar, and she conceived. (Genesis 16:4, KJV)

And when Shechem the son of Hamor the Hivite, prince of the country, saw her, he took her, and *lay with* her, and defiled her. (Genesis 34:2, KJV)

> And it came to pass, when Israel dwelt in that land, that Reuben went and *lay with* Bilhah his father's concubine. (Genesis 35:22, KJV)

> If a man be found *lying with* a woman married to an husband, then they shall both of them die. (Deuteronomy 22:22, KJV)

Isn't it interesting that intimacy without relationship is described as two people merely lying with one another? They are in fact perpetrating a lie which the world calls "making love." What Hagar, Sarah's maidservant, conceived when Abraham lay with her has caused troubles and war up to the present day because that union was nothing more than man's effort to produce God's promise. And man's efforts outside of covenant relationship with God, independent of God's guidance and blessing, will never produce any good thing. Lying together does not promote "knowing" one another, contrary to popular belief. The deception of the enemy is so subtle. Intimacy without covenant is a lie. God does not lie to us; He calls us to come into the full knowledge of who He is so that we can trust Him and conceive good things.

Now please! Do not go off on a tangent

and run around saying that I said God had sex with Mary. *That is not what I am saying.* I am addressing the principle of intimacy. All of us who believe that the Bible is the written Word of God believe in the virgin conception. We believe Mary was overshadowed by the power of the Holy Spirit in the same way that Adam became a living soul by the breath of God. Mary conceived Jesus by that same breath, which brings life to the soul of every man and woman who drinks it in and allows him or her to be filled to overflowing with the very life of God.

GETTING IN SYNC

The mystery of becoming one with another person lies in the degree of intimacy you are willing to explore with that person. The more you know of him and the more time you spend with him, the more that person begins to rub off on you. You begin to absorb parts of his nature, and vice versa. I have a very special friend. When the two of us get together, people say it's like seeing and hearing everything in stereo. We have a lot of the same inflections. When we catch ourselves bursting into laughter at the same time or crossing our legs at the same time, we can't help but giggle because we are so delighted to be one in our sisterhood. Oh, to have that type of relationship with God! To be so in sync with His Spirit that we speak in stereo with His voice! That's what Jesus did.

> Jesus gave them this answer: "I tell you the truth, the Son can do nothing by himself; he can do only what he sees his *Father* doing, because whatever the *Father* does the Son also does." (John 5:19)

> Don't you believe that I am in the *Father,* and that the *Father* is in me? The words I *say* to you are not just my own. Rather, it is the *Father,* living in me, who is doing his work. (John 14:10)

When this type of closeness exists between friends, it is easy to trust each other implicitly. You know your friend has your heart, and vice versa. There is a knowing between the two of you. You sense the timing of the other person and rest in following that rhythm without question.

When I was working in advertising, the significant man in my life was a film director whom I hired quite often to shoot commercials for me. I always had a sense of peace when I worked with him because I knew we had the same vision. We liked the same things. We were connected. I would stand at one end of the set watching a scene and think to myself, "Hmm, they need to release the pigeons before he walks by." Before I could complete the thought in my head, I would hear him say, "They need to release the pigeons before he walks by." It would happen this way time and time again. The more I worked with him, the more I released projects to him and stayed out of the way. I trusted him to bring to life what was in my head. We had open communication. We shared and exchanged thoughts, ideas, our hearts, our dreams. We understood each other. I had faith in him. Therefore I could let go and allow him to do his thing and trust it to be right.

Knowing God in that way is crucial to having faith in God. When we know His character and His heart, we can believe even the seemingly ridiculous. I always chuckle when people say, "Put God in remembrance of His Word." As if He forgot! No, it is *we* who need to put *ourselves* in remembrance of His Word. It is for *our* sakes that we are to meditate on His words all the day long. To write them on our hearts, our foreheads, and our forearms, even as the priests of old did. Then, when He doesn't appear as *we think* He ought, *when* we think He ought, we will not panic. We will draw upon the things we know about Him and stand firm until He comes, doing what He said He would surely do. Sometimes when we think we are waiting too long, He is trying to get us more truly in sync with His heart. As we go through changes while waiting on God, I believe that He waits too. He waits for us to come up to a higher level of trusting Him. It's safe to say that none of us trusts Him as much as we should, no matter how great a level of faith we profess to possess. One trial is usually enough to prove it.

WHEN GOD STAYS AWAY

Mary and Martha sent a message to Jesus that their brother Lazarus was ill. The Scriptures say that Jesus stayed away *on purpose.* He actually waited for Lazarus to die! Then He announced to His disciples that Lazarus was asleep and that He wanted to go wake him up. The disciples thought this meant that Lazarus was taking a nap and recuperating, but Jesus went on to explain to them that, in earthly terms, Lazarus was dead. Lazarus was dead and Jesus was glad! Why? Because now He would have an opportunity to glorify His heavenly Father and prove that He had been sent by God.

Can you imagine the looks the disciples exchanged on that one? I love that about God. He refers to death as sleep — a temporary thing that does not interrupt life. We on earth see death as a permanent thing. The end. But God views it as a rest between breaths. A comma between earth and heaven! How much less we would grieve over the departure of loved ones if we could fully grasp this concept.

As Jesus approached the place where Lazarus lived, his sister Martha came out to greet Jesus and said, "If you had been here, Lazarus would not have died." Martha and Mary's unbelief made Jesus weep. His tears are often interpreted as grief over Lazarus's death, but Jesus had expressly stated that Lazarus was only sleeping. Jesus' statement reveals that the source of His tears was their unbelief. He had been with them so many times and shared so much, and still they did not understand all that He had taught them. They still couldn't conceive of what the Father was capable of doing through Him on their behalf. How much more does our lack of faith hurt the heart of God? Yet isn't that what we say to Him? "Where were you? If you had been here, this mess would not have occurred!" And then I think of Joseph going off to Egypt, sold into slavery, and the Bible says, "But the Lord was with Joseph." Then again, as he is thrown into prison, wrongly accused of rape, "But the Lord was with Joseph." If Joseph really was highly favored by God, how could these terrible things happen? Could it be that God knew He could trust Joseph to triumph in his trial and glorify Him? But when we're put through trials of our own, triumphing over them and glorifying God do not occur to us. I have a better understanding of why we miss opportunities like Joseph's when I consider what Jesus said to Martha next (in Michelle paraphrase): "I'm here now, and it's not over."

What Jesus really said was, "Your brother will rise again." Martha should have been able to accept that, coming from Jesus. After all, she herself had boldly proclaimed to Him that, even though it was late in the game, she knew God would give Him anything He requested. Yet when Jesus says, "Your brother will rise again," Martha is quick to reply that she knows he will rise in the resurrection at the *last day.* But that is *not* what Jesus said!

We can't get mad at Martha because we do the same thing. We put God in a box and put a lid on our faith because we don't know everything we need to know about

Him. We, too, are quick to utter religious confessions and memorized scriptures by rote without examining their meaning. But Jesus is more patient than we are.

> Jesus said to her, "I am the resurrection and the life. He who believes in me will live, even though he dies; and whoever lives and believes in me will never die. Do you believe this?"
> "Yes, Lord," she told him, "I believe that you are the Christ, the Son of God, who was to come into the world." (John 11:25–27)

Again she misses the point. She doesn't make the connection between Jesus and the *present* situation. She puts His answer off into the future, a place where she won't have to exercise her faith in the moment. She has already determined everyone's fate based on her own finite understanding. Perhaps this is why we are not to lean to our own understanding, but rather to trust in God. Yet we put our faith in a cave and roll stones across the entrance, stifling the liberty that trusting God affords us.

> But some of them said, "Could not he who opened the eyes of the blind man have

kept this man from dying?"

Jesus, once more deeply moved, came to the tomb. It was a cave with a stone laid across the entrance. "Take away the stone," he said.

"But, Lord," said Martha, the sister of the dead man, "by this time there is a bad odor, for he has been there four days."

Then Jesus said, "Did I not tell you that if you believed, you would see the glory of God?" (John 11:37–40)

Ah, but perhaps this is where the disconnect occurs! Perhaps it is our *own* glory that we seek and not the *glory of God* in our everyday experiences. We would like to be comfortable, presenting a perfect image of perpetual victory to those around us and taking the credit. *Look at what a good little Christian I am. I am so tight with God that nothing touches me. I never have a problem. I possess the type of faith that can run though a troop and leap over a wall! Aren't I great?* All right, I'll start the confession — I've been guilty of this.

TAKING THE FAITH ROUTE

While I was struggling to recover from an injury I received when hit by a car (I was on foot), a friend said to me after my third surgery, "You haven't been healed because you don't have enough faith." I was furious. I retorted, "If it was just about faith, I would never have been hit in the first place. I never in my wildest dreams believed that God would allow something like this to happen to me!" And yet He did. Has this cost me my faith? No. I am following God's instructions and continuing to get better as I walk in obedience. Whenever I lag behind in the things He has told me to do, my injuries flare up. My faith and cooperation with God's instruction are a crucial part of the process of my physical healing. For some, He merely speaks the word and a quick work of healing is done. That's called a miracle. For others of us, the healing is a process because of what God wants to accomplish in our lives.

Listen, my sons, to a *father's instruction;*
  pay attention and gain understanding.
    (Proverbs 4:1)

A wise son heeds his *father's instruction.*
(Proverbs 13:1)

Whoever gives *heed* to *instruction*
  prospers,
  and blessed is he who trusts in the

LORD. (Proverbs 16:20)

Faith and obedience must walk hand in hand in order to reach the promise. Faith believes that the Father's instructions are right and willingly follows them, regardless of what our eyes see. Faith trusts the Father even when He leads us down a road that seemingly isn't taking us where we want to go.

Have you ever been given instructions to a place you've never been before? After driving for a while you begin to grow apprehensive if you don't see any markers along the way confirming that you're on the right track. You begin to doubt the instructions. You pull off to ask additional directions, or you call the person to make sure you are still heading down the right path. You find out that you are and are instructed to proceed. Your next question probably is "How far am I away from you? How much longer should it take me?" We feel more comfortable when we have a sense of the time frame surrounding our situation.

Well, sometimes God doesn't give us the time frame or the rationale for the route He has placed us on, and panic sets in. We worry. We fret. *Is He really going to do what He said?* We begin to poll our friends for reassurance. We turn off the path in search of a shortcut and become more turned around. Not so with Mary. She took God and His word without doubt. She asked how His promise would be accomplished and the answer came back, "By my Spirit." And that was enough for her. Her quiet trust supplied a fertile place for God to plant His promise. Her faith equipped her to birth the fruit of her expectations, and she was blessed.

THOUGHTS TO PONDER

- Where do you really place your trust?

- Is your faith in God contingent upon what you see, hear, or feel?

- What evidence do you need to believe what God says to you?

- Are you following God's instructions?

- What is the level of your intimacy with God? Do you truly know Him, or are you embracing a lie?

- Are you in sync with God's Spirit? How do you know?

6. How Does Your Garden Grow?

DETERMINING YOUR HARVEST

And she cried out with a loud voice, and said, "Blessed among women are you, and blessed is the fruit of your womb!"

Luke 1:42 (NASB)

It is said the fruit that grows closest to the vine is the sweetest. That makes sense to me. That which is closer to the source of nourishment is in a better position to receive the nutrients necessary for its enrichment. It would have first dibs on all the goodies, so to speak. The fruit further away would get the leftovers. I don't know about you, but I'm not fond of warmed-over goods. I like my food fresh, hot off the press. Kind of like information. The closer you are to the original story, the better chance you have of possessing the facts.

Likewise, when we get God's Word firsthand, the revelation is powerful, life-changing. One word from God is enough to renew your mind. Transform your life. Make you look different. Walk in a different way. Do something you've never done before. If you see the words on the page as nothing more than arranged letters, that's not enough to revolutionize your world. But when you get in God's face and allow Him to breathe on the Word you've absorbed, it comes to life and bears fruit!

A seed looks like absolutely nothing until it's pressed into fertile soil and watered. It sits for a while looking the same, and then it dies. Just when you think it's over, something happens. The pressure of what is deep within it breaks open that ol' dry, dead shell. New life bursts forth. It begins to grow roots and grab hold of the earth around it to anchor itself. Once the seed has taken a firm grip, it extends itself upward and reveals what has been inside of it all along — scrumptious fruit for others to behold, partake of, and enjoy. Are you aware of the joy that can be found in feeding others with what God has planted inside of you? Truly, producing fruit is the greatest part of the blessed life.

The Lord Jesus himself said: "It is more *blessed* to *give* than to receive." (Acts 20:35)

I love to give things away, anything from a word of encouragement to a gift I know someone will enjoy. I love seeing the look that crosses recipients' faces as they receive. I am fed as I feed others. When I withhold from others, I rob myself of joy. Because being fruitful is an important part of the call God has placed on the lives of all who know Him, it stands to reason that after the Fall in the Garden of Eden, the desire to be fruitful became the focal point of human effort. In their quest for knowledge, Adam and Eve became self-centered instead of God-centered. They had the knowledge but not the ability to produce what God had produced so easily: Eve would bear children in difficulty, and Adam would sweat to reap what had once literally fallen into his hands before. Their relationship would also suffer as selfish ambition drove them to try to control each other. The man and the woman were not cursed; their ability to be fruitful apart from God was cursed.

HANG IN THERE

But Jesus would come onto the scene through the womb of Mary. God would once again be the originator of the fruit, and the curse would be broken as His Son was broken for us! The fruit of Mary's womb was blessed, and now His life within us will produce fruit as long as we cling to Him in an intimate embrace.

> Remain in me, and I will remain in you. No branch can *bear fruit* by itself; it must remain in the vine. Neither can you *bear fruit* unless you remain in me.
> I am the *vine;* you are the *branches.* If a man remains in me and I in him, he will bear much fruit; apart from me you can do nothing. (John 15:4–5)

Here is where our war with new age religion begins. New age religion teaches that *you* are your *own* source, that *you* are the one who makes things happen, that *you* control your destiny. There is some truth in this way of thinking in that you choose whether or not to cooperate with God. Because God has given us free will, our decisions do indeed set our course. But new-age philosophy suggests that you are entirely the captain of your own ship. You are a little god. Your *own* god. Nothing could be further from the truth. There is only one God, and He will not share His glory with another. Yet He will allow you to build your own personal kingdom and then watch it topple because no foundation except the Solid Rock is stable.

When we stand on God's promises, abide in Him, and allow Him to be the source of our life's fruit, whether attitudinal or material, we thrive. We prosper. It's all good! *Good fruit.* God is delighted with good fruit. Why? Because it fosters spiritual germination and health in all who partake of it. Producing life in others. Multiplying. Producing more fruit after its own kind — meaning more believers living completely sold-out lives for God. We should be adding to the kingdom, as God's good fruit in us attracts others who seek nourishment. What was God's first command to Adam? "Be fruitful and multiply." This command is issued to every believer.

> You did not choose me, but I chose you and appointed you to go and *bear fruit* — *fruit* that will last. Then the Father will give you whatever you ask in my name. (John 15:16)

> So, my brothers, you also died to the law through the body of Christ, that you might belong to another, to him who was raised from the dead, in order that we might *bear fruit* to God. (Romans 7:4)

And we pray this in order that you may live a life worthy of the Lord and may please him in every way: *bearing fruit* in every good work, growing in the knowledge of God. (Colossians 1:10)

We were chosen to bear fruit. God planted His Spirit within us that we might produce good works that glorify Him. He wants us to bear fruit that makes the sacrifice of Jesus worthwhile.

Have you ever put in a good word for someone, gone the extra mile to pave the way for an opportunity for them? When they do a good job and the person to whom you recommended them comes back to thank you for the reference, you feel as if your efforts were worth your while. On the other hand, if the person turns out to be a disappointment or a disgrace to you, it is easy to wonder why you ever bothered. Do you think Jesus looks at you and says it was worth all the trouble He went through to die for you? Is your life producing things that make Him glad He endured the shame of the cross because of the joy you now bring to Him through the fruit of your life? Or are you experiencing spurts of growth, mere samplings of what could be, but no fruit that lasts?

Passing Fruit Inspection

What type of fruit lasts? The fruit of the Spirit at work in your personal life and in the souls of others — souls drawn to the kingdom because of what your life testifies about God. Souls called into His marvelous light will live eternally in His presence. His life in you is supposed to produce more life. More fruit. And lush fruit draws God's indulgence. Jesus said that when you are fruitful the Father will give you whatever you request. How can He guarantee such a thing? Because He knows that when you are truly bearing fruit you won't ask for anything that won't produce more fruit. You will be so tapped into the vine that you will know instinctively what is not conducive to your continued growth, and you won't even go there. You will be sold out to your sole purpose — glorifying God.

This is to my Father's glory, that you *bear* much *fruit,* showing yourselves to be my disciples. (John 15:8)

We make God look good when we bear fruit. We affirm where we truly stand and to whom we belong. Why should God bless people who make Him look bad? I have never witnessed a parent reward a child for embarrassing him or her in public. Unfruitful Christians are a disappointment to God and an embarrassment to His kingdom. Unfruitful in attitude. Unfruitful in deeds. Both should cause us to hang our heads in shame.

Think of how you have felt during the publicized fall of any great man or woman of God. Their bad fruit leaves a lot of explaining for you to do to those around you who are not Christians. It sets the Christian community back for a minute. We all struggle collectively to recover, hoping the memory of this disgrace will quickly fade so we can get back to witnessing effectively. We are deeply grieved over this poor advertisement for the kingdom, and we realize that now our job has become more difficult. Yet we can't draw back, for to do so would be to stifle the part of our very nature that lives to share Christ's life with others. When you abide in the vine, such sharing comes as naturally as breathing. It is an act of worship to God to reproduce what He has given you. This is your reason for being. Your very purpose, the fulfillment of which brings a smile to

God's face and great blessings to your life.

It is important to note that unfruitful Christians are not victorious Christians because they do not attract the blessings of God. Some may say, "Well, isn't fruit itself a blessing?" My answer is that the fruit of *your* fruit — the byproduct of your original fruit — is the blessing. Stay with me here. You are told to be fruitful and multiply. So multiply your fruit. Your first fruit goes to God in response to His command, which is to produce the fruit of the Spirit that draws others to Him:

Now he who supplies seed to the sower and bread for food will also supply and increase your store of seed and will enlarge the harvest of your righteousness. You will be made rich in every way so that you can be generous on every occasion, and through us your generosity will result in thanksgiving to God.

This service that you perform is not only supplying the needs of God's people but is also overflowing in many expressions of thanks to God. Because of the service by which you have proved yourselves, men will praise God for the obedience that accompanies your confession of the gospel of Christ, and for your generosity in sharing with them and with everyone else. (2 Corinthians 9:10–13)

Your obedience sets a multiplication factor in motion: Your fruit produces and multiplies more fruit for the kingdom. God then blesses your obedience, which causes you to experience an overflow. The overflow is what blesses *you.* The overflow is the extra-dimensional blessing of God, which you receive because the fruit of the Spirit is evident in your life first. This pleases God and promotes you with man. Are you getting this? Lush fruit gets God's attention and blessings, but He turns His face away from what does not please Him.

Unfruitfulness is not a pretty picture in God's eyes. Small wonder Jesus was so upset with that old tired fig tree. It was defying its reason for existing by being unfruitful.

Early in the morning, as he was on his way back to the city, he was hungry. Seeing a fig tree by the road, he went up to it but found nothing on it except leaves. Then he said to it, "May you never bear fruit again!" Immediately the tree withered. (Matthew 21:18–19)

Whoa! Now that's deep. Some Christians are like that — all foliage and no fruit. God isn't interested in the fancy garnish for show; He wants to sample and partake of the fruit of our lives. When He visits us and finds our fruit bitter or nonexistent, He removes our ability to produce more of the same. God cannot allow fruitlessness to abound. An overgrowth of fruitless branches will sap all the life out of the plant and out of the ground it is planted in. They leave no room or opportunity for the good fruit to spring forth. And that's a no-no. So in essence Jesus was saying (in Michelle paraphrase), "Look, if you're just going to stand around being unproductive, there is no reason for you to be here."

Then he told this parable: "A man had a fig tree, planted in his vineyard, and he went to look for fruit on it, but did not find any. So he said to the man who took care of the vineyard, 'For three years now I've been coming to look for fruit on this fig tree and haven't found any. Cut it down! Why should it use up the soil?'

" 'Sir,' the man replied, 'leave it alone for one more year, and I'll dig around it and fertilize it. If it bears fruit next year, fine! If not, then cut it down.' " (Luke 13:6–9)

God will do whatever He can to help jumpstart the bearing of fruit in our lives. If we don't respond, however, we will find ourselves cut off from opportunities that were once available to us in order to make room for those who will be more productive. This brings us back to operating according to our purpose. Our purpose is to be fruitful by utilizing our gifts and talents to bless people around us, and then to allow that fruit to be the catalyst that draws them to God and multiplies the kingdom.

In the same way, let your light shine before men, that they may see your *good* deeds and praise your Father in heaven. (Matthew 5:16)

Live such *good* lives among the pagans that, though they accuse you of doing wrong, they may see your *good* deeds and *glorify* God on the day he visits us. (1 Peter 2:12)

The servant who knows his master's will and does not get ready or does not do what his master wants will be beaten with many blows. But the one who does not know and does things deserving punishment will be beaten with few blows. From everyone who has been *given much, much* will be demanded; and from the one who has been entrusted with *much, much* more will be asked. (Luke 12:47,48)

For everyone who has will be given more, and he will have an abundance. Whoever does not have, even what he has will be taken from him. (Matthew 25:29)

In the last scripture above, so goes the story of the unproductive servant who was given a talent and did not use it (Matthew 25:14–30). The good master had distributed talents among his workers according to what he knew to be their ability. Two of the servants invested theirs wisely and used them to gain a greater return for the master. But the third servant buried his and gave the original talent, a little crusty and mildewed from being hidden, back to the master. This did not bring accolades from his superior. Rather, the master took the unused talent from the unproductive servant and gave it to the one he knew would use it. Likewise, God is a wise investor.

PROVING YOUR WORTH

No matter our station in life, we must use what we have at our disposal. Saints cannot afford to sit around looking for a handout. That is not how we get blessed or gain favor. We must put to work the talents that God has placed within us. Invest your gifts wisely by blessing others with them — then watch the doors fly open, ushering you into the presence of great blessings.

But what is your gift? I will say this in every book I write if I have to: Your gift is the thing you do well because it is second nature to you. Others notice and celebrate what you do, even though it may seem like nothing to you. That's your gift. Some have the gift of cooking, cleaning, hospitality, organization, decoration, working with children — you name it — not everyone does it well. In Proverbs 18:16 (NASB), we are told that our gifts make room for us. In other words, your gift, when set before those who need what you have to offer, opens the door to favors and blessings. No job should be viewed as despicable or undesirable. Every job, whether seemingly menial or noteworthy, fills a need. Can you imagine what the world would be like if no one cleaned the rest rooms in public facilities? They would be filthy, and disease would run rampant! Some people are good at cleaning and have prospered from doing it by establishing cleaning companies or doing it themselves for clients. What is your gift? What are you good at? Be fruitful and use it for God's glory.

GOING WITH THE FLOW

Let's take a look at the life of Joseph. He went from being the favorite in his father's house, pampered on every side, to being a slave in a foreigner's house. You don't think he rose to the position of overseeing Potiphar's house in a day, do you? Absolutely not! Israelites were like dogs in the eyes of the Egyptians, who fancied themselves far more sophisticated and advanced than any other society in the earth. No, Joseph started with the most menial of tasks. He applied himself to these drudgeries, performing them with a spirit of excellence, to the glory of God, and God honored him by causing everything he touched to prosper. So of course Joseph got promoted.

You may know the rest of the story. Potiphar's wife took a liking to him, and when he refused to respond to her advances, she accused him of rape and had him thrown into jail. But even there he decided to be the best convict that he could be. Again God honored him, and Joseph was promoted. I love how Jacob, Joseph's father, described Joseph's response to these difficult situations:

> Joseph is a fruitful vine,
>> a fruitful vine near a spring,
>> whose branches climb over a wall. . . .
> because of your father's God, who helps
>> you,
>> because of the Almighty, who blesses
>> you
> with blessings of the heavens above,
>> blessings of the deep that lies below,
>> blessings of the breast and womb.
> Your father's blessings are greater
>> than the blessings of the ancient
>> mountains,
>> than the bounty of the age-old hills.
> Let all these rest on the head of Joseph,
>> on the brow of the prince among his
>> brothers.
>
> (Genesis 49:22,25–26)

I just love that passage! Jacob praises the fact that Joseph drew his strength from the Spirit of God and survived — no, *overcame* — his circumstances. He was anchored in his relationship to God, the true vine, drawing from His living waters to sustain himself in tough times and situations. Joseph set his sights on maintaining a godly attitude and being an excellent servant, though surely he must have chafed under his seeming reversal of fortune. He decided to learn the necessary lessons and come out the victor. He put his hand to the grindstone and used what he had — his ability to serve — where he was. He flourished in the midst of his trial and, by God's grace, made something out of the lot that had been given him. And because of Joseph's obedient and willing attitude, God blessed him. He himself proclaimed, "God has made me fruitful in the land of my affliction."

Fruitful people allow themselves to be purged of all that is not needed to produce what God has called them to. Fruitful people are overcomers no matter what! They can take a licking and keep on ticking, as the old Timex advertisement said. Why? Because fruitful people continue to cling to the vine and draw strength from it. They know their ultimate assignment is to glorify God. And they know who alone can help them accomplish that end.

Surely God is my *help;*
    the *Lord* is the one who sustains me.
                        (Psalm 54:4)

My help comes from the LORD,

141

the Maker of heaven and earth.

(Psalm 121:2)

But let's talk once more about that fruit. What kind of fruit does God like? What type of fruit does He smile upon and bless? Fruit that is borne from the seed God Himself plants within us through the deposit of His Holy Spirit. As His own Spirit works within us, as we yield to the lessons He teaches and cooperate with His instructions, we cultivate a crop that is pleasing to God. But if we resist His Spirit, we sow an entirely different crop in our field. Again, the choice is ours to choose kindness over insensitivity, goodness over cruelty, love over bitterness, gentleness over harshness. God gives us the option between yielding to the works of the flesh or allowing the fruit of the Spirit to bloom within us. He equips us with everything we need to do what pleases Him, but He won't force us to produce. If we truly love Him, we will choose the fare He likes.

But the fruit of the Spirit is love, joy, peace, patience, kindness, goodness, faithfulness, gentleness and self-control. (Galatians 5:22–23)

How I struggled with this verse when I first

came to the Lord! I tried to behave like all the wonderful Christians around me, but I just could not be like them. Finally in the midst of my despairing to the Lord, He spoke to me and said, "Michelle, I didn't call you to be a cookie-cutter Christian. I don't want you to mimic others and try to be like everyone else. I want you to be you and to allow Me to be who I am in you. If you would allow Me to operate through you, using your unique personality, we could be quite a team." Well, that set me free. I allowed Him to adjust my habits (and even my wardrobe) instead of adjusting myself to the example of others. My life and character were transformed as I studied God's Word and renewed my mind with His perspective. I responded to His voice as He instructed me on what was good and what was unbecoming, and it was easy to obey because His instructions were so loving!

Once I let go of trying to toe the line in my own flesh, I found myself flowing in God's love, joy, peace and all of the above a whole lot more easily. I allowed His Spirit to rise up inside of me. I gave Him permission to overtake my flesh and cause me to be fruitful. Just like Mary. But every time I took the reins back into my own hands, I stumbled into error and felt the strain of dead works done in the flesh.

Working It Out

Because it's true that God lives in us and produces love, that the joy of the Lord is our strength, that He promises to give us the peace of God that surpasses all understanding by Christ Jesus, that patience does its own perfect work in us if we let it, then why do we grunt, groan, work, and stress? We are told to simply abide in Him. Relax, relate, release, and go with the flow of His Spirit. Leave the driving to Him, in a sense, and you will arrive at the destination of fruitfulness.

Pack up your stuff and get in the car, but don't grab the wheel! Don't be Sarah, Abraham's wife in the book of Genesis, who tried to make God's promises happen and added confusion to the plan. Stay sensitive to His leading and don't run ahead of the program. But don't lag behind either. Give God something to work with. That something would be *you* — yielded, available, and ready to be used. Allow *Him* to open doors of opportunity for blessing. It's your job to be equipped and prepared to embrace whatever He brings your way. When I wrote my first book, I had no idea where to begin to get it published. I just knew that it would one day be in print. As I wrote my manuscript, opportunities came my way, and I was ready to present something when asked what I had to offer. I did my part; God did His. The end. By the Holy Ghost.

Mary didn't have to do anything to conceive the seed that bore God's firstfruit. She simply said yes to God. She didn't try to help God; she merely cooperated. There is a difference. She didn't go off in search of a partner to guarantee her pregnancy. No, she rested in what she was told and waited on God. She yielded to Him her flesh and the limitations of her understanding. He was able to work with a surrendered vessel. Because she presented to Him a heart that was pliable in His hands, He was able to plant what He wanted in her life. He blessed His living Word within her womb. She received it and allowed it to become a perfect work in her. And the fruit of her womb was blessed.

THOUGHTS TO PONDER

- Have you taken stock of your fruit lately? What's it like? Do you bear more foliage or more fruit?

- Are you nurturing life in others around you? Are their lives different because of you?

- When do you try to be fruitful in the flesh versus allowing the Spirit to have control?

- What are your talents or gifts? Are you using them to bless others?

- What type of advertisement are you for the kingdom of God?

7. STANDING FOR SOMETHING, FALLING FOR NOTHING

CHOOSING THE PATH OF GREATEST REWARD

> But the angel said to her, "Do not be afraid, Mary, you have found favor with God. You will be with child and give birth to a son, and you are to give him the name Jesus. He will be great and will be called the Son of the Most High. The Lord God will give him the throne of his father David, and he will reign over the house of Jacob forever; his kingdom will never end."
>
> Luke 1:30–33

Looking back on heroes of old, one is struck by their determination to stand firm in the face of great opposition and misunderstanding. These were the ones who kept their heads when around them everyone else was losing theirs. They did not waffle at difficulty or lose heart in the face of adversity. They had a vision in mind, a great cause. Usually it involved the saving of a nation. Such heroes were willing to give their lives for what they believed in. People like William Wallace of Scotland, Joan of Arc of France, Gandhi, Martin Luther King Jr., and many others gladly gave their lives in an effort to redeem the lives of others. Some did not live to see what their efforts wrought, but their sacrifices were worth it because embedded in their hearts was belief in their mission. For them, abandoning the cause would have been worse than death.

Today, when political candidates run for office, debates rage over their stand on the issues. We are quick to criticize them if they seem to shift and change their opinions to please special-interest groups. Our disdain for them escalates if they seem indecisive about issues. We decide they cannot be trusted. No trust, no vote. No vote, no victory for that candidate. Why? Because we've been taught that the person who doesn't stand for something will fall for anything. I think that boils down to being double-minded. In the eyes of man or of God, double-mindedness is not a good quality.

He who doubts is like a wave of the sea, blown and tossed by the wind. That man should not think he will receive anything from the Lord; he is a double-minded man, unstable in all he does. (James 1:6–8)

THE BLESSING BUSINESS

When it comes to the issue of blessings, God searches our hearts to see where we stand. Where do we stand in Him? Where do we stand on kingdom issues? His evaluation determines what He can trust us to possess. Obviously Mary could be trusted with His Son. God knew, based on Mary's heart condition, that she would raise Jesus in the right fashion and groom Him for His life mission. She would not be selfish but would remember that He was God's Son first. Jesus was not born to give Mary emotional comfort or to validate her as a woman. He was born to redeem the souls of mankind. In order for her to be able to release Him to His mission, God had to be her all-consuming passion. God, not her son, had to be the One who filled her heart to overflowing. She had to be consumed with God's desire for the salvation of the world. She had to be in agreement with His plan. Yes, for this very special assignment God searched the hearts of countless women and found Mary's heart not wanting for anything. All of this is not to say that Mary was perfect by any stretch of the imagination. After all, she was human, but the bottom line was her heart condition. It is my belief, whatever her mistakes, that she kept short accounts with God and did not abuse His grace. When God looked at her heart He found a heart sold out to Him and so He took up residence there. In order to be blessed above measure, we must deal with our hearts and decide where we stand.

Come near to God and he will come near to you. Wash your hands, you sinners, and purify your hearts, you *double-minded.* (James 4:8)

Why is being double-minded associated with impure hearts? Because the heart is the seat of the will, the place where we come to conclusions and make decisions. The heart influences our every move. Depending on whom or what we love most, we choose our course of action. We operate according to either a selfish strategy or a heavenly agenda.

Do not store up for yourselves treasures on earth, where moth and rust destroy, and where thieves break in and steal. But store up for yourselves treasures in heaven, where moth and rust do not destroy, and where thieves do not break in and steal. For where your treasure is, there your heart will be also. . . .

No one can serve two masters. Either he will hate the one and love the other, or he will be devoted to the one and despise the other. You cannot serve both God and Money. (Matthew 6:19–21,24)

Those whose hearts are God-centered, who live with kingdom purpose at the forefront of their thoughts, are blessed and highly favored to eat from the fat of the land.

The heart is deceitful above all things and
    beyond cure.
    Who can understand it?
"I the LORD search the heart
    and examine the mind,
to reward a man according to his
    conduct,
    according to what his deeds deserve."
                                    (Jeremiah 17:9–10)

Let's look at this heart thing in every context, from emotional to physical to material blessings. Consider Abraham, an extremely wealthy man. God could trust him with wealth because Abraham was sold out to God. He was not a hoarder. Can God trust you with money? Do you still go through a battle when it's time to give your tithes and offerings? Do you still quibble over whether to tithe your gross or your net? I'm just trying to make a point, not offend you. Abraham gladly gave to Melchizedek, the first high priest mentioned in Scripture, a tithe off all he had acquired after winning a tremendous battle. Even when dividing the land between Lot and himself so they could all live peaceably, Abraham did not insist on the best for himself. Instead, he allowed Lot to choose the better area. Abraham continued to trust that God would bring him into the fullness of His inheritance, and Lot's choices could not stop that from happening. In Abraham's mind, God was well able to guard His interests, keep His promises, and fulfill His kingdom agenda. After all, Abraham was merely being obedient to God's order to move out and possess the land. It was *God,* not Abraham, who wanted to establish a nation. Abraham was simply walking in cooperation with God. The bottom line was that Abraham had no agenda other than God's.

HEART'S DESIRES, HEAVEN'S INQUIRIES

Now look at Hannah, who so dearly wanted a child (1 Samuel 1). She also came to the place of releasing her selfish agenda. Perhaps she thought long and hard on a comment her husband, Elkanah, made. He had inquired of her, "Why are you downhearted? Don't I mean more to you than ten sons?" Elkanah gave her a double portion to offer to the Lord just because he loved her, not because of anything she did. In fact, by the worldly standards of the day she was a failure not worthy of a reward. Elkanah's other wife, Peninah, had borne him several children, but Hannah had not birthed one. Elkanah did not care about Hannah's performance; he only saw her heart and loved her. Likewise, I think God looks at our heart condition and loves us, bestowing double portions on those whose hearts long to produce fruit not for our own personal gain but for the kingdom.

Hannah focused on the reason for her desire and chose to make the only sacrifice that would truly be a sacrifice to her. She vowed to release her firstborn into the service of the Lord. She chose to give that which was dearest to her back to Him! Can you imagine waiting years for a son, only to finally get one and have to leave him at the temple? Yet that was exactly what Hannah did. She gave God her first fruit, and He in turn gave her a rich harvest, a crop of children in addition to the one she had given over to Him for the furtherance of His purposes.

Hannah had come to the place of realizing that having children was not about gaining personal satisfaction or even validation as a woman in the eyes of her husband and society. Her first call was to produce a child to the glory of God. She did that by releasing Samuel to be groomed as a mighty prophet for the Lord. And for this offering to the Lord, she gained the regard of God and was richly blessed above and beyond what she could have asked or imagined.

Just as Elkanah asked Hannah, God asks us the question, "Don't My love and My purposes mean more to you than the blessings you long for?" Whatever is on our wish list — be it riches, love, prominent position — we must be willing to render these things back to the Lord. Then and only then can He trust us with them. When He finds a heart that can truthfully say, "Yes, Lord, I'm willing to sacrifice everything for your sake," then He pours out such a wealth of blessings that we cannot contain them all. If we are double-minded about our commitment to God and the furtherance of His kingdom, our vats will dry up.

What about David? His mind was consumed with using his great wealth to build a temple for God. Yet God would not allow him to build it because he had been a man of war and had blood on his hands. The Lord allowed David to contribute goods for the building of the temple and continued to bless David with material goods to overflowing *because he knew where David's heart was.* David's heart was consumed with pleasing God, with lifting Him up for all to see. David's passion went beyond leading Israel; David's passion was to establish God's kingdom on earth. David wanted to give God His due — a place designated for worshiping Him — and in David's heart even that wouldn't have been enough. Although David was not able to carry out this desire, God honored David's heart toward Him. Even after David had acquired houses, lands, gold, and more, God was his first love.

FOR THE LOVE OF MONEY

Money and power truly reveal our hearts. Position, status, and wealth have been the downfall of many a great man and woman of God. With these things in hand, they have gotten off of their knees and onto their own course, forgetting all the wonderful plans they had to glorify God if only they had enough money or influence to do so.

Solomon was guilty of this. He started off so well. He had seen what God had done for his father, David. Now that the throne belonged to him, he purposed to carry on in the tradition of his father and be a worshiper first and a king second, totally relying on the guidance of the Lord.

At Gibeon the LORD appeared to Solomon during the night in a dream, and God said, "Ask for whatever you want me to give you."

Solomon answered, ". . . give your servant a discerning heart to govern your people and to distinguish between right and wrong. For who is able to govern this great people of yours?"

The Lord was pleased that Solomon had asked for this. So God said to him, "Since you have asked for this and not for long life or wealth for yourself, nor have asked for the death of your enemies but for discernment in administering justice, I will do what you have asked. I will give you a wise and discerning heart, so that there will never have been anyone like you, nor will there ever be. Moreover, I will give you what you have not asked for — both riches and honor — so that in your lifetime you will have no equal among kings." (1 Kings 3:5–6,9–13)

But with the acquisition of these things, Solomon also acquired more opportunities to be distracted by ungodly women and all the material things his wealth could afford him. His heart turned away from the purposes of God toward his own designs, and he fell. He began to worship the gods of his foreign wives and offended God. On that note, he also fell out of favor with God. He ended his days sighing, "Vanity of vanities! All is vanity" (Ecclesiastes 1:2, NASB). If all we heap up for ourselves does not have God's favor and blessing, it becomes an empty acquisition that cannot be fully enjoyed.

The lust of the eyes, the lust of the flesh, and the pride of life are the original sins still at work in our lives today. The Holy Spirit is also at work, searching the hearts of all those who profess to love God: Who can be trusted among us with the blessings we ask for? And yet God desires to bless us and shower His favor on us. So determined is He to bless us that He is willing to break us first, as he did with Joseph.

Yes, God was going to promote Joseph, but only when Joseph was ready to handle the promotion. I heard a preacher once say that God is ready to bless you when you are ready to be blessed. Now that is deep. I'll repeat it again: God is ready when you are ready, when you finally have His heart toward the matters set before you. Joseph understood that his newfound position as the right-hand man to Pharaoh was not about him. It wasn't about saying, "Nah, nah, na, na, nah" to his brothers. It was about God placing him in a position where he was able to carry out God's agenda: saving the nation of Israel. Why do you want what you want? Why do you dream of what you dream of? Think about it.

Because it is God who blesses with wealth, let's think about why He would. So we can buy more shoes? (That's *my* weakness! The Lord knows I love a beautiful pair of shoes!) No! Absolutely not! As my mother would say whenever I left food on my plate, "There are children starving in Ethiopia and other portions of the world." So why would He bless us with wealth? Why would He put large sums of money into our hands? Because He wants us to distribute it to those in need.

"Bring the whole tithe into the *storehouse, that there may be food in my house.* Test me in this," says the LORD Almighty, "and see if I will not throw open the floodgates of heaven and pour out so much blessing that you will not have room enough for it." (Malachi 3:10)

God wants provision to be available to those who need to see His benevolence manifested in their lives. What a privilege it is when you can be a partner with Him in this! This is one of the ways we glorify God, and He blesses us in return. We cannot beat God in our giving. Neither can we deny that blessing His children is the desire of His heart. His Word on why He chooses to give or withhold is clear.

> When you ask, you do not receive, because you ask with wrong motives, that you may spend what you get on your pleasures. (James 4:3)

> Religion that God our Father accepts as pure and faultless is this: to look after *orphans* and *widows* in their distress and to keep oneself from being polluted by the world. (James 1:27)

Isn't that interesting? What kind of pollution is He talking about? The pollution of selfish gain. Don't be like the world, hoarding your blessings for yourself. Share your wealth. Feed others. Jesus clearly responded to Peter's claims that he loved Him with "Feed my sheep." Use both faith and material helps. Jesus could well have said, "If you love Me, please Me by doing what is important to Me. Make Me look good. Make Me desirable to those who don't know Me by making My care for them evident in your giving. Give of yourselves, give of what you have."

It Is Better to Give Than to Receive

One day I was in a hurry, trying to get out of town for a speaking engagement. As I drove my car down the street, a young lady crossed my path and I almost collided with her. I was upset with her for not realizing that I had the green light. She should not have been walking across the street at that time. I wondered aloud what was the matter with her and continued to the gas station to fill up for the journey. As I got back into the car, I noticed that this same young lady had circled back to the gas station and crossed in front of my car to ask the customer in front of me for money. The person ignored her, but I felt a tug in my spirit to give her some money. I called her over to the car and gave her a twenty-dollar bill.

Do you know what she said? She said, "Are you a Christian?"

"Yes," I said.

"Thank you for the money," she said, "but could you please pray for me?" Well, I began to pray over that girl right there and then as others in the gas station looked on. She went away praising God, rejoicing in the fact that He cared for her. It was a God moment. I was happy I could give her more than money, and I thought to myself as I drove off, "Truly this is what the Christian life is all about. God, grant me more opportunities like that one." He had chosen to use me as a vessel to glorify Him.

When I consider those in the world who have an abundance of wealth, most of those people make major contributions on behalf of children or the unfortunate. From people like Oprah Winfrey to Bill Gates, Christians and non-Christians alike flourish. Why? Because although they have acquired a lot of things for themselves, they are faithful in giving to others. They abide by the principle of sowing and reaping.

I was talking with a wealthy friend of mine one day, and we were discussing a designer line of clothing. I was complaining about the exorbitant prices of the articles, although I knew these things were well within my friend's reach. But then she said something that rocked my world. She said, "I agree with you, and though I love her designs I just couldn't spend God's money like that." Wow! God's money. In her mind her money did not belong to her. I have to admit I had never looked at finances in that light, but the more I thought about it, I realized her perspective was right on. I began to think of my bank account differently. God had left it in my care, and He trusted me to use it wisely. My friend and I went on to discuss being a wise steward over that which God has given us. I walked away with a greater sense of purpose and a renewed understanding of true stewardship in light of kingdom business.

It's All or Nothing

Looking at the life of Jesus, we see the ultimate illustration of giving everything and gaining the world. Jesus loved not His own life, but gave it willingly for the sake of others. For the sake of the kingdom. Therefore God made Him Lord over all.

The Father loves the Son and has placed everything in his hands. (John 3:35)

Jesus was willing to be misunderstood in

order to carry out the desires of the Father. A life of selflessness is not without opposition. Just as the devil confronted Jesus and tempted Him to take self-preserving measures, the enemy of your soul will come to taunt you, to tell you that you are a fool, that your giving is in vain and unappreciated. Yet you must persevere in your principal quest: to do the Father's bidding. Your efforts will not go unrewarded.

> But seek first his kingdom and his righteousness, and *all* these *things* will be *given* to you as well. (Matthew 6:33)

You must be willing to follow Jesus down the path of sacrifice in order to gain the greater blessings that await those who choose His way. Mary said yes to God knowing that it would cost her something, that it could in fact cost her everything! She had no idea how Joseph would take the news that she was pregnant, pregnant with the Son of God. How does one explain such a thing? She had to have considered that he might not believe her. If he didn't believe her, the consequences could be grave indeed. She could be accused of fornication and stoned to death. Yet sharing the angel's message was a chance she would take to birth, literally, the purposes of God. If Joseph did not choose to join her, so be it. Though it could cost her reputation, family, and all that she held dear, so be it. God's will be done above all things. She was willing to take the chance. This fierce allegiance to the purposes of God was exactly what He was looking for.

In our quest to fulfill God's call on our lives, we will likely be misunderstood along the way. We will be challenged by people to use our gifts and resources in ways other than the way God has asked of us, but we must remain true to our call in order to know the blessed life. Some might challenge your tithing. Your celibacy. Your refusal to give up on a difficult marriage. Some might challenge your sacrifice of a high-profile job for the sake of ministry. Whatever it is that causes you to be peculiar in the eyes of others, if God has called you to it, persevere in it; your reward is on the way. God is watching how you handle your circumstances. And whatever the circumstances, we must make a stand for the purposes of God. His desires must be our desires; His priorities, our priorities. When our hearts are in the right place, God can trust us to be wise stewards over what He gives — and give He will!

Whoever can be trusted with very *little* can also be trusted with much, and whoever is dishonest with very *little* will also be dishonest with much. (Luke 16:10)

"Well done, my good servant!" his master replied. "Because you have been trustworthy in a very small matter, take charge of ten cities." (Luke 19:17)

Yes, God is watching. Watching how you behave. Watching how you spend what you have. Watching how you spend your time. Watching what you give to others. How you handle authority. How you submit to those over you. If you can submit, God can trust you to lead. If you give out of your need, He can trust you to give out of plenty.

Are you getting the picture? If God can trust you to be a living sacrifice, proving what is His good, acceptable, and perfect will, He will take your sacrifice and exchange it for incredible blessing. Mary gave what she had to God. Herself. And she was blessed.

THOUGHTS TO PONDER

- What motivates your decisions and choices?

- Are your aspirations good ideas or God ideas?

- What would God say about how you spend your time? Your money?

- Can God trust you with power? Money? Position?

- How do your desires fit in with kingdom business? Are you concerned about what God is concerned about?

8. What's in a Name?

LETTING YOUR REPUTATION WORK FOR YOU

But why am I so favored, that the mother of my Lord should come to me?

Luke 1:43

Shakespeare wrote, "What's in a name? That which we call a rose by any other name would smell as sweet." Perhaps that's true, but names do seem to bear a lot of weight at least in our floral selections. Discriminating flower shoppers know of one rose in particular whose reputation precedes it: the American Beauty. When you want to present your best or really make a statement, a dozen of these gorgeous red flowers will always impress.

Why is a good name so important? Because it defines, simply and succinctly, who we are. When I left the ad agency I worked for, I never had to call anyone to secure work. I didn't realize how the work I'd done up to that time had set the stage for my life as a freelancer. When the buzz that I was self-employed hit the street, the phone began to ring. "So-and-so said you were just the person I needed for this project. Are you interested?" "I heard you are really good at this." "I hear you're the one to call." My name had become associated with excellence in my field, and I never even knew that anyone was paying attention! I had cultivated a good reputation in advertising circles, not because I had been networking, but because I had applied myself to being superb at my craft. This was my way of glorifying God in the workplace. When people asked me how I came up with my ideas, I'd say, "Well, I simply pray and wait for God's creativity to operate through me." Some looked at me quizzically. I'm sure they were thinking there had to be more to it than that. But believe me, there wasn't.

FIRST IMPRESSIONS ARE LASTING ONES

A good name creates favor for you and opens the door for countless blessings. This is why it is so important to always walk in righteousness and excellence. We never know who is watching us or in what situations our reputation will pave the way for promotion or demotion.

When a man's ways are pleasing to the
   LORD,
   he makes even his enemies live at
   peace with him.

(Proverbs 16:7)

When Joseph received news of Mary's pregnancy, he found himself torn. I believe the godly life she had led caused him to seek a way to protect her rather than to expose her, though he couldn't reconcile how she could be pregnant without human contact. He knew that Mary was a woman after God's own heart, a woman who would not wander beyond the righteous boundaries of God's law. Therefore his heart was open to instruction from the angel who confirmed that, indeed, Mary's pregnancy was a holy event and that Joseph should proceed with his marriage plans.

After he had considered this, an angel of the Lord appeared to him in a dream and said, "Joseph son of David, do not be afraid to take Mary home as your wife, because what is conceived in her is from the Holy Spirit. She will give birth to a son, and you are to give him the name Jesus, because he will save his people from their sins."

169

All this took place to fulfill what the Lord had said through the prophet: "The virgin will be with child and will give birth to a son, and they will call him Immanuel" — which means, "God with us."

When Joseph woke up, he did what the angel of the Lord had commanded him and took Mary home as his wife. (Matthew 1:20–24)

Now that's what a good name will do for you! Mary had lived a faultless life before God, so the insinuations of the enemy were not able to stick to her. God came to her defense, and Joseph rose to the occasion by standing beside her as her covering and husband.

My son, do not forget my teaching,
    but keep my commands in your heart,
for they will prolong your life many years
    and bring you prosperity.
Let love and faithfulness never leave you;
    bind them around your neck,
    write them on the tablet of your heart.
Then you will win favor and a good name
    in the sight of God and man.
(Proverbs 3:1–4)

When God is on your side, what can man

do to you? Who can say no to you when God says yes? A clean conscience and right-standing with God are the prerequisites for a sparkling reputation and a good name. If you want a good long life and prosperity, cultivate a good name.

> A *good name* is more desirable than
>   great riches;
>   to be esteemed is better than silver or
>   gold.
>
> (Proverbs 22:1)

> A *good name* is better than fine perfume.
> (Ecclesiastes 7:1)

A good name cannot be spent, it will not tarnish, and, like perfume, it lingers long after you've left the room. Have you ever been in a room with someone who has on a wonderful fragrance? When he or she leaves, the memory of that person remains with you. You almost want to follow in order to continue the pleasant experience. Like that kind of perfume, our name should bring a smile to the faces of God and man when mentioned. And when people think highly of you, they are willing to extend a favor on your behalf.

THE BENEFITS OF HEARSAY

Ruth was minding her own business, gleaning in the fields of Boaz, when she caught his eye. When he inquired after her identity, her good name spoke on her behalf, and he made special concessions to make sure she had what she needed.

At this, she bowed down with her face to the ground. She exclaimed, "Why have I found such favor in your eyes that you notice me — a foreigner?"

Boaz replied, "I've been told all about what you have done for your mother-in-law since the death of your husband — how you left your father and mother and your homeland and came to live with a people you did not know before. May the LORD repay you for what you have done. May you be richly rewarded by the LORD, the God of Israel, under whose wings you have come to take refuge."

"May I continue to find favor in your eyes, my lord," she said. "You have given me comfort and have spoken kindly to your servant — though I do not have the standing of one of your servant girls." (Ruth 2:10–13)

There is no deep spiritual principle here, just good godly sense. Notice I didn't say common sense because sense is not common. When people think highly of you, they will do good for you, even when others accuse you of wrongdoing.

I think of Jacob's son Joseph, accused of rape by Mrs. Potiphar. Due to the integrity that Joseph had always displayed to Potiphar, Joseph had a good name. Oh, in order to keep the peace at home, Potiphar had to address what his wife had told him, but he could not get past what he knew to be true of Joseph. So Potiphar put Joseph in the king's prison instead of ordering the usual death penalty for such a crime. And it was Potiphar who placed the Pharaoh's wine steward and chief baker under Joseph's care in the prison. These two events, plus Joseph's ability to tap into the spirit of God and interpret these men's dreams, gained him release from prison and promotion to the right-hand man of the Pharaoh of Egypt.

MAKING A NAME FOR YOURSELF

Even the heathens knew the importance of names. When Daniel went into the employ of the king of Babylon, the king changed Daniel's name to Belteshazzar, after a Babylonian god. But Daniel held fast to his

Hebrew name, refusing to change the confession of faith that it was. I find it interesting that despite his name change everyone still continued to call him Daniel! — so great was his stand and lack of compromise. Because of his excellent service to the king, no one bothered to dispute him. Daniel (meaning "God is my judge") survived four administrations of Babylonian government because of his good name.

Now think about how unusual that is. Governments and corporations are famous for cleaning house whenever a new leader comes on the scene. Newcomers usually clear out the old administration and bring in all of their own people. But Daniel's reputation for wisdom and integrity preceded him. Incoming kings actually chose Daniel for chief administrative services. King Darius, the third king Daniel served, was so impressed with Daniel that he placed him over the entire empire. Of course this did not sit well with the other administrators and princes at all.

Now Daniel so distinguished himself among the administrators and the satraps by his exceptional qualities that the king planned to set him over the whole kingdom. At this, the administrators and the satraps tried to find grounds for charges against Daniel in his conduct of government affairs, but they were unable to do so. They could find no corruption in him, because he was trustworthy and neither corrupt nor negligent. Finally these men said, "We will never find any basis for charges against this man Daniel unless it has something to do with the law of his God." (Daniel 6:3–5)

So they conspired against Daniel and devised a law against prayer that they knew he would break. Everyone knew Daniel was a praying man. So they bamboozled the king into writing a decree against prayer. Then they lay in wait.

When they caught Daniel offering his usual supplications to the Lord, they were quick to run and report him to the king. But an unusual thing happened.

When the king heard this, he was greatly distressed; he was determined to rescue Daniel and made every effort until sundown to save him.

Then the men went as a group to the king and said to him, "Remember, O king, that according to the law of the Medes and Persians no decree or edict that the king issues can be changed." So the king gave the order, and they brought Daniel and threw him into the lions' den. The king said to Daniel, "May your God, whom you serve continually, rescue you!" (Daniel 6:14–16)

Now when you are known as a man or a woman who continually serves God, guess what? God's name is on the line too. And you had better believe God is able to show up and show Himself to be strong on your behalf. He will move the hearts of those who opposed you and set you up for victory. He will have those who opposed you cheering you on. He Himself will come down and be your buckler and your shield, your strong defense. He will grant you the power to be an overcomer despite the circumstances. That's just a natural part of the blessed life.

Then the king returned to his palace and spent the night without eating and without any entertainment being brought to him. And he could not sleep.

At the first light of dawn, the king got up and hurried to the lions' den. When he came near the den, he called to Daniel in an anguished voice, "Daniel, servant of the living God, has your God, whom you serve continually, been able to rescue you from the lions?"

Daniel answered, "O king, live forever! My God sent his angel, and he shut the mouths of the lions. They have not hurt me, because I was found innocent in his sight. Nor have I ever done any wrong before you, O king."

The king was overjoyed and gave orders to lift Daniel out of the den. And when Daniel was lifted from the den, no wound was found on him, because he had trusted in his God.

At the king's command, the men who had falsely accused Daniel were brought in and thrown into the lions' den, along with their wives and children. And before they reached the floor of the den, the lions overpowered them and crushed all their bones.

Then King Darius wrote to all the peoples, nations and men of every language throughout the land:

"May you prosper greatly!

"I issue a decree that in every part of my kingdom people must fear and reverence the God of Daniel.

"For he is the living God
    and he endures forever;

his kingdom will not be destroyed,
  his dominion will never end.
He rescues and he saves;
  he performs signs and wonders
  in the heavens and on the earth.
He has rescued Daniel
  from the power of the lions."

So Daniel prospered during the reign of Darius and the reign of Cyrus the Persian. (Daniel 6:18–28)

See what I mean? A good name is powerful, more powerful than bribe money or anything else you could think of to use as leverage in the natural world. Your good name will cause people to praise God's name. Why? Because they can see the evidence of Him at work in your life as you seek to honor Him in all that you do.

IT'S ALL IN A NAME
In the end our names or our reputations are really all we have that completely represents who we are. Our name encapsulates our personal legacy, which will remain to speak of our character and integrity long after we have departed. This is why God chooses to swear by His own name.

> When God made his promise to Abraham, since there was no one greater for him to swear by, he *swore* by *himself.* (Hebrews 6:13)

Our name is our confession. What we confess is what we are. Our words have power. The power of death and life is in our tongues, according to the book of James. That's why I always urge those I know to be careful what they name their children. My name, *Michelle,* means "Who is like God?" That is, "one who stands behind and practices absolute truth." My middle name, *Ayodele,* means, "Joy arrives in the home." Now those are two good daily confessions for my life. They keep me remembering the call of God on my life. Every time someone calls my name, that person reinforces my identity and God's call: "Hey, you who stands behind and practices absolute truth, you who carries joy — how are you today?" I've got to line up my life with that because, with the pronouncement of my name, the air is charged with who I am supposed to be and how I am supposed to live!

Psychologists have found that children with unusual names are more prone to juvenile delinquency because they are constantly teased about their names. I would dare to go a step further and add the spiritual implication that, if a child's name doesn't mean anything, he or she will be more likely to have a sense of meaninglessness that provokes him or her to cause trouble.

God deliberately chose to name those who would be instrumental in His plan. The given names described the character and attributes of the man or woman God had chosen. At times the Lord changed an individual's name because a transformation had taken place in that person's life. Abram (exalted father) was changed to Abraham (father of many nations). Sarai (princess) became Sarah (noblewoman), and Jacob (supplanter), Israel (prince). These people had come into the fullness of what God had called them to be and were identified as such.

Since no single name is sufficient to describe God, He chose to call Himself "I Am," because He is all things. Even Jesus could not be described by just one name.

Behold, a virgin shall be with child, and shall bring forth a son, and they shall call his name Emmanuel which being interpreted is, God with us. (Matthew 1:23, KJV)

For unto us a child is born, unto us a son is given: and the government shall be upon his shoulder: and his name shall be called Wonderful, Counsellor, The mighty God, The everlasting Father, The Prince of Peace. (Isaiah 9:6, KJV)

Isn't that incredible? God is so many things that He requires a myriad of names. Think of all the things we call Him: Jehovah Jireh (our provider), Jehovah Shalom (He is our peace), Abba Father, Yahweh. And that's just the beginning of all His names! Each of these describes but one feature of many belonging to our complex God, who encompasses more than we will ever be able to imagine. And still He is our loving Father. Our God. Our King. Our confidence is in His name because it is the embodiment of what He has promised to be for us.

I will praise you forever for what you have
    done;
    in your *name* I will hope, for your *name*
    is *good.*
    I will praise you in the presence of
    your saints.
(Psalm 52:9)

I will sacrifice a freewill offering to you;
I will praise your *name,* O Lord,
for it is *good.*

(Psalm 54:6)

There is authority in the name of Jesus because He has been proclaimed Lord and King. We are able to stand firm before the enemy of our souls because we have the assurance that at the name of Jesus, all things must come into submission to His Lordship. In other words, He has our back!

Therefore God exalted him to the highest place
and gave him the name that is above every name,
that at the name of Jesus every knee should bow,
in heaven and on earth and under the earth,
and every tongue confess that Jesus Christ is Lord,
to the glory of God the Father.

(Philippians 2:9–11)

God's name proclaims His sovereignty. What does your name proclaim about you? The mere mention of certain names elicits a quick response: awe, respect, laughter, disdain. Our hearts open or shut at the sound of a person's name.

When others hear your name, do you think the words *faithful, honest, responsible, loving, kind,* and *dependable* come to their minds?

Consider someone like Jacob, whose name meant "supplanter." He connived his way through the early years of his life, but his true identity caught up with him when he needed a blessing from God. "What is your name?" God asked him. Jacob had to confess who he truly was, a supplanter, and only then did God change his name and transform him into a man of honor. Jacob became Israel, "prince," and the father of the tribes of that nation which would affect the world for all eternity. Wow! If our names have been tarnished, truly God is able to redeem our past failures and ruined reputations as we come clean with Him, allowing Him to wash us and make us new creations in Him. He is willing to do so because He fully understands the importance of a good name.

The reaction people have to your name can affect your blessings. That's why this discussion of names brings us full circle to our relationship with God. Do you walk in a godly fashion and, by so doing, place yourself in right standing with God and others? Favor with God affects your favor with man. You need that favor for open doors, for effectual opportunities to prosper in your calling and giftings. You need that favor in order to be blessed. You see, part of the secret of getting blessed is giving your heavenly Father something to work with. Why not start with a good name? Mary had a good name. It gave her favor with God and with Joseph, and she was blessed.

Thoughts to Ponder

- What does your name mean? Are you the embodiment of your name? Do you take your name's confession over your life seriously?

- How do you think people respond when they hear your name?

- What standards have you set for yourself in order to cultivate a godly reputation?

- Do people know that you are a Christian even when you don't tell them?

- What is the one descriptive word you would like placed by your name if it were in the dictionary?

9. A WORD IN TIME

UNDERSTANDING THE POWER
OF SILENCE

But *Mary* treasured up all these things and *pondered* them in her heart.

Luke 2:19

When God speaks, the universe listens. But sometimes He speaks only to you.

Can you keep a secret? Sometimes being able to keep a secret is important to receiving God's blessings. Let me explain by first asking a question. Have you ever been promised a great deal by someone and been so excited about it that you just had to tell everybody? I'll bet everybody wanted to know why they weren't getting the same deal, and they started raising sand about it. What happened? Either your deal got put on hold until the furor died down, or it was withdrawn completely in order to keep the peace.

Words spoken out of season can get us in trouble. Sometimes you have to keep to yourself the details of those great and wonderful promises, whether from God or someone else, until the appointed time. Remember, we are partners with God in this blessing thing. You can make it easy, or you can make it more difficult than it has to be.

Not everyone is going to be happy about the things God has promised you. Satan certainly won't be. He will raise his ugly head to question you and try to dislodge your faith. Others will be just plain jealous because God didn't promise them the same thing. People who wait on God's promises may be viewed as unrealistic dreamers. And people don't like dreamers. Dreamers make people uncomfortable, perhaps because dreamers expose a lack of vision and a sense of purposelessness that other people may be feeling. Joseph found this out the hard way.

Now Israel loved Joseph more than any of his other sons, because he had been born to him in his old age; and he made a richly ornamented robe for him. When his brothers saw that their father loved him more than any of them, they hated him and could not speak a kind word to him.

Joseph had a dream, and when he told it to his brothers, they hated him all the more. (Genesis 37:3–5)

You know the rest of the story. The brothers focused on Joseph's dream even more than he did, I think, and they were so incensed that they sought his harm.

> Then he had another dream, and he told it to his brothers. "Listen," he said, "I had another dream. . . ."
>
> When he told his father as well as his brothers, his father rebuked him and said, "What is this dream you had? . . ." [Joseph's] brothers were jealous of him. . . .
>
> They saw him in the distance, and before he reached them, they plotted to kill him.
>
> "Here comes that dreamer!" they said to each other. "Come now, let's kill him and throw him into one of these cisterns and say that a ferocious animal devoured him. Then we'll see what comes of his dreams." (Genesis 37:9–11,18–20)

Joseph had spoken too soon. Although he didn't know it, his dreams would not be realized for years. Now, mind you, God used the evil plot of Joseph's brothers to position Joseph exactly where he needed to be in order for his dream to be fulfilled. We will never know how God would have gotten him to Egypt any other way, but that's beside the point. The bottom line is that sometimes we bring unnecessary complications into our lives by speaking out of time. I find it interesting that when his dreams were fulfilled, Joseph wasn't as quick to reveal his identity to his brothers. He had learned a thing or two about timing.

Even God doesn't tell us everything at once. Although He already knows all the details of our lives, He gives us only as much as He knows we can handle at any given time. Too much information at the wrong time is not a good thing. It leaves too much room for error, misunderstanding, confusion, and strife of various kinds. Sometimes you just have to keep things to yourself until they come into full manifestation. The enemy of your soul will use others to try to steal, kill, and destroy the dream God has placed in your life. Even after the dream has been birthed, he keeps on trying! But we can sometimes prevent the abortion of God's dreams by learning how to hold our words for the right season.

There is a time for everything,
   and a season for every activity under
    heaven: . . .
   a time to be silent and a time to

speak. . . .

He has made everything beautiful in its time. He has also set eternity in the hearts of men; yet they cannot fathom what God has done from beginning to end.

(Ecclesiastes 3:1,7,11)

The eyes of all look to you,
and you give them their food at the
proper time.
You open your hand
and satisfy the desires of every living
thing.

(Psalm 145:15–16)

Many of us are so quick to blab it and grab it that we end up grabbing the wrong thing. The opinions of others misguide us. Therefore, it is best to quietly wait on the Lord.

Now that word *wait* is not a passive word. Waiting can be quite active. Wait on the Lord to take care of what He said while you delight yourself in serving Him. Keep moving forward toward His promise. Do what it takes to be in position to receive His blessing. The best position to be in is as close to God as you can get, right smack dab in the center of His will, doing what He's called you to do. You take care of His business and

He will take care of yours. God tells us secrets so we will draw closer to Him to hear and see the rest, not so we will burst into action trying to bring about what He has spoken or to convince others of what He said. The proof will be in the pudding soon enough.

WHAT YOU SAY IS WHAT YOU GET?

Truly the power of life and death is in the tongue. Have you ever shared a secret longing with others only to have them destroy your hopes? They spoke doubt and death to your dream. They took the joy out of it and killed it for you. Perhaps you walked away resolved to no longer pursue your dream. You convinced yourself that what they said made sense. You disregarded the power of God to do the impossible. Small wonder that, when it comes to those things crucial to God's purposes, He will take drastic measures to prevent the vision from fading. He knows what our mouths do; therefore He will either not tell us what He is going to do, or He will arrest us by His Spirit to keep what He has spoken under wraps. We must be sensitive to the leading of the Spirit when this occurs, recognizing the right moment to speak up.

When the angel told Zechariah, the husband of Mary's cousin, Elizabeth, that they would have a son in their old age who would be the forerunner of Jesus, the poor old man had a hard time believing.

Zechariah asked the angel, "How can I be sure of this? I am an old man and my wife is well along in years."

The angel answered, "I am Gabriel. I stand in the presence of God, and I have been sent to speak to you and to tell you this good news. And now you will be silent and not able to speak until the day this happens, because you did not believe my words, which will come true at their proper time."

Meanwhile, the people were waiting for Zechariah and wondering why he stayed so long in the temple. When he came out, he could not speak to them. They realized he had seen a vision in the temple, for he kept making signs to them but remained unable to speak. . . .

When it was time for Elizabeth to have her baby, she gave birth to a son. . . .

On the eighth day they came to circumcise the child, and they were going to name him after his father Zechariah, but his mother spoke up and said, "No! He is to be called John."

They said to her, "There is no one among your relatives who has that name."

Then they made signs to his father, to find out what he would like to name the child. He asked for a writing tablet, and to everyone's astonishment he wrote, "His name is John." Immediately his mouth was opened and his tongue was loosed, and he began to speak, praising God. (Luke 1:18–22,57,59–64)

How's that for keeping a person out of the way? Zechariah was not able to speak until he was able to confess the Word of God about the matter. Notice that Elizabeth had no problem aligning herself with God's chosen name for the baby. She was adamant and would not be moved by the crowd.

If you must share what God has revealed to you, make sure you choose someone who is able to match your faith. As inspiring minister Tim Story says, "Look for your Elizabeth." Mary knew whom to seek out when she was overwhelmed with her miraculous situation. She sought out the companionship and encouragement of Elizabeth, and Elizabeth was able to exhort Mary because she was experiencing her own miracle!

You've got to have someone in your life

who is able to relate to your experience and partner with you in faith. Those who have not been where you're going will have difficulty finding the path and urging you onward. They will be unable to appreciate your experience.

KEEPING IT UNDER WRAPS

To share your dream or promise with someone who has no concept of the miraculous is like casting your pearls before swine. Expect no words of encouragement or any other good thing. Those who have not experienced the favor of God will not be able to join you in faith. In fact, they will downright hurt your feelings.

> Do not give dogs what is sacred; do not throw your *pearls* to pigs. If you do, they may trample them under their feet, and then turn and tear you to pieces. (Matthew 7:6)

Mm-hm, they'll trample your dream and not be satisfied to do just that. They will add insult to injury by telling you that you think more highly of yourself than you ought. That you're being a bit too "high sadiddy" (that's "uppity" in urbanese). After all, why should God bless you like that when they haven't been blessed that way? Well, the answer to that is simply, "Because I expect more from God." Or even better, because you've been working to apply principles to your life that put you in line for a blessing.

So again I say, if you just *must* tell somebody, make sure it's someone who can handle the information in a godly fashion. Even so, God will sometimes require you to do as Mary did and ponder what He has told you in your heart. Even if others receive a witness in their heart concerning God's promise to you and they confirm what has been resting in your spirit, even then continue to guard it.

And there were shepherds living out in the fields nearby, keeping watch over their flocks at night. An angel of the Lord appeared to them, and the glory of the Lord shone around them, and they were terrified. But the angel said to them, "Do not be afraid. I bring you good news of great joy that will be for all the people. Today in the town of David a Savior has been born to you; he is Christ the Lord. This will be a sign to you: You will find a baby wrapped in cloths and lying in a manger." . . .

When the angels had left them and gone

into heaven, the shepherds said to one another, "Let's go to Bethlehem and see this thing that has happened, which the Lord has told us about."

So they hurried off and found Mary and Joseph, and the baby, who was lying in the manger. When they had seen him, they spread the word concerning what had been told them about this child, and all who heard it were amazed at what the shepherds said to them. But Mary treasured up all these things and pondered them in her heart. (Luke 2:8–12,15–19)

When God has spoken a word to you, He will send others to confirm it. Allow Him to select those people. They will be people who are in the Spirit. They will be people who anxiously await the fulfillment of God's agenda, not their own. They are not selfish or self-consumed. The desires of God matter most to them. Their will is lost inside His; therefore, they are not inclined to think negatively about a person who is being set up for promotion or a blessing. They keep kingdom business in full view, seeing it as a blessing for the body and not for just one individual.

Now there was a man in Jerusalem called

Simeon, who was righteous and devout. He was waiting for the consolation of Israel, and the Holy Spirit was upon him. It had been revealed to him by the Holy Spirit that he would not die before he had seen the Lord's Christ. Moved by the Spirit, he went into the temple courts. When the parents brought in the child Jesus to do for him what the custom of the Law required, Simeon took him in his arms and praised God, saying,

"Sovereign Lord, as you have promised,
    you now dismiss your servant in peace.
For my eyes have seen your salvation,
    which you have prepared in the sight of
    all people,
a light for revelation to the Gentiles
    and for glory to your people Israel."

The child's father and mother marveled at what was said about him. (Luke 2:25–33)

When God has spoken, many of us are not confident that we have heard *His* voice. We seek validation and find ourselves as invalids instead, paralyzed by the unbelief or disdain of others. But God will select an unselfish encourager for you. One who knows how to pray and to travail with you until the time for the manifestation of the promise is upon you. When you are believing for the incredible, extraordinary blessings of God, chances are you're going to have a long labor in the birthing process. You need a spiritual midwife to coach you through, to tell you when to wait and when to push.

Birthing the Vision

If you've ever seen a mother in her eighth or ninth month of pregnancy, you may have heard "I am ready for this baby to come out!" That woman has carried and incubated that child to the birthing point, and now she's ready to deliver it. But guess what? That child isn't coming out until he or she is good and ready!

God's blessings and promises are like that. Others who induce labor for whatever reason typically find that the pain of the delivery process is intensified. Their bodies are unprepared for delivery, and it is literally a shock to the system. The body is hostile to the disturbance. When we try to make things happen either through our actions or the things we say, I believe it sends shock waves through the spirit realm that cause unnecessary tension or pressure. Our efforts will affect people negatively because we are out of order. But the mother — as well as the servant of God — who simply lets nature take its course, though not escaping pain, fares better than the one who induced the delivery.

Prosperity theologies may have added fuel to this fire. These urge Christians to "name it, claim it, and frame it." They say that confession is everything, and if you can't confess it, you can't get it. We must find the balance in this line of thinking. What we must confess daily is *who God is and what He is able to do,* not the specific expectation of blessing, because that type of confession puts God in a box of our own making. And He will not abide there. After all, what if He wants to do more than you're confessing?

Jesus spoke constantly of the Father, His abilities, and the things that were already established in the heavenlies. Then He opened His hands and simply watched for God to move in any way He desired. Of course, Jesus was so close to His Father that He knew the specifics of what the Almighty would do. At the appropriate time the Lord's plans would be revealed. Until then, however, Jesus tucked the details away in His heart until every piece was in place, set in position for the fulfillment of what God had decreed. Then Jesus released it, giving life to the promise. When we wait on the Lord for the birthing of blessings, we will echo those in the book of Acts on the day of Pentecost who said, "This is what was spoken of . . ." (2:16, NASB).

Timing Is Everything

God waits to reveal His plans. He is not willing to be interrupted or circumvented by either our flesh or the natural urge we have to make things happen. Throughout the Old Testament He gives us glimpses of a Savior. But after the Savior bursts onto the scene, He reveals yet another aspect of His plan: to invite Gentiles into the lineage of Abraham, Isaac, and Jacob. We get hints of this intention in the Old Testament, but in the New Testament God lays it out plainly through the life and writings of Paul. Paul is God's Elizabeth, ready to partner with Him in this undertaking.

In reading this, then, you will be able to understand my insight into the mystery of Christ, which was not made known to men in other generations as it has now been revealed by the Spirit to God's holy apostles and prophets. This mystery is that through the gospel the Gentiles are heirs together with Israel, members together of one body, and sharers together in the promise in Christ Jesus. . . .

Although I am less than the least of all God's people, this grace was given me: to preach to the Gentiles the unsearchable riches of Christ, and to make plain to everyone the administration of this mystery, which for ages past was kept hidden in God, who created all things. His intent was that now, through the church, the manifold wisdom of God should be made known to the rulers and authorities in the heavenly realms, according to his eternal purpose which he accomplished in Christ Jesus our Lord. (Ephesians 3:4–6,8–11)

Can God keep a secret or what? From the beginning God was plotting and planning the salvation of the *world,* giving hints along the way that could not be fully comprehended. I have this picture in my mind of all the angels in heaven saying, "What is God up to? What is He doing? Why is the Lamb going down to earth? Why is God allowing His Son to be killed? What is this all about?" Then all of a sudden — *bam!* The entire picture is revealed. Christ dies, is resurrected, and ascends back to heaven with the keys of death and hell in His hands. And all of heaven has one giant "Ah! Now I see!" moment. Satan couldn't mess up the plan because, for one thing, He didn't even know it. God didn't utter a word, He just did His thing, and now we are all blessed because of it. We have favor because of the blood of Jesus. As many a preacher has said, if Satan had known what the crucifixion would have accomplished, he would never have had Jesus killed. Remember, silence is your friend. A word out of season can be your worst enemy and rob you of your blessing.

The book of Nehemiah documents Nehemiah's return to Jerusalem to rebuild its wall. After securing written documentation that confirmed his right to proceed, he set out to do what God had laid on his heart. With wise foresight, he had chosen to keep his plans to himself until he arrived. He traveled by night to inspect the ruins and, after surveying and estimating the extent of the work to be done, met with the leaders to outline a strategy. By the time Jerusalem's enemies got wind of what was happening, it was too late. The plans were already underway, and their opposition was thwarted.

So do you feel like you will just burst with anticipation of what God is going to do in your life? If He said it, He will do it. So for your own sake, before you explode, write it down. The written word has power and is subject to no one.

Then the Lord replied:

"Write down the revelation
  and make it plain on tablets
  so that a herald may run with it.
For the revelation awaits an appointed
    time;
  it speaks of the end
  and will not prove false.
Though it linger, wait for it;
  it will certainly come and will not delay."

(Habakkuk 2:2–3)

For no word from God shall be void of power. (Luke 1:37, ASV)

Seek validation and confirmation only from the Spirit of God. When He is the One who has spoken the promise, He will surely bring it to pass. The gates of hell cannot prevail against the blessings He has stored up for you, but waiting wisely for their delivery is key. Mary didn't run around screaming to the world, "My baby is the Son of God, and He's going to save everybody!" No, she rested in the knowledge of the things that had been told to her, pondering them in her heart, and she was blessed.

- What has God promised you? Do you believe Him?

- What instructions has He given you concerning the promise? Are you actively pursuing Him for more instruction?

- Can God trust you with His secrets?

- Do you trust God to deliver what He has promised?

- Are you willing to wait on the delivery of God's promise? What steps of preparation will you take?

- Are you willing to do the work to birth God's promise when the time comes? To what extent?

10. The Power of Submission

LEARNING HOW TO GET TO THE TOP

And Mary said:
"My soul glorifies the Lord
and my spirit rejoices in God my Savior,
for he has been mindful
of the humble state of his servant."
Luke 1:46–48

I sat and listened to my friend express her disappointment. "God has never blessed me," she said. The words sent chills down my spine. I stifled the urge to reply, "How can you say that? You are sitting before me in perfect health. You are not homeless. We just finished a fabulous lunch. How could you put your lips together to utter such a thing?" But because I was cognizant of the pain that had forced these words out of the basement of her heart, I remained silent, waiting until a better time to speak reason to her. For now I would allow her to feel what she felt without feeling judged as well.

My friend's disappointment was real. It could not be denied, and yet I had a different perspective on her life. I saw before me someone I loved very much who was writhing in her own self-involvement. Her life had always been about what she wanted from God, never about what God wanted from her. And so God waited for her to give her heart to Him so that He could fill it. I wonder why it wasn't clear to her that she was her own worst enemy. I knew she had dreams she had never pursued because she was unwilling to commit to doing the extra work required to gain the extra-dimensional blessings of God. Yet she desired them and felt *entitled* to them. But a basic life only gets us the basic blessings at best. Now was not the time for me to share these observations with her. There's a time for everything, including loving correction.

I walked away questioning myself and the condition of my own heart. Did I regard God as a sort of Santa Claus? Or was He more like a slot machine? If I put in a token of obedience, would I expect a prize to automatically drop into my hands? Depending on our own experiences with our earthly father, other men, or authority figures in our lives, our view of our heavenly Father may be limited and incorrect. Our experience might be as basic as "If I do this, you will reward me with that" — Pavlov's dog theory on a human level.

But God doesn't practice behavior modification techniques with us. We cannot manipulate Him. To feel that we are here for our own benefit and that God exists to give us the desires of our heart will get us nowhere fast in the blessing department.

> Thou art worthy, O Lord, to receive glory and honour and power: for thou hast *created* all things, and for thy *pleasure* they are and were *created.* (Revelation 4:11, KJV)

We have to remember that we are here *for God.* For *His* purposes and *His* pleasure. As we bring pleasure to His heart, He opens the windows of heaven and pours out more blessings than we have room to receive. From our hearts to our tithes to our talents to our time, all that we are and all that we have belongs to the Lord. Mary was willing to give God the use of her life, no matter what it might cost her: the wrath of Joseph, the misunderstanding and judgment of her family and community, the loss of freedom that having a child would bring, *her very future.* She put aside her personal desires to fulfill the will of the Father. She was willing to do the work that the call on her life required come pain, shame, or lack of free time . . . whatever! She was up to the task. That is the heart of a true servant, a servant who is destined to be blessed above the norm.

> Therefore, I urge you, brothers, in view of God's mercy, to offer your bodies as *living* sacrifices, holy and pleasing to God — this is your spiritual act of worship. (Romans 12:1)

Someone once said that the only problem with a living sacrifice is that it keeps crawling off the altar. But a true living sacrifice is one that is living and breathing unto God and is dead to its own desires. When we wipe clean the slate of our lives, erasing our own agenda, and allow God to write what He wants on the board, we enter into what I call the eye-has-not-seen, ear-has-not-heard, neither-has-it-entered-into-the-hearts-of-man-the-things-that-God-has-prepared-for-him zone. In short, we enter the above-all-you-can-ask-or-imagine dimension. You have let God out of the box of your assumptions. The extra-dimensional blessings are not for the lazy, the faint at heart, or the selfish.

When we take the focus off of ourselves and redirect it toward Him, God shows up and performs extraordinarily. When we let Him out of our box, He brings us boxes of His own filled with delights and incredible surprises. But these special gifts are reserved for those who are more enthralled with the Giver than the gifts. These special treats are reserved for those who put His wishes above their own. They have surrendered their will to embrace His and to all that His will requires of them.

Delight yourself in the LORD
    and he will give you the *desires* of your
    heart.

(Psalm 37:4)

"If you keep your feet from breaking the
    Sabbath
    and from doing *as you please* on my
    holy day,
if you call the Sabbath a delight
    and the LORD'S holy day honorable,
and if you honor it by not going your own
    way
    and *not doing as you please* or speak-
    ing idle words,
then you will find your joy in the LORD,

and I will cause you to ride on the
heights of the land
and to feast on the inheritance of your
father Jacob."

The mouth of the LORD has spoken.
(Isaiah 58:13–14)

Time and time again the promises of God
are clearly stated: As we seek to give God
joy, by being busy about the furtherance of
His plan, by using our abilities to be His
hands at work in the earth to fulfill the
needs of others, then the reward of our self-
sacrifice will be receiving the desires of our
hearts. And let me remind you that as we
lose ourselves in pleasing Him our desires
change. They are transformed to match His
desires for us because we are finally able to
rest in the knowledge that He knows what
is best for us. And trust me, we're not talking about oatmeal here! He knows what will
bring us complete satisfaction.

It is the blessing of the LORD that makes
rich,
and He adds no sorrow to it.
(Proverbs 10:22, NASB)

I love the title of C. S. Lewis's book

Surprised by Joy. That pretty much sums it up. I am learning more and more that I am not aware of what would really make me happy. As I survey the life that the Lord has given me and the things that now bring me the most joy, I am forced to admit that none of those things was on my original wish list. Fancy that! Who would have thunk it? Indeed, the Creator knows what would make His creation the happiest. But we have to get ourselves out of the way in order to receive this revelation.

THE HEART OF A SERVANT

Think about how you feel when you've received good service at a restaurant. When your server has paid extra attention to the details of your meal and your comfort. You want to leave a good tip to show your appreciation. On the other hand, if you had lousy service, you are probably tempted to leave a little *written* tip saying, "When you give better service, you'll get the type of tip you like." Instead, you'll probably leave something out of obligation, but not what you would have given if you had been served well.

What is considered good service? I find it interesting that the biblical kings surrounded themselves with eunuchs. Though castrating the men they drafted for service seems cruel, I think there was more to it than removing the temptations of the harem. The thought was that eunuchs would have no personal drives or desires of their own. Therefore, their entire focus would be serving and pleasing the king. They would anticipate the desires of the king and serve him without any agenda of their own. They would serve without thought of reward. They would not be distracted by the pull of their own flesh, which had been put to death. They would live only to be in the presence of the king.

When I visit my father in Ghana, West Africa, the house stewards illustrate this kind of service. Upon my arrival, I find my room prepared. The air conditioner is on, the room has been sprayed for mosquitoes and the linens are turned down. In the morning when I go downstairs, my breakfast has already been started; they've heard me stirring. I sit at the table and out it comes — all of my favorite morning fare. The cook knows what I like. Once I overheard the steward telling him to go easy on the pepper because I don't like a lot of it. The entire time I'm there I am surrounded by people who seek to make my stay enjoyable. They look out for me. They anticipate my needs and seek my comfort. If I try to lift a finger to iron a dress or do anything domestic, I am quickly shooed away with the words, "Oh no, madam, I will do that."

By now you're probably wondering why I come back home. I wonder that sometimes myself, but back to the point: I am served well. I am humbled by their giving attitude, and I always make sure that I give them good gifts before I leave. They are always grateful, but I know that their service is not based on the anticipation of a reward. It is because they take their positions of service seriously and they have a heart focused toward me. They miss me when I'm gone and await my return with gladness.

This gives me insight into the heart of God and what moves Him to bless us. God looks for the heart of the eunuch in us, and He makes generous promises to those who put aside their own desires to seek His pleasure. This means pressing past what our flesh views as inconvenient or uncomfortable. Anyone who has died to any life of his own for the sake of the one he serves is a servant in the truest sense.

For this is what the LORD says:

"To the eunuchs who keep my Sabbaths,
  who choose what pleases me
  and hold fast to my covenant —
to them I will give within my temple and
  its walls
  a memorial and a name
  better than sons and daughters;
I will give them an everlasting name
  that will not be cut off."

(Isaiah 56:4–5)

Better than sons and daughters! Do you see that?! Surely that is favor — a name that represents carte blanche for now and eternity! Yet it seems difficult for us to accept that only when we release everything do we truly gain everything.

As Jonah sat in the belly of the whale, he came to the conclusion that "those who cling to worthless idols forfeit the grace that could be theirs" (Jonah 2:8). As I take note of those people in Scripture who prospered and were blessed mightily, one theme rings true: They all had a do-or-die mentality. They were willing to risk it all to attain a greater prize. They were willing to let go of the familiar in many cases, do what they did not want to do, press past their comfort level, and risk what they did not know in order to see what God would do.

213

God called Abraham out from a place where he was settled, well-off, and respected and then instructed him to go to a place he had never been. By blind faith, Abraham chose to forsake all. He followed the finger of God and became a very wealthy man, the father of many nations, and one of the pillars in the hall of faith. Lot, who went with him, did not fare as well. He did not have the heart of a servant. While his attitude should have been to follow Abraham, serve him, and develop the same type of relationship he had with God, Lot's self-centeredness soon eclipsed his call. Asking Abraham to give him a plot of land so that he could pursue his own well-being, he set off on a path that led to his undoing. Abraham had to rescue him a couple times. Who was serving whom here? Who got blessed? Abraham, of course.

On the other hand, Lot's home was destroyed, and his wife was turned to a pillar of salt. To add further injury to all of this, his own daughters seduced him in his sleep! (They had learned this type of behavior in the land Lot had chosen.) This incestuous moment gave birth to the Moabites and Ammonites, who later became enemies of

Israel. A self-serving attitude always leads to destruction.

In sharp contrast to Lot is the example provided by the life of Elijah the prophet and his trainee Elisha (2 Kings 2). Elisha wanted the anointing that rested on Elijah and was willing to go the extra mile to get it. Now Elijah was training a whole company of prophets, but Elisha was the only one who pressed past the basic requirements to gain an extra portion.

> Then Elijah said to him, "Stay here; the LORD has sent me to the Jordan."
>
> And he replied, "As surely as the LORD lives and as you live, I will not leave you." So the two of them walked on.
>
> Fifty men of the company of the prophets went and stood at a distance, facing the place where Elijah and Elisha had stopped at the Jordan. Elijah took his cloak, rolled it up and struck the water with it. The water divided to the right and to the left, and the two of them crossed over on dry ground.
>
> When they had crossed, Elijah said to Elisha, "Tell me, what can I do for you before I am taken from you?"
>
> "Let me inherit a double portion of your spirit," Elisha replied.
>
> "You have asked a difficult thing," Elijah

said, "yet if you see me when I am taken from you, it will be yours — otherwise not."

As they were walking along and talking together, suddenly a chariot of fire and horses of fire appeared and separated the two of them, and Elijah went up to heaven in a whirlwind. Elisha saw this and cried out, "My father! My father! The chariots and horsemen of Israel!" And Elisha saw him no more. Then he took hold of his own clothes and tore them apart.

He picked up the cloak that had fallen from Elijah and went back and stood on the bank of the Jordan. (2 Kings 2:6–13)

This type of all or nothing attitude is what separates the mighty from the marginal. Fifty men hung back where it was comfortable (no extra effort required), while Elisha dogged Elijah's steps, determined to grasp the blessing! On which side of the river do you stand? Are you following after God at all costs, living up to the calling on your life and your gifts, or are you standing back, first waiting to see what He will do for you? Are you satisfied with a sample of God's blessings, or do you want the double portion? You know what this really comes down to? Loving God more than anything else and wanting what He is holding in His hands more than anything you can grasp for yourself by your own efforts. When you want supernatural blessings and abundance, you have to be willing to stretch beyond all that you hold dear or find familiar. You must be willing to do the work, go the extra mile. You must be willing to lay your entire life on the line for the prize.

Let us fix our eyes on *Jesus,* the author and perfecter of our faith, who for the *joy* set *before him* endured the cross, scorning its shame, and sat down at the right hand of the throne of God. (Hebrews 12:2)

Do nothing out of selfish ambition or vain conceit, but in humility consider others better than yourselves. Each of *you should look not only to your own interests, but also to the interests of others.*
　Your attitude should be the same as that of Christ Jesus:

Who, being in very nature God,
　did not consider equality with God
　　something to be grasped,
but made himself nothing,
　taking the very nature of a servant,
　being made in human likeness.

And being found in appearance as a
   man,
   he humbled himself
   and became obedient to death — even
   death on a cross!
Therefore God exalted him to the highest
   place
   and gave him the name that is above
   every name.

                           (Philippians 2:3–9)

Contrary to the world's system, in God's kingdom the way up is down. Even Jesus had to be willing to sacrifice His very life in order to be blessed with us as His prize. Now I just heard somebody say, "We're no prize," but we are to Him. So great was His love for us that He was not willing to see any of us perish, so He made the ultimate unselfish move in order to save us and preserve us for Himself. We, like Jesus and the saints of old, must not draw back from the concept of laying our personal desires and our lives on the line to take hold of the promises of God.

They overcame him [Satan]
   by the blood of the Lamb
   and by the word of their testimony;
   they did not love their lives so much

as to shrink from *death.*

(Revelation 12:11)

In It but Not of It

The three Hebrew boys in the book of Daniel didn't care what anybody had to say when the king confronted them about whom they were going to worship. They were not willing to compromise themselves for earthly favor and blessing. Losing their lives meant nothing in the face of doing something that would betray the heart of the God they served. They were bold in their refusal to compromise. Though they worked for the most powerful monarch on the face of the earth at the time, they were always cognizant of whom they truly served.

Shadrach, Meshach and Abednego replied to the king, "O Nebuchadnezzar, we do not need to defend ourselves before you in this matter. If we are thrown into the blazing furnace, the God we serve is able to save us from it, and he will rescue us from your hand, O king. But even if he does not, we want you to know, O king, that we will not serve your gods or worship the image of gold you have set up." (Daniel 3:16–18)

How could God ignore such unwavering faith?! As King Nebuchadnezzar had them thrown into the fiery furnace, the Lord Himself met them there. He walked with them through the fire. And when they were pulled out, their garments didn't even smell of smoke. God's presence in the furnace was more than an answer to the youths' bold proclamation. This special visitation would further the purposes of God and make an irrefutable impact on King Nebuchadnezzar and the nation he "ruled."

Nebuchadnezzar then approached the opening of the blazing furnace and shouted, "Shadrach, Meshach and Abednego, servants of the Most High God, come out! Come here!"

So Shadrach, Meshach and Abednego came out of the fire, and the satraps, prefects, governors and royal advisers crowded around them. They saw that the fire had not harmed their bodies, nor was a hair of their heads singed; their robes were not scorched, and there was no smell of fire on them.

Then Nebuchadnezzar said, "Praise be to the God of Shadrach, Meshach and Abednego, who has sent his angel and rescued his servants! They trusted in him and defied the king's command and were willing to give up their lives rather than serve or worship any god except their own God. Therefore I decree that the people of any nation or language who say anything against the God of Shadrach, Meshach and Abednego be cut into pieces and their houses be turned into piles of rubble, for no other god can save in this way."

Then the king promoted Shadrach, Meshach and Abednego in the province of Babylon. (Daniel 3:26–30)

Now *that's* what I'm talking about! God was glorified by the faith of Shadrach, Meshach, and Abednego, their enemies were destroyed, and they were crowned with favor and blessed with promotions. Remember, "Whoever tries to keep his life will lose it, and whoever loses his life will preserve it" (Luke 17:33).

Are you still lost in the land of "What am I going to get out of it?" Or have you yelled the war cry "Whatever the cost, I'm willing to pay it in order to gain God's best and richest for my life"?

THE WAY TO A MAN'S HEART
Like Esther, we must have an "If I perish, I perish" attitude if we truly want to get the

King's attention and see our desires fulfilled. Of course, that's a lot easier to achieve when our desires are honorable ones. Remember, your favor and blessings affect the kingdom at large.

> [Mordecai] sent back this answer [to Esther]: "Do not think that because you are in the king's house you alone of all the Jews will escape. For if you remain silent at this time, relief and deliverance for the Jews will arise from another place, but you and your father's family will perish. And who knows but that you have come to royal position for such a time as this?"
> Then Esther sent this reply to Mordecai: "Go, gather together all the Jews who are in Susa, and fast for me. Do not eat or drink for three days, night or day. I and my maids will fast as you do. When this is done, I will go to the king, even though it is against the law. And if I perish, I perish." (Esther 4:13–16)

You might be wondering where I'm going with this. Here's what I want you to get: Esther pressed her way into the king's court to beg for the life of others. When she finally finds herself in his presence, he is so pleased to see her that he offers her up to half of the kingdom.

But by now this girlfriend has completely gotten over herself. She stays focused on the needs of others. She invites the king to dinner, serves him, waits for him to ask her what she needs — and then she does something not many desperate women I know would do. She stifles her request and invites him to another dinner. She bides her time, allowing the king to indulge in her adoration of him before broaching the subject of her wants. Once the king has been thoroughly satisfied and is literally bursting at the seams to bless Esther with something, she submits her need to him. Not only does he give her what she has asked for, but he gives her above and beyond her wildest dreams. The king wipes out Esther's enemies, reverses their plot against her and the Jews, takes all of their property and possessions, gives them to Esther, and promotes her uncle Mordecai! Her selflessness and servant's attitude got her everything she wanted, plus some stuff she hadn't thought of.

One thing that struck me was how Esther worded her petition to the king. It speaks volumes about how far many of us have strayed in our prayer life.

Then the king extended the gold scepter to Esther and she arose and stood before him.

"If it pleases the king," she said, *"and if he regards me with favor* and *thinks it the right thing to do, and if he is pleased with me,* let an order be written overruling the dispatches that Haman son of Hammedatha, the Agagite, devised and wrote to destroy the Jews in all the king's provinces." (Esther 8:4–5)

When was the last time you prayed in such a way that acknowledged the Lord's sovereign choice? I remember the old folks who used to say, "I'm going to do so and so, Lord willing." But, sadly, we've gotten past that. Now the attitude for many is that God just ought to do as we ask. Never mind if it is a bad idea. Never mind that it doesn't fit into His kingdom agenda. Never mind that we have unfinished business with Him we need to settle first. We want what we want.

But Esther submitted her desire before the king. She submitted herself to his wisdom and judgment. She yielded to how he felt about the matter. She did not assume anything. When was the last time you asked God to judge your request? Esther recognized the king had a choice in the matter, and he acted on her behalf. How could he harden his heart against one who was so humbly submitted, even to the point of death? Wow! That is truly a compelling example for us, though the bottom line is clear: When nothing else matters more to us than what pleases God, He is more than willing to extend His favor and shower us with blessings from on high.

Which brings us full circle back to Mary. Mary surrendered everything to become a willing and cheerful servant, and she was blessed.

THOUGHTS TO PONDER

- What is your attitude toward servant-hood? Do you serve God cheerfully or only when it suits your interests?

- How dear to your heart are the things that you cling to? Are you willing to surrender your life to God's decisions even if they don't coincide with yours?

- Do you give God a choice in the matter when you submit your requests to Him? What do you think He would do if you did?

- Do you understand how using your

gifts and talents tie into serving God?

- What dream has He given you that you haven't pursued because of the work involved? Have you replaced God's abilities with your insecurities?

11. No Rest for the Weary?

ALLOWING GOD TO PLAN HIS WORK AND WORK HIS PLAN

Mary stayed with Elizabeth for about three months and then returned home.

Luke 1:56

If you are anything like me, you have probably thought, "How could Mary take a vacation at a time like this?" Didn't she wonder what Joseph was thinking? It's not as if she could call him on the phone and find out! What transpired while she was away? What kind of reception would she encounter when she returned? Would they all be waiting at the city gate to stone her to death? Shouldn't she get back home quickly and try to explain her circumstances? In spite of the thoughts that could have been swirling through her mind, Mary clung to her confidence that God was able to handle perfectly all things concerning her.

What do you do when God has promised you something so incredible that you yourself have no power to bring it to pass? What do you do when the call on your life might cause you to be misunderstood, judged, ridiculed, or resented? All you can do is *rest* in the Lord and in the power of His might, not yours. By His Spirit the things God has promised will be accomplished. You must simply await His cues and not move before then, no matter how long the wait. "But I've got to do something, Michelle!" you say, though you don't know just what. After all, what do you do when there's *nothing else* you can *do?* The answer comes back from God: rest. "But . . . but . . . ," you say. There, there, I do understand!

And I also know that we live in a society that doesn't allow rest because our worth is determined by what we *do.* However, God does not call us to *do* anything; He calls us to *be.* Being is far more difficult for most of us. "So what do I do while I am simply *being?*" you might be wondering. Well, God has several suggestions.

Now then, *stand still* and see this great thing the LORD is about to do before your eyes! (1 Samuel 12:16)

You will not have to fight this battle. Take up your positions; *stand* firm and see the

deliverance the LORD will give you. . . .
Do not be afraid; do not be discouraged.
(2 Chronicles 20:17)

Some *trust* in chariots and some in
  horses,
  but we *trust* in the name of the LORD
  our God.
(Psalm 20:7)

Be still, and *know* that I am God;
  I will *be* exalted among the nations,
  I will *be* exalted in the earth.
(Psalm 46:10)

This is what the Sovereign LORD, the Holy
One of Israel, says:

"In repentance and rest is your salvation,
  in quietness and *trust* is your strength,
  but you would have none of it."
(Isaiah 30:15)

Trust in the LORD and do good;
  dwell in the land and enjoy safe
    pasture.
Delight yourself in the LORD
  and he will give you the desires of your
    heart.
Commit your way to the LORD;

trust in him and he will do this:
He will make your righteousness shine
   like the dawn,
   the justice of your cause like the
   noonday sun.
Be still before the LORD and wait
   patiently for him.

(Psalm 37:3–7)

See? There's plenty for you to do. Be still, stand firm, trust God, delight yourself in the Lord, commit your way to Him, and wait patiently for Him to do His thing.

TAKE FIVE

For musicians, a rest is a beautiful thing. It is the pause that affords them the opportunity to catch their breath and continue the melody or to shift tempos and create new moods in the piece they are playing. For athletes, rest is crucial. It is a time of restoration and rebuilding of strength in preparation for the next round. Their rest is necessary for victory. For a farmer, giving the fields rest makes the difference between good crops and mediocre ones, life and death.

When a farmer plows for planting, does
   he plow continually?

Does he keep on breaking up and har-
rowing the soil?

(Isaiah 28:24)

Be patient, then, brothers, until the Lord's
coming. See how the *farmer* waits for the
land to yield its valuable crop and how
patient he is for the autumn and spring
rains. (James 5:7)

For six years you are to sow your fields
and harvest the crops, but during the
seventh year let the land lie unplowed and
unused. Then the poor among your people
may get food from it, and the wild animals
may eat what they leave. Do the same
with your vineyard and your olive grove.
Six days do your work, but on the seventh day do not work, so that your ox and
your donkey may rest and the slave born
in your household, and the alien as well,
may be refreshed. (Exodus 23:10–12)

But in the seventh year the *land* is to have
a sabbath of *rest,* a sabbath to the LORD.
Do not sow your fields or prune your
vineyards. (Leviticus 25:4)

Why is rest so vital to the land and the seed?
Because if you relentlessly turn the soil, the

rich nutrients embedded deep within it become exposed to and depleted by the elements. Also to keep planting continually in the same field sucks the life out of the earth. The crops are not as lush, sweet, or nutritious. God knew that even the land needs to regain its strength in order to yield good fruit. For all things, there is serious merit in rest.

Even God rested. Does that mean He was inactive? I don't believe so. I picture him sitting back and allowing everything He had put in place to settle into the divine order He had ordained. I imagine Him taking a deep breath and, as He exhales, seeing that breath give the finishing life-giving touches to all His creation.

What you must know in order to really rest is that while you are resting, God is still busy on your behalf. Esther retired for the night after her first banquet with the king, but he was unable to sleep. God troubled him in the night in order to make it clear to him who was truly on his side in the kingdom. This episode set the king up to show favor to Esther the next day when she appealed to him for the lives of her family and her people.

Similarly, when Ruth informed Boaz that she was in need of a redeemer and then returned home, Naomi told her to simply bide her time. Boaz would not rest until the matter was settled. Sure enough, Boaz headed straight for the city gate to negotiate with the next of kin in line for Ruth's hand. In the end Ruth was blessed with not only a wealthy and loving husband, but also with a place in the lineage of Christ.

As I write this I chuckle. I am watching with trepidation the 2000 presidential returns. It is a close race, and I am concerned about the candidates' platforms. So why the chuckle? It never fails — the minute you learn a principle, you will be tested on it. By now I should know the drill. I have to stop and remind myself that regardless of who wins, the just will live by faith, the simple faith that God is in control. Ultimately, only one truly sits on the throne and commands the affairs of men and women alike.

The bottom line: Even when we don't see anything with our natural eye, God is still at work.

He also said, "This is what the kingdom of God is like. A man scatters seed on the ground. Night and day, whether he sleeps or gets up, the seed sprouts and grows, though he does not know how. All by itself the soil produces grain — first the stalk, then the head, then the full kernel in the head. As soon as the grain is ripe, he puts the sickle to it, because the harvest has come." (Mark 4:26–29)

However, as it is written:

"No *eye* has *seen,*
   no ear has heard,
no mind has conceived
   what God has prepared for those who
      love him."
(1 Corinthians 2:9)

While some trust in the arm of flesh, those who believe must trust the Spirit of God to bring the seed of our dreams and our faith to life.

Let the beloved of the LORD *rest* secure
   in him,
   for he shields him all day long,
   and the one the LORD loves rests
   between his shoulders.
(Deuteronomy 33:12)

In other words, don't fret! God's got it! God's got *you!* Your desires and longings are safe and secure in the breast of God.

How should I rest? you might be wondering. Here's the answer that may make you quake: Simply take a deep breath and let go. Chances are that the things God has promised you are so huge and overwhelming there is absolutely nothing you can do to bring them to pass. You have no choice but to continue on right where you are, with nothing more than the expectation of things to come from God.

GIVE IT A REST

As Abraham set out for a land he knew nothing of, and though he was walking, he rested in the promise that God would prosper him and bring him to a place that was greater than where he had been. However, when it came to the matter of fatherhood, Abraham struggled. Why? Because he was distracted by his own flesh and his own abilities. Anytime we stop to evaluate our own abilities, we will be unable to rest. There is little we can truly accomplish in our own strength. In the long run it is far easier to admit this than to spend our energy proving it to ourselves! When we attempt to "help" God carry out His plans and refuse to rest in His ways and His timing, we make drastic mistakes that can have far-reaching consequences.

The irony in all of this is that God is not moved by our self-centered efforts. He merely waits until we have exhausted ourselves. When we finally throw our hands up in dismay, He says, "Good, you are finally out of the way."

Rest must use faith as a pillow. When we lay down our own efforts and stop trying to make things happen, then we sink into our pillow of faith, safe and secure in His abilities, and allow God to take up our part. In our weakness He reveals His strength. He longs to have the elbowroom to perform the miraculous in our lives. The reason we struggle so with the issue of rest is because it makes us feel helpless. To rest is to place yourself at the mercy of God.

I recently experienced this in a dramatic way. If you have read my other books, you are aware of this part of my testimony. One day as I was walking across the street, a man driving a delivery van stepped on the gas as I stepped in front of his vehicle. To make a long story short, I suffered a severe injury to my knee. A major tendon was completely severed. Five years later, after I had three operations, underwent the trial of literally learning to walk again, and spent a year-and-a-half more in bed than out of it, my lawsuit saw the inside of a courtroom. It was a trial made for television. The defense was ruthless because they had no defense. The driver admitted his negligence and guilt. My doctor and therapist testified to the seriousness of my injury. My employer confirmed my inability to work. After attempting to cause a mistrial, the defense attacked me and distracted the jury from my permanently damaged knee by concentrating on my lifestyle. They sneered as they told the panel that I had gained an extraordinary life as the result of my accident.

They pointed to the fact that I had completed my first book while I was lying in bed and, as a result, had secured a new career for myself. They told these men and women that I now led the glamorous life of an author who had penned nine more books in three years, flown around the country speaking, and co-hosted a television show. Since I had done so well for myself, they concluded, I should not be compensated because I had not really suffered at all. I sat there thinking of the excruciating pain I had endured after each surgery and throughout my rehabilitation — of how, despite my new life, I struggled with a leg that would never be the same again. I thought of the pain I still experience and how it now takes double the effort to do what I could easily do before the accident. I thought of my therapist telling me, "Because of the trauma associated with your injury, your leg will never have the strength it had before." I felt helpless as my attorney said the words "We rest our case." I was now at the mercy of the jury.

As we waited for the verdict, the defense offered a settlement that was unacceptable to my attorney. By her calculations the worst I would get from the jury would be equal to what they offered. I sought the counsel of others and they agreed. And so we waited. Finally we were summoned back to the court. The jury had been swayed to be hostile. Though they acknowledged that the driver was guilty of hitting me and compensated me for my medical fees, they did not feel that I should be awarded anything substantial for my pain and suffering. In the end they awarded me less than the insurance had offered to settle for. The judge was mortified, as was the man who had hit me. My attorney was stunned, and even the defense team was surprised. To be perfectly honest, I stood there trying to find God and get an explanation. How do you rest at a time like this? How do you continue to feel blessed and highly favored when things aren't going the way you think they should?

How would I express to my attorney my faith in God's goodness after an outcome like that? What would I say to the man who had hit me? As I listened to his heartfelt apology, I told him I had never held him responsible for my pain and asked him if he believed in God. Yes, he said, he did. I asked him if he knew the story of Joseph. He said he had read it in the Koran. He was Muslim. I told him I felt the words of Joseph were apropos to my situation. What was meant for evil had been turned around for my good. It was true. I had sustained an injury with lasting consequences. But during that time of rest and healing I had stepped into the center of God's will for my life. I had never been still enough prior to the accident to complete what He had called me to do, but adverse circumstances brought me to a place of yielding. Now I'm living the life of my dreams. It was true: I had gained an extraordinarily blessed life because of this trial.

THE KINDNESS OF STRANGERS

Perhaps the lesson for me that day was never to place my confidence in man but always to rely on God. Indeed He had taken care of me and even prospered me during my convalescence. I thought back to the time of my accident. Two weeks before it occurred, I had acquired a freelance contract on a retainer basis. I was to be paid a certain amount every month whether or not I worked. God, in His omnipotent foresight, had looked down the road, anticipated my need, and secured my provision for this difficult time. With a grateful heart I was able to count my blessings that had not decreased during that time but had increased instead. It was a miracle, so *totally* a God thing that I could not have planned it better myself!

The Lord had proven to me that I could rest in Him for not only what I required but also for what I desired — *and above and beyond!* As I shared this with the driver who had hit me, he gazed at me in amazement. I continued, "Hey, there are people out there who don't have a leg. I'm happy to be limping. It could be worse." He could not understand why I was not bitter. I had to chuckle at the irony of the whole situation. The defense was right: I was so blessed that I didn't need men to bless me! My God was completely able, all by Himself, to arrange for me to receive anything I needed. Who knows why things turned out the way they did? Perhaps this man's salvation was at stake. But since God doesn't waste anyone's life or time, I think the end of the story is yet to be revealed.

I remember the Israelites, who were afraid to allow the land to rest every seven years in accordance with God's command. Four hundred and ninety years later, as they headed to Babylon, God tallied up their years of disobedience and determined that they must spend seventy years in captivity in order for the land to have the full rest it was due. God will get you to rest one way or the other. And it's all for your own good. A failure to rest leads us into the bondage of self-effort, which usually yields only deep hurt and disappointment. Whether you war for the blessing of getting married, starting a ministry, obtaining a dream, succeeding in your career, attaining financial success — whatever it is that you are trying to accomplish in your own strength — it's time to stop and rest in order to be blessed.

> There remains, then, a Sabbath-rest for the people of God; for anyone who enters God's rest also rests from his own work, just as God did from his. (Hebrews 4:9–10)

As we cease our labors and wait for God to make His entrance, we must believe His promises no matter what we see or hear. Sometimes His promises seem too incredible to believe, and we stumble over them in pursuit of our own goals and dreams. We can't stand the suspense!

When the Lord commanded Israel to allow the land to rest, He also reassured the people that they shouldn't worry about what they were going to eat. He promised them that He would make the land produce enough food to cover the year that they didn't plant and the year of sowing and reaping. But that was just too hard for the Israelites to believe. What if God didn't keep His promise and they starved? No, no, no, they had better take matters into their own hands and keep right on planting. And so in the end they didn't get to plant anything for seventy years. At least not in Israel. Despite all of their doubt and disobedience, the Lord urged them to get back on track.

This is what the LORD says:

"Stand at the crossroads and look;
    ask for the ancient paths,
ask where the good *way* is, and *walk* in it,
    and you will find rest for your souls."
                                    (Jeremiah 6:16)

At every step along the way, God will always require us to take a season of rest before moving to the next level. Take the time to remember His first word to you. Regain your strength, rearrange your priorities, and get further instructions for the next phase. You will never be able to move forward without the Word of God, without the prompting of the Holy Spirit saying, "Go this way, I'm right behind you." Otherwise you will end up under a broom tree like Elijah, running from the threats of the enemy, too spent and tired to remember God's promises (1 Kings 19).

Mary did not forget. She took God's promise and ran with it. She did her part and left the balance to God. He took care of the seemingly impossible. This young woman accepted God's Word and rested in the knowledge that what He had said He was able to perform, regardless of what anyone might say or do. He would take care of His own and guard His promises jealously; therefore, no harm would come to her. She would see the fulfillment of His plan birthed in her own life. She felt safe and secure under His watchful eye. Mary rested, and she was blessed.

THOUGHTS TO PONDER

- Do you trust God to carry out His promises in your life?

- Do you feel the need to help Him bring His word to pass? When things aren't going the way you imagined they would, do you doubt His word to you?

- Do you question God's goodness? Or do you trust the way He takes you?

- Do you leave God options for your life?

- Do you feel paralyzed by rest? Why? Do you believe that God is still working long after you have stopped striving?

- How can you refresh yourself while you wait on Him?

12. LIVING WITH OPEN HANDS

MASTERING HOW TO CATCH THE RAIN

"I am the Lord's servant," Mary answered. "May it be to me as you have said."

Luke 1:38

Can we talk about the blessedness of being completely open to whatever God wants to do with you? That is an incredible place to be. I remember when I first came to the Lord. I decided that I didn't want to be one of those "weird" Christians. I understood that we were a peculiar people, but I didn't want to be strange. However, I was in quite a dilemma. One part of me wanted to be whatever God wanted me to be, but another part of me was afraid to find out what that would be. I didn't want to end up on some television show with over-the-top hair and outrageous makeup looking ridiculously sanctified. I wanted to be cool and saved at the same time. Somehow I didn't see those two things merging.

I was at war within.

Whenever I felt myself being stretched, I was quick to clamp down and short-circuit my growth. I didn't want to know more. I wanted to stay the same. So stay the same I did — until I got good and bored with being stagnant. I tell you, sometimes when God says, "Okay," it's *not* a good thing. A good friend of mine once told me, "Until the pain of staying the same is greater than the pain of change, you won't change." When God said "okay" to my desire to not change, I got so sick of me I was ready for whatever He wanted to do. Then I was pleasantly surprised to find that I liked the things He had in mind. But I must admit that I remained suspicious for quite a while, thinking He was buttering me up with all the things He knew I liked before He pulled a fast one on me. I kept glancing at the mirror out the corner of my eye to see if He was rearranging my hair.

But the longer I walked with God, the more I came to realize that He had fabulous taste and incredible ideas. Every time I surrendered to Him and allowed Him to do His thing in my life, I ended up saying, "Wow! I couldn't have come up with that in a million years!" I found out that the happiest place to be was in the center of His perfect will. The doors and opportunities that were opened to me were in accordance with His kingdom plan, but my joy was the icing on the cake. What a powerful combination: His will, my fulfillment.

I Did It My Way

So many miss the potential for blessings by clinging to their own ideas, goals, and desires. They bang their heads against the wall over and over again and come to the conclusion that God is cruel. As I wrote in my devotional *His Love Always Finds Me,* "In straining to hear You, my questions drown out Your answers and I accuse You of not listening. In grasping to receive Your blessing, my hands get in the way and I drop Your promises." Meanwhile God sits pointing to the yield sign and the detour up ahead that leads to a better way.

God loves us so much that He presses past our outer countenance; He looks in our heart and sees that our desire is really what He wants. He gently nudges us into the right spot by allowing failure and the passage of time to bring us to our knees at the place where He waits, ready and willing to meet us and guide us back onto the right track.

Whether you turn to the right or to the left, your ears will hear a voice behind you, saying, "*This* is the *way; walk* in it." (Isaiah 30:21)

In his heart a *man plans* his course,
  but the LORD determines his steps.
                                        (Proverbs 16:9)

Many are the *plans* in a *man's* heart,
  but it is the LORD's purpose that
  prevails.
                                        (Proverbs 19:21)

GOD'S SIGHT IS FORESIGHT

Thank God His purposes prevail! When I was in college, I fell in love with a very handsome young man. He was my sun, my moon, my everything. But neither of my fathers, Mr. Hammond or Mr. McKinney, could stand him. They prevailed upon my mother to get me to end the relationship. Well, talk about a modern-day *Romeo and Juliet*! My, my, my — the drama of it all. The tears, the pleadings, the clandestine meetings, the railings at the unfairness of life, and the cruelty of my parents. I concluded that they had never been in love and therefore would never understand that life just wasn't worth living if I couldn't see the light of my life. Finally I was shipped off to another college in another city. Time and distance did what my parents could not, and eventually his golden halo melted into an ordinary Afro.

Seven years later this man resurfaced, still professing his love for me at a time when I was open and vulnerable. He expressed the desire to see me and talk about getting back together. By then, however, I had become a Christian. The Lord warned me to flee his advances, and though I didn't understand why at the time, I'm glad I did. Years passed, and his life went from bad to worse, to the type of life I would not have wanted to share. About a week ago I learned he had murdered an eighty-year-old man by bludgeoning him to death with a two-by-four. What a shock! I could not picture this man doing such a thing. Who knew he had such a violent temper — and whether I would have been a victim of it? God did. God, in His infinite mercy, shielded me from danger even when I did not know Him. May His name be praised! What if I had insisted on my own way? Where would I be today? The thought is not one I care to consider.

TO BE OR NOT TO BE
I believe that as we walk before God with

open hands and allow Him to take and give as He pleases, we will walk between the raindrops more often than not. For every time that I have failed to yield to His still, small, and gentle voice, I've regretted it. Every time I please myself first, I end up not so pleased at all. Although God delights in us coming to Him as children, He also exhorts us to grow up, to be perfect — not in the sense of perfectionism, but in the sense of being mature.

> *When* I was a *child,* I talked like a *child,* I thought like a *child,* I reasoned like a *child.* *When* I became a man, I put childish ways behind me. (1 Corinthians 13:11)

> Be perfect, therefore, as your heavenly Father is perfect. (Matthew 5:48)

Is it a Catch-22 situation? While Jesus tells us we must be like children, He also tells us to grow up. *Well, which one is it, Jesus?* It's important to understand that in the first case He was discussing our belief system. A little child believes anything adults say, and God is delighted when we have *childlike faith* in what He says. However, *childish behavior* is characterized by selfishness, petulance, wanting to have one's own way, not accepting correction willingly, and throwing manipulative tantrums. In contrast, maturity teaches us to be open to correction, change, and options, to be both flexible and generous.

> Brothers, stop thinking like children. In regard to evil *be* infants, but in your thinking *be* adults. (1 Corinthians 14:20)

> Jesus answered, "If you want to *be perfect,* go, sell your possessions and give to the poor, and you will have treasure in heaven. Then come, follow me." (Matthew 19:21)

Maturity teaches us that God's pleasure becomes our pleasure. His pleasure is to use you; in return you will be blessed. I think of Mary saying, "Yes, Lord, completely yes," harboring no agenda of her own. Hers would be a lifelong call, first as a woman of God, then as a mother, then as a wife.

As a mother, Mary would have to be willing to surrender her child to the world and watch Him die. Mothers have a difficult time releasing their children, and yet Mary walked with the understanding that although Jesus was her son, truly He was not. She was merely the vessel chosen to raise

Him and give Him back to God. And, actually, that is all any parent is called to do.

I believe the prophecy of future pain that Mary received in the temple applies to every parent. A sword pierces the hearts of parents several times throughout life as they watch their charges go through the difficult passage from infant to adult. Even so, they must release their children into the hands of God and dare to believe that He is able to keep that which is committed to Him. I know that it is difficult to believe, but He loves your children more than is humanly possible — more than even you do! And He longs for their victory far above your greatest longing. I believe that on the day Mary encouraged Jesus to perform His first miracle, she watched Him with a divided heart. Part of her was proud of what He had become; the other part knew it was time to cut the apron strings.

HOTEL, MOTEL, HOLIDAY INN

Besides yielding to God in her parenting, Mary the wife yielded to her husband's correction. I find it interesting that prior to Mary's marriage, the angel spoke first with her and then with Joseph. After she became his wife, however, all angelic instructions were given to Joseph. Mary submitted to him as unto the Lord. This was a good thing, a life-saving thing. Can you imagine what would have happened if she hadn't submitted?

You'll recall that shortly after Jesus was born, Herod decreed all newborns up to the age of two be killed, so fearful was he that a king had been born to replace him. The angel told Joseph to take Mary and flee to Egypt. What if she had put her hand on her hip and said, "I'm not going anywhere. God didn't tell me that. He talks to me, too, you know. I want to go home and show my baby to my family and friends, thank you." The outcome would have been quite different, to say the least. Mary's obedience meant a blessing to them all.

Living life with open hands demands that we be prepared for sudden changes. Sometimes God wants to change the route of our lives for our own protection and for increased blessings. Think of Mary and Joseph as they traveled to Bethlehem and, after an especially wearing day, finding no room at the inn. I've got to pause here and consider my own irritation when I arrive at a hotel after traveling all day, only to find that my reservation has been lost somewhere in the computer. I have to take a deep breath and exercise self-control when I would rather fuss and ask, "What *is* the problem? You knew I was coming. Why don't you have your act together? Can't you see that I'm exhausted? *Where* is the manager?!"

Taking the temperature of our impatient microwave generation, I imagine the Mary of today saying, "Look, don't you know I'm carrying the Son of God? I'm a VIP! I think you'd better look again and find me a room *some*where in this joint 'cause I'm not taking no for an answer." But the real Mary settled gratefully and gracefully into a stable for the night. Mary did not view her circumstances as a reason for preferential treatment. She continued in humility, simply considering it an honor to be of service to her Lord. She chose to make the best out of an undesirable situation. Perhaps there was a good reason for her not to stay at the inn. We will never know in this life. But Mary certainly didn't learn any lessons the hard way that night.

But, unlike Mary, when we decide how things should go and how we should be treated, we get in trouble. We will always think that we are due something more than what we have received, and from time to time, that expectation becomes a stumbling block to our spiritual and natural growth. So many people in ministry today fall prey to the devices of the enemy, who whispers the same thoughts that once assaulted his own mind and cost him his heavenly post. They begin to think that they are worthy of praise, honor, and special treatment. This way of thinking leads them to exercise liberties that cause them to fall. No matter how coveted a position we find ourselves in, we must continue to see ourselves as servants of the Most High God, accepting each accolade with the utmost of humility, offering the praise back to Him who truly deserves it. After all, it is not by our own works that we achieve anything lest we find occasion to boast. It is totally by the grace of God that we find ourselves where we are. If this is our attitude, we, like Mary, will gracefully accept every situation we find ourselves in, trusting God and His purposes to triumph on every occasion.

WHERE HE LEADS ME . . .

As we look down the Hall of Biblical Fame in search of inspiring characters who were blessed above measure, one thing rings true: These people opened their hands to God. People like Abraham. Truly Abraham was open. He had to be. He had no idea where he was going! But God knew. I will be the first to admit it: I hate change — hate it, hate it, hate it! And doesn't it seem as if the minute you settle into a groove and get comfortable, God comes along and says, "Okay, it's time to pull up the stakes and move on"?

"But wait a minute, God!" you say. "I was just getting comfortable." God knows that "comfortable" is a dangerous place. The more comfortable we become, the less dependent on God we become. And so He shakes up the mix of our lives and keeps us moving. When we arrive at the destination He has selected, we rejoice. "Gee, Lord!" we exclaim, "You should have told me — I would have done this sooner." Well, that's exactly why He didn't. You would have moved ahead of His plan and missed it. God wants us to be open to His voice and His leading every step of the way. He will always lead us down the right path.

> The LORD is my shepherd, I shall not be
>   in want.
>   He makes me lie down in green
>   pastures,
> he leads me beside quiet waters,
>   he restores my soul.
> He guides me in paths of righteousness
>   for his name's sake. . . .
> You anoint my head with oil;

my cup overflows.
Surely goodness and love will follow me
    all the days of my life,
and I will dwell in the house of the LORD
    forever.

                            (Psalm 23:1–3,5–6)

All these *blessings* will come upon you and accompany you if you obey the LORD your God. (Deuteronomy 28:2)

Sheep are devout followers of the shepherd. They are totally dependent, obedient, and trusting. Where he leads, they follow. The few who are inattentive and misguided wander off and are devoured by wolves or fall off cliffs. But those who follow the shepherd's path are led to the best areas of pasture and the clearest brooks; they spend their days in peace. These are the blessings that are so taken for granted. Yet provision and peace are lacking in the lives of many who stray from His path. They have provided for themselves but have no peace. Some have peace but struggle with provision. The Good Shepherd offers both.

The Shepherd's path leads to blessings, unlimited provision, and rest. But that's just half of it. Do you know what it is like to be followed by goodness? To have blessings chasing after you? This is a phenomenal thought. Many feel they have to run after a good blessing, but no — God said His blessings would run after you if you follow Him! I like the sound of that.

Living the Good Life

Have you ever known someone who just seems to lead a serendipitous life? Good things just come their way. Their conversation always goes something like this: "I was walking down the street minding my own business, and I happened to run into so-and-so. We were standing there talking when I happened to mention this and that, and so-and-so said, 'I just met someone who could help you with that.' We ended up stopping off to have a cup of coffee and discuss it further. We were sitting there when this *very* person walked in — can you believe it? So my friend mentioned my need, and this person told me he was just thinking that someone needed to do what I wanted to do. And *just* like that he told me he would give me everything I needed to make it happen! *Just like that!*"

Meanwhile, you're standing there saying to yourself, *How does this sort of thing happen to this person all the time?* I'll tell you how: Such people are open to the possibilities God sets before them. They embrace the possibilities and run with them, but not too fast. They don't want to miss God's next turn. As they go, the pieces of their lives fall into place because they have stronger belief in the power of God than in their own ingenuity. They are fully cognizant of the fact that they, in and of themselves, don't make anything happen. They wake up in the morning ready to go with the flow. They are open to the moment. They live in the moment. They are not myopic. They are open to change. They are ready to go wherever the Spirit of the Lord takes them that day. (The result of this attitude toward life holds true for unbelievers as well as believers. Unbelievers just give credit to forces such as luck, a higher power, or whatever suits their fancy. But those who come to know the Lord look back in hindsight and acknowledge that God was wooing them to His side as He sprinkled blessings along the path leading them to His throne.)

Getting back to Abraham: He was willing to sacrifice his only son, Isaac. He was willing to give up the child of promise if that was what God wanted. Of course, God stopped him and provided a ram in a thicket for the sacrifice, but the test revealed where

Abraham's heart was. Where is your heart? Do you just want what you want? Do you fail to ask God what He thinks about it because you fear He'll tell you it's a bad idea? Oh yeah, we go to the land of I Want from time to time, but we need to leave that country *real* fast. There are giants in that land who will have you for dinner. In God-First country, however, there is great safety and blessing. Because Abraham's heart matched the heart of God the Father (who was also willing to sacrifice His Son for our sakes), Abraham was made the father of many nations. He could be trusted with blessings because he did not rejoice in the gift more than the Giver. And that is what being blessed really boils down to.

> For where your *treasure* is, there your *heart* will be also. (Matthew 6:21)

Is your heart wrapped around the blessings or wrapped up in the Blesser? You've got to have your priorities straight. God will not give you anything that will distract you from Him. And when we grasp things for ourselves, they might come into our hands, but they may not remain there for long. And when they come by self-propelled means and do remain, the inevitable pain that results doesn't make the prize worthwhile. Anything that does not come in accordance with God's timing or purpose brings hard lessons with it. Trust me, every good thing is not a blessing if you're not ready to receive it. It's like putting a two-year-old child behind the wheel of a Porsche and allowing him to drive. Both would be destroyed. This is why God would like us to release to Him both the timing and the manner in which we will be blessed. He chooses well, my friend. Allow Him to select your presents.

TAKING GOD OUT OF THE BOX

God has never given me a blessing I didn't like. I went to New York one year to visit a friend and buy a ring for myself in celebration of my birthday. My friend and I went from store to store looking at different baubles. She was quite a connoisseur of jewelry, diamonds in particular, and found something wrong with everything I selected. After a long day, I returned home bone weary and disappointed that I had nothing on my finger.

Later, after dinner, we were going through some photo albums of hers when I spotted a ring in one of the pictures that made me exclaim. On that note she jumped up and said, "Oh, now you've ruined my surprise." She disappeared for a moment and returned bearing a small silver platter with a little velvet box on it. She presented it to me, saying, "While we were out today, the Lord told me to give you this." My jaw dropped as I opened the box. It was that very ring I had admired in the photograph, far more beautiful than anything I had seen that day. I burst into tears, overwhelmed by the generosity of my friend, but even more so at the attentiveness of God. He knew all along what I would like and had chosen to *give it* to me. I often wondered what would have happened if I had insisted on buying one of the other rings. I think I would have missed out on a rich blessing: experiencing God's love for me and witnessing the depth of my friend's affection. Both were humbling.

Oh, if only we would close our eyes and open our hands! Did you ever play that game as a child? You never could be certain what your friends would put into your hands. Would it be a marble? A piece of candy? A leaf? A worm? Ew! This uncertainty will always remain when we are dealing with human beings, but we can always count on our heavenly Father to deliver incredible gifts.

Which of you, if his son asks for bread, will give him a stone? Or if he asks for a fish, will give him a snake? If you, then, though you are evil, know how to give good gifts to your children, how much more will your Father in heaven give good gifts to those who ask him! (Matthew 7:9–11)

Every *good* and *perfect gift* is from above, coming down from the Father of the heavenly lights, who does not change like shifting shadows. (James 1:17)

God is not moody, loving us one day and raging against us the next. He does not change His good intentions toward us. Daily He extends new mercies and looks for our open hands, into which He wants to deposit invaluable, immeasurable blessings. He is always faithful to deliver on His promises.

We tend to be suspicious of God because we see Him through the haze of what our own hearts are capable of. *We* change our minds. *We* feel stingy or generous on any given day depending on how others treat us. *We* are reserved with others based on past hurts and disappointments. But His ways are not our ways; His thoughts are not our thoughts. God keeps short accounts.

He does not superimpose the past over the future. He is able to let bygones be bygones. So no matter what you have done, He is ready to start anew. He's ready to start blessing you all over again. Don't you just love that about Him?

THE SECRET RECIPE FOR BLESSING

As our conversation draws to a close, let's review the pictures of reality we've covered. Surely the pages of biblical history are clear: Those people who were blessed the most were broken the most; they sacrificed the most. They opened their lives to God so that He could shape and mold them in preparation for the blessings to come. What are you willing to let drop from your outstretched hands? Your heart? Your life? The thing dearest to you? Everything? Can you be like Hannah, who gave the very son she longed for back to God and then received many children in return? Can you be like the mother of Moses, who placed him in a basket and set him afloat in the Nile, trusting that God would keep him? She received him back as a mighty leader. Can you be like David, who refused to seize the throne of Israel himself and instead left the timing of his coronation completely up to God? He refused to kill the very enemy who hunted him day and night for years! As evil as King Saul was, and as justified as David would have been in killing him while he had the opportunity, David released Saul to be dealt with by God.

> Abishai said to David, "Today God has delivered your enemy into your hands. Now let me pin him to the ground with one thrust of my spear; I won't strike him twice."
>
> But David said to Abishai, "Don't destroy him! Who can lay a hand on the LORD's anointed and be guiltless? As surely as the LORD lives," he said, "the LORD himself will strike him; either his time will come and he will die, or he will go into battle and perish. But the LORD forbid that I should lay a hand on the LORD's anointed. Now get the spear and water jug that are near his head, and let's go." (1 Samuel 26:8–11)

The list continues: Three Hebrew boys willingly walked into the fiery furnace and came out promoted. Jesus, the author and finisher of our faith, was insulted, bruised, broken, and crucified before He was exalted. He not only opened His hands, He opened His arms, His life, His everything. When He could have defended Himself, He did not; instead He went as a lamb to the slaughter, not saying a word.

Are we there yet? Are we willing to be in communion with Christ's suffering so that we may be blessed to reign with Him? Are you willing to be broken, given away, and blessed in order to acquire something greater? Some days I say yes. Thank God I'm saying it more often than I used to.

COME OUT WITH YOUR HANDS UP

When we sing the words to that old song, "I'm Yours, Lord, everything I am, everything I've got. I'm Yours, Lord, try me now and see. See if I can be completely Yours," we must be careful. Do we really live what we sing? "I surrender all. All to Thee, my blessed Savior, I surrender all." Do we really? If we were to tally the number of times we say no to God versus the number of times we say yes, which would be greater? Surrender yourself. Get your hands in the air, up and open in demonstration that you are neither hiding nor holding anything. What is in your hands at this very moment? Will it hinder you from getting what you truly want from the Lord?

A certain Hollywood screenwriter is said to have written many scripts, but no one ever liked any of them. After suffering from deep disillusionment, this man left California and went to live in a small town. He started noticing the incredible racial harmony of the people who lived there. He began to ask questions and was told that the harmony was the result of certain things that had transpired in the lives of the local high-school football team and the impact it had on the community. He went in search of the coaches and other involved parties and began conducting interviews. He then wrote the story and headed back to Hollywood. No one wanted to buy the rights to the story or give him the money to develop it. So he wrote the screenplay himself. He sent it out to everyone he could think of; no one wanted it. Once again he threw his hands up in the air and retreated. About that time he received a call. A powerful producer wanted to do a football film. The rest is now history. *Remember the Titans* opened to much acclaim.

The moral of the story? Your hopes might not pan out the way you want them to; *they could turn out to be even better.* Once you let go, that is. As a child, I wanted to be a rock star when I grew up — a combination of Diana Ross and Barbra Streisand. Can you imagine that? I sang my way through high school, beauty pageants, plays, and home-grown bands. I prepared myself for stardom, but it never happened. Oh, I got glimpses of it, but it never happened. I came close, but not quite. I had all the right connections and entrées. I even got a music publishing deal with a major music publishing company, but I never held that brass ring.

Instead I ended up in the world of advertising. Ironically, I got to do all the things I wanted to do and enjoyed much more financial stability. I ended up writing and producing jingles and singing them myself! I created television commercials, produced them, and met and worked with a myriad of stars. I had tickets to every event they had tickets to. The Grammys, the Oscars — you name it, I went. So what was I missing? Absolutely nothing, and I was probably staying out of a heap of trouble to boot. In retrospect I now see that that type of life would not have made me happy. Why? Because I would have ignored the greater call on my life to be a writer. I would not have discovered this precious gift that gives me so much joy while it hopefully blesses others.

I had started my life off one way, but it ended up completely different than I thought it would, and I'm loving every minute of it. I studied to be an art director but ended up writing. I started off writing commercials and ended up writing books. I started off writing books and ended up speaking all over the place. I started off speaking and ended up singing as well! I even got the television show thrown in!

Are you getting this? Do you see how God brought me full circle? When life refused to work the way I wanted it to, I surrendered all that I held dear and decided to put one foot in front of the other, use the resources presently available to me, and go where He led. He led me to the very center and fulfillment of my dreams. He got what He wanted out of me and then added what I wanted as well. I didn't get the leftovers; I got the mother lode! I feel so blessed every day that I am alive. I feel the umbrella of His favor over me even in the moments of my life that try my faith. I know that He is faithful and that each trial that comes my way is just a test. It, too, shall pass, because I am determined to pass the test and get to the good part of kingdom living. I know what I have been called to do for Christ. I count it such a privilege to be able to utilize all of my gifts to bless others. To live and work for God is the ultimate blessing, no matter what your profession or walk of life.

TAKING OFF THE LIMITS

God is limitless. This is a resounding fact. However, for a myriad of reasons, sometimes we unintentionally limit ourselves, as well as His ability to work in our lives. It is within our power, via our choices, to cast off the limits and give God free reign in our lives. If God is limitless, we can be too. I have learned that He is not obligated to bless you in the way that you think you should be blessed, but He is motivated to bless you as much as you allow Him to. Mary the mother of Jesus knew that. As a single woman I am blessed by the fact that when Mary received this awesome call from the Lord she was a single woman. She was betrothed to Joseph, but their vows had not been consummated yet. She belonged completely to God. She was totally *available* to God. He was her focus and her center. Whither God went, she went also. Nothing stood between them. She didn't have to check with anyone else. The affairs of her life were between her and God. And so it was that she was the chosen one. Because of Mary, we have all been blessed. Now, because of her Son, Jesus, we can all qualify to be blessed and highly favored. Because of God's love for mankind we are *all* called to bear Christ to the world!

If Mary were to be the feature of a special biography program today, I believe the reporter would introduce her with something like this: "Today we would like to take a look at the life of the only person in the Bible greeted with the impressive salutation 'blessed *and* highly favored.' As we consider her life, several things will become evident about this extraordinary woman. She lived a life of purity and had an incredible relationship with God. She was extremely sensitive spiritually and possessed remarkable faith. The fruit of her life was as obvious to others as her refusal to compromise on ungodly issues. Her reputation was as flawless as her sense of discretion. This was a woman who did not insist on her own way. Instead, she was at peace with God's decisions for her life. She was open and completely available to go wherever the Spirit of God led her. Truly she was favored. Truly she was blessed. She herself uttered the very words that would be repeated throughout the ages when others referred to her: 'From now on all generations will call me blessed' (Luke 1:48)."

THOUGHTS TO PONDER

- Do you consider yourself completely available for God to use as He pleases?

- What areas in your life do you still reserve for yourself?

- What do you think God would do with your life if you let Him have his way completely?

- Should He come calling with some amazing assignment for your life, are you ready? Are your hands open? Are you willing to see the task through to completion no matter what the cost?

- How would you like God to use you? What would you like a biographer to say about you?

- What would you like your lasting impact on others to be?

A PRAYER FOR BLESSING

Dear Lord,
As I seek to cleanse my hands, O God, purify my heart and make me acceptable in your sight.

I pray that You would look upon me and bless me. As I humble myself before You, exalt me and let Your favor go before me. Spread Your goodness before me. May it accompany Your mercy as it follows me in accordance with Your promises. Lord, cause Your face to shine upon me. Let Your blessings overtake me.

Grant me peace with all who would set their face against me as I walk in peace and fellowship with You. Let no weapon formed against me succeed.

Equip me with the strength to do your will.

Bless the work of my hands and cause me to prosper in all my ways, even as my soul prospers. Order my steps on paths of promotion as I acknowledge You. Grant me the power to gain wealth as I surrender my all to You.

Most of all, I pray that You grant me wisdom. The wisdom to seek You above all things. Teach me to be a wise steward of all You grant, and let each blessing that You render be an occasion to further glorify Your name in the earth.

In the matchless and wonderful name of Jesus.

Amen.

If you would like to correspond
with Michelle
in response to her books,
contact her at:

Michelle McKinney Hammond
c/o HeartWing Ministries
P.O. Box 11052
Chicago, IL 60611-1722
E-mail: hartwingmin@yahoo.com
Web site:
http://www.mckinneyhammond.com or
http://www.heartwing.com

For speaking engagements, contact:
Speak Up Speaker Services
1-888-870-7719

ABOUT THE AUTHOR

Michelle McKinney Hammond is founder of HeartWing Ministries and is a vibrant author and animated speaker who makes biblical principles practical for every-day living. She is a featured speaker at the Women of Virtue conferences and is sought after regularly for women's retreats and church services. Michelle is also co-host of the Chicago-based syndicated TV talk show *Aspiring Women* and the author of nine books, including *Single, Sassy, and Satisfied; Secrets of an Irresistible Woman;* and *In Search of the Proverbs 31 Man.*